Hero Myths

HERO MYTHS
A Reader

Edited by *Robert A. Segal*

Copyright © Blackwell Publishers Ltd 2000
Editorial matter and organization copyright © Robert A. Segal 2000

First published 2000

2 4 6 8 10 9 7 5 3 1

Blackwell Publishers Ltd
108 Cowley Road
Oxford OX4 1JF
UK

Blackwell Publishers Inc.
350 Main Street
Malden, Massachusetts 02148
USA

British Library Cataloguing in Publication Data

A CIP catalogue record for this book is available from the British Library.

Library of Congress Cataloging-in-Publication Data has been applied for

ISBN 0–631–21514–X (hbk)
ISBN 0–631–21515–8 (pbk)

Typeset in 10 on 12 pt Sabon
by Kolam Information Services Pvt Ltd., Pondicherry, India
Printed in Great Britain by MPG Books Ltd, Bodmin, Cornwall

This book is printed on acid-free paper

CONTENTS

CONTENTS

ACKNOWLEDGMENTS

The editor and publishers gratefully acknowledge the following for permission to reproduce copyright material:

1   Sigurd: *The Saga of the Volsungs: The Norse Epic of Sigurd the Dragon Slayer* (trans. Jesse L. Byock). Copyright © 1990 The Regents of the University of California.

2   John Henry: Brett Williams, *John Henry: A Bio-Bibliography.* Copyright © 1983 by Greenwood Press, Westport. Reproduced with permission of Greenwood Publishing Group, Inc., Westport, CT.

3   Finn mac Cool: *Essential Celtic Mythology: Stories that Change the World*, retold by Lindsay Clarke (Thorsons Publishing, HarperCollins Inc., 1997).

4   Duke of Wellington: *Myths of the English*, ed. Roy Porter (Polity Press, Cambridge, 1992).

5   George Washington: Barry Schwartz, *George Washington: The Making of an American Symbol* (The Free Press, New York, 1987).

6   Robin Hood: Henry Gilbert, *Robin Hood* (Ware: Wordsworth Classics, 1993, Wordsworth Press).

7   Coyote: A. L. Kroeber and E. W. Gifford, *Karok Myths* (ed. Grace Buzaljko). Copyright © 1980 The Regents of the University of California.

8   Maui: Martha Beckwith, *Hawaiian Mythology* (University of Hawaii Press, 1970).

9   Christopher Columbus: Claudia L. Bushman, *America Discovers Columbus: How an Italian Explorer Became an American Hero* (University Press of New England, 1992).

10   Penthesilea: *Apollodorus: The Library*, from *Apollodorus*, vols. I and II (reprinted by permission of the publishers and the Loeb Classical Library from *Apollodorus: The Library*, Volumes I and II, trans. J. G. Frazer, Cambridge, Mass.: Harvard University Press, 1921). Penthesilea: *Herodotus: The Histories* (trans. Aubrey de Sélincourt, revised A. R. Burn) (Penguin Books, Harmondsworth, 1972, reprinted 1975).

11   Eve: *The New Oxford Annotated Bible with the Apocrypha: Revised Standard Version* (eds. Herbert G. May and Bruce M. Metzger) (Oxford University Press, 1977). Scripture quotations are from the Revised Standard Version of the Bible, copyright © 1946, 1952, 1971 by the Division of Christian Education of the National Council of the Churches of Christ in the USA. Used by permission.

12   Prometheus: *Hesiod*, trans. Richmond Lattimore (The University of Michigan Press, Ann Arbor, 1959, reprinted 1973).

13   Oedipus: *Sophocles I: Oedipus the King* (trans. David Grene) from *The Complete Greek Tragedies* (eds. Grene and Lattimore) (The University of Chicago Press, Chicago, 1942).

14   Job: *The New Oxford Annotated Bible with the Apocrypha: Revised Standard Version*, (eds. Herbert G. May and Bruce M. Metzger) (Oxford University Press, 1977). Scripture quotations are from the Revised Standard Version of the Bible, copyright © 1946, 1952, 1971 by the Division of Christian Education of the National Council of the Churches of Christ in the USA. Used by permission.

15   Joan of Arc: Frances Gies, *Joan of Arc: The Legend and the Reality* (copyright © 1981 by Frances Gies. Reprinted by permission of HarperCollins Publishers, Inc.).

16   Galileo: Bertolt Brecht, *Plays, Volume I: The Life of Galileo*, trans. Desmond I. Vesey (Methuen, 1955/60, reprinted 1961/3).

17   Arjuna: R. K. Narayan, *The Mahabharata: A Shortened Modern Prose Version of the Indian Epic* (Heinemann, 1978).

18   Gilgamesh: *The Epic of Gilgamesh*, trans. N. K. Sandars (Penguin Books, Harmondsworth, 1972).

19   Sisyphus: Albert Camus, *The Myth of Sisyphus and Other Essays*, trans. Justin O'Brien (Vintage Books, New York, 1942/1955, from *The Myth of Sisyphus and Other Essays* by Albert Camus, trans. Justin O'Brien. Copyright © 1955 by Alfred A. Knopf, Inc. Reprinted by permission of the publisher and Hamish Hamilton Ltd, London).

20   Don Quixote: Miguel de Cervantes, *The Adventures of Don Quixote* (trans. J. M. Cohen) (Penguin Books, Harmondsworth, 1951, reprinted 1982).

21   Davy Crockett: Constance Rourke, *Davy Crockett* (Harcourt, Brace, 1934).

22   Elvis Presley: Patsy Guy Hammontree, *Elvis Presley: A Bio-Bibliography*. Copyright © 1985 by Greenwood Press, Westport. Reproduced with permission of Greenwood Publishing Group, Inc., Westport, CT.

The publishers apologize for any errors or omissions in the above list and would be grateful to be notified of any corrections that should be incorporated in the next edition reprint of this book.

INTRODUCTION

THE "GREAT MAN" VIEW OF HISTORY

It is a truism in the twentieth century that impersonal forces, not individuals, make history. It was equally a truism in the nineteenth century that heroic individuals were believed to make history. The epitome of this nineteenth-century outlook was Thomas Carlyle (1795–1881), whose biographies and histories were devoted to demonstrating the power that heroes had had or could yet have. Carlyle's best-known book on heroes, *On Heroes, Hero-Worship, and the Heroic in History* (1841), celebrates eleven disparate figures grouped into six categories: the hero as divinity (Odin), the hero as prophet (Mahomet [Mohammed]), the hero as poet (Dante, Shakespeare), the hero as priest (Martin Luther, John Knox), the hero as man of letters (Samuel Johnson, Jean-Jacques Rousseau, Robert Burns), and the hero as king (Oliver Cromwell, Napoleon).[1]

Carlyle opens his book with a statement that has come to epitomize the "Great Man" view of history: "For, as I take it, Universal History, the history of what man has accomplished in this world, is at bottom the History of the Great Men who have worked here. They were the leaders of men, these great ones; the modellers, patterns, and in a wide sense creators, of whatsoever the general mass of men contrived to do or to attain; all things that we see standing accomplished in the world are properly the outer material result, the practical realisation and embodiment, of Thoughts that dwelt in the Great Men sent into the world: the soul of the whole world's history, it may justly be considered, were the history of these" (*On Heroes, Hero-Worship, and the Heroic in History*, p. 1). Heroes are saviors: "In all epochs of the world's history, we shall find the Great Man to have been the indispensable saviour of his epoch; – the lightning, without which the fuel never would have burnt" (*On Heroes, Hero-Worship, and the Heroic in History*, p. 13).

1

Yet for all the credit that Carlyle accorded heroes, they were for him as much at the mercy of history as in control of history. Carlyle praises heroes for above all their insight into the course of society rather than for the direction they impose on it. Unlike ordinary humans, who mistake appearance for reality, heroes see beyond appearance to reality: "A Hero, as I repeat, has this first distinction, which indeed we may call first and last, the Alpha and Omega of his whole Heroism, That he looks through the shows of things into *things*" (*On Heroes, Hero-Worship, and the Heroic in History*, p. 55).

Sometimes Carlyle does declare that heroes can alter history. For example, in his earlier *French Revolution* (1837)[2] he writes of Mirabeau, whose death in 1791 was mourned by all of France, that "had Mirabeau lived, the History of France and of the World had been different" (I, p. 444). But once Mirabeau dies, "the French Monarchy may now therefore be considered as, in all human probability, lost" (I, p. 455). Carlyle castigates the hapless King Louis XVI less for failing to fend off revolution than for failing to recognize its coming. Conversely, Oliver Cromwell is lauded less for bringing about the English Revolution than for grasping its imminence and acting accordingly.[3] Heroes do not ultimately impose their will on history. They subordinate themselves to history, the course of which is set by God.

Furthermore, the period determines the kind of hero needed and even possible. The hero as divinity could arise only in a pre-scientific age, presupposing as it does the "pagan" belief in the immanence of divinity in the physical world and in humanity. While there have long been kings, kings as heroes are distinctly modern, needed as they are to overcome the wide modern divide between the spiritual and the material realms. By contrast, the hero as poet can arise in any age (see *On Heroes, Hero-Worship, and the Heroic in History*, p. 78). Still, heroes of thought as well as of action can save society, and Carlyle was writing to inspire men of letters to do so.

As stereotypical of the nineteenth century as Carlyle's preoccupation with heroism was, Carlyle saw himself as a stalwart defender of heroism in a skeptical age: "I am well aware that in these days Hero-worship, the thing I call Hero-worship, professes to have gone out, and finally ceased. This, for reasons which it will be worth while some time to inquire into, is an age that as it were denies the existence of great men; denies the desirableness of great men. Show our critics a great man, a Luther for example, they begin to what they call 'account' for him; not to worship him, but to take the dimensions of him, – and bring him out to be a little kind of man! He was the 'creature of the Time,' they say; the Time called him forth, the Time did everything, he nothing – but what we the little critic could have done too! . . . The Time call forth? Alas, we have known Times *call* loudly enough for their great man; but not find him when they called!" (*On Heroes, Hero-Worship, and the Heroic in History*, pp. 12–13). For all Carlyle's emphasis on the role the times play, he is still crediting heroes with great accomplishments.[4]

Even if Carlyle saw himself as bucking a trend, he was hardly the sole Victorian advocate of heroism, and the Victorian period has even been called an age of "hero worship."[5] At the same time Carlyle was castigated by his contemporaries, not merely by successors, for his stance. His most vitriolic critic was the pioneering sociologist Herbert Spencer (1820–1903), for whom the attribution of decisive events to the talents of individuals rather than to the fundamental laws of physical and social evolution was a hopelessly primitive, childish, romantic, and unscientific outlook.[6] Spencer ascribes the popularity of the Great Man approach to the "universal love of personalities," to the satisfaction of "an instinct not very remotely allied to that of the village gossip," and to the preference for explanations "easy to comprehend" (*Study of Sociology*, pp. 32–3).

Spencer argues that unless one deems the appearance of a great man a supernatural event, the appearance must itself be explained as the product of society at a certain stage of development. As he puts it in a passage that today sounds shockingly offensive, "True, if you please to ignore all that common observation, verified by physiology, teaches – if you assume that two European parents may produce a Negro child, or that from woolly-haired prognathous Papuans may come a fair, straight-haired infant of Caucasian type – you may assume that the advent of the great man can occur anywhere and under any conditions. . . . But if all biological science, enforcing all popular belief, convinces you that by no possibility will an Aristotle come from a father and mother with facial angles of fifty degrees, and that out of a tribe of cannibals, whose chorus in preparation for a feast of human flesh is a kind of rhythmical roaring, there is not the remotest chance of a Beethoven arising; then you must admit that the genesis of the great man depends on the long series of complex influences which has produced the race in which he appears, and the social state into which that race has slowly grown" (*Study of Sociology*, pp. 34–5). Rather than the cause of society, a great man is the product of society. In Spencer's famous summary phrase, "Before he [the great man] can re-make his society, his society must make him" (*Study of Sociology*, p. 35). The changes any great man makes are marginal and are only the direct causes of change. The ultimate causes are the ones that produced the great man himself: "So that all those changes of which he is the proximate initiator have their chief causes in the generations he descended from" (*Study of Sociology*, p. 35). Mocking

Carlyle, Spencer declares that if you wish to understand social change, "you will not do it though you should read yourself blind over the biographies of all the great rulers on record, down to Frederick the Greedy and Napoleon the Treacherous" (*Study of Sociology*, p. 37) – two of Carlyle's favorite heroes.

Spencer's metaphysical counterpart in the rejection of the influence of great men on history was the philosopher G. W. F. Hegel (1770–1831). While Hegel, unlike Spencer, praises the hero, he praises him for embodying the World Spirit in its predestined course of development. Hegel's great man can be motivated by private gain yet still be serving society. Or he can have "insight" into the times like Carlyle's heroes, yet still be oblivious to the overall direction of the history he is serving. As Hegel writes of Caesar, "In accomplishing his originally negative purpose – the autocracy over Rome – he at the same time fulfilled the necessary historical destiny of Rome and the world. Thus he was motivated not only by his own private interest, but acted instinctively to bring to pass that which the times required. It is the same with all great historical individuals: their own particular purposes contain the substantial will of the World Spirit. They must thus be called 'heroes' . . . Such individuals have no consciousness of the Idea as such. They are practical and political men. But at the same time they are thinkers with insight into what is needed and timely. They see the very truth of their age and their world, the next genus, so to speak, which is already formed in the womb of time."[7] While Hegel, writing before Carlyle, might have commended Carlyle for emphasizing the hero's insight, he would probably have belittled Carlyle for making the hero the cause rather than the manifestation of change.

The twentieth century has spawned still stronger skepticism toward the impact of individuals, even in the face of the seemingly all too real impact of dictators like Hitler and Stalin.[8] Defenders of heroism nevertheless remain. Perhaps best known is the philosopher Sidney Hook, author of *The Hero in History* (1943).[9] Hook argues for a sensible middle ground between crediting heroes with everything, which he assumes Carlyle to be doing, and crediting them with nothing. Unlike Carlyle, Hook is concerned only with heroes of action. He distinguishes between "eventful men," whose actions happen to change history, and "event-making men," whose actions are *intended* to change history. Eventful men have no special insight, and someone else in their place might have done the same. By contrast, event-making men, like all of Carlyle's heroes, alone have the insight leading them to make the decisions they do. Despite his use of the term "men," Hook includes females in both groups – for example, Catherine II of Russia as an event-making woman. Because only event-making men and women act on the basis of their talents, only they deserve the epithet "hero": "This distinction tries to do justice to the general belief that a hero is great not merely in virtue of what he does but in virtue of what he is" (*The Hero in History*, p. 154).

While granting that Carlyle was writing as a moralist, and while faulting those who take him to have asserted that "all factors in history, save great men, were inconsequential" (*The Hero in History*, p. 14), Hook still maintains that, "literally construed, Carlyle's notions of historical causation are clearly false, and where not false, opaque and mystical" (*The Hero in History*, p. 14). Hook thus grants that "the Spencerians, the Hegelians, and the Marxists of every political persuasion" have been right to reject his "extravagance" (*The Hero in History*, p. 15). But Hook contends that their denial of any role to individuals has been equally "extravagant."

On the one hand Hook concedes that movements like the Renaissance, the Reformation, and the Industrial Revolution were more than the handiwork of great men. Similarly, he concedes that no one could have prevented World War I: "no matter what *individuals* had occupied the chancellories of Europe in 1914, the historical upshot of commercial rivalries, Germany's challenge to British sea power, chauvinist resentments in western Europe, the seething kettle of Balkan intrigue, would very probably have been much the same" (*The Hero in History*, p. 18).

On the other hand Hook asserts that individuals can make a difference. It was not inevitable that World War I would be fought the way it was. It was not inevitable that Hitler would be successful as Chancellor: "he was victorious not merely because of the widespread economic misery produced by the crisis. His political skill in unifying the right, ranging from Junker to industrialist to the frightened middle classes, together with Hindenburg's support, played an important part" (*The Hero in History*, pp. 115–16). Hook credits Lenin with the success of the Russian Revolution: whatever social unrest already existed in Czarist Russia, Lenin "capitalized" on it. Hook refuses to reduce individual decisions to expressions of the times. Decisions stem from the character of the agents.

Hook thus proposes a compromise between the extremes of Carlyle and of Spencer. But in fact he is close to Carlyle, for whom heroes do not create a new world *ex nihilo* but instead act in accordance with the times. Carlyle does, however, venture far beyond Hook in his admiration for heroes, an admiration that amounts to worship.

HEROES AND GODS

Carlyle outright declares that heroes are not merely celebrated but "worshiped": "in all times and places, the Hero has been worshipped" (*On*

Heroes, Hero-Worship, and the Heroic in History, p. 15). Still, he see-mingly does not mean literal worship. His heroes are not gods. Of the eleven discussed in *On Heroes*, the sole exception is Odin, who after death was deified by his followers. Carlyle attributes the deification partly to the boundlessness of his followers' reverence: Odin's followers "knew no *limits* to their admiration of him" (*On Heroes, Hero-Worship, and the Heroic in History*, p. 25). But more mundanely, he attributes the transformation to the loss of records that would have kept Odin tethered to humanity: "Why, in thirty or forty years, were there no books, any great man would grow *mythic*, the contemporaries who had seen him, being once all dead" (*On Heroes, Hero-Worship, and the Heroic in History*, pp. 25–6). For Carlyle, subsequent heroes have remained mere humans because records have survived. Consequently, "the Hero [as prophet] is not now regarded as a God among his fellow-men; but as one God-inspired, as a Prophet." The hero as divinity is gone forever: "in the history of the world there will not again be any man, never so great, whom his fellowmen will take for a god" (*On Heroes, Hero-Worship, and the Heroic in History*, p. 42).

Aptly, Carlyle uses the term "mythic" synonymously with "divine": "were there no books, any great man would grow *mythic*." For even if most heroes are not divine, those heroes whose stories constitute myths are. Hero myths are stories about divine heroes – divine in effect, whether or not formally. To be sure, in the academic study of myth it is conven-tional to distinguish mere heroes, however glorious, from gods. It is even commonplace, especially among folklorists, to categorize the stories about most heroes as legends *rather than* myths.[10] Yet contrary to con-vention, heroism can blur the line between the human and the divine – not by demoting gods to humans but by elevating humans to gods. More precisely, heroism, when recounted in myth, retains the distinction between the human and the divine but singles out the hero for making the leap from the one to the other.

Usually, the gap between the human and the divine is insurmountable, especially in Western religions. The most egregious sin in the West is the attempt by humans to become gods, epitomized by the vain efforts of Adam and Eve and of the builders of the Tower of Babel. The hiatus between the human and the divine applies as fully to polytheistic religions as to monotheistic ones. For ancient Greeks, those who dared to seek divinity were doomed for their *hubris*. Those who directly challenged the gods were often consigned to eternity in Tartarus.

The West does permit exceptions. In the ancient world the greatest exception was Heracles (Hercules), who, though Zeus' son, was still mortal, yet accomplished superhuman feats of strength, outmaneuvered death in his last three main feats, and was rewarded with immortality for his yeoman service. Still, to some ancient writers such as Herodotus Heracles' very stature meant that he had been born a god. The Greeks did establish cults to worship human heroes, but only after their deaths, when heroes had transcended ordinary constraints.[11] In the West the grandest exception to the divide between humanity and divinity is, of course, Jesus. Yet even his capacity to be at once fully human and fully divine is taken to be a paradox, and a paradox difficult to maintain in practice. Throughout its history, Christianity has often veered between making Jesus merely an ideal human being, as in the Victorian period, and making him a sheer god, as in ancient Gnosticism.[12]

Rather than trying to dissolve the gap between the human and the divine, hero myths transform humans into virtual gods by conferring on them divine qualities.[13] The qualities can range from physical attributes – strength, size, looks – to intangible ones – intelligence, drive, integrity. One measure of the humanity of Carlyle's heroes is the limit of their power: to the extent that they cannot alter history, they are only human. The difference between humans and gods may be of kind: gods often can fly, can change shape, and live forever. Or the difference may be of degree: gods typically are bigger, stronger, sexier, and smarter than humans. But even a difference of degree still puts divinity beyond the reach of most. If anyone can aspire to become a Hollywood star, the few who make it are fittingly called "gods." Classic Hollywood stars were drawn from the handsomest and the most beautiful. Even today, with a wider array of types, the biggest box office draws, male and female alike, look the part on screen. Thus it comes as a shock to learn that in person Mel Gibson is not very tall.

Carlyle himself acknowledges the divine aura of his human heroes. While "it was a rude gross error, that of counting the Great Man a god," yet "it is at all times difficult to know *what* he is" (*On Heroes, Hero-Worship, and the Heroic in History*, p. 42). While claiming that we have advanced beyond the "pagan" practice of deifying humans, he acknowledges that we no longer do so only because our conceptions of God "are ever rising *higher*" rather than because "our reverence for these [heroic] qualities ... is getting lower" (*On Heroes, Hero-Worship, and the Heroic in History*, p. 84). Of Napoleon, he asks, "is he not obeyed, *worshipped* after his sort, as all the Tiaraed and Diademed of the world put together could not be?" (*On Heroes, Hero-Worship, and the Heroic in History*, pp. 84–5). Of Burns, he writes that listeners felt "that they never heard a man like this; that on the whole, this is the man! In the secret heart of these people it still dimly reveals itself ... that this rustic, with his black brows and flashing sun-eyes, and strange words moving laughter and tears, is of a dignity far beyond all others, incommensurable with all others" (*On Heroes, Hero-Worship, and the Heroic in History*, p. 85). Of Dante and Shakespeare, Carlyle asks, "have we not two mere Poets, if not deified, yet we may say beatified? Shakespeare and Dante are Saints of Poetry" (*On Heroes, Hero-Worship, and the Heroic in History*, p. 85). For Carlyle, hero worship is the source of all religion, including Christianity: "Hero-worship, heartfelt prostrate admiration, submission, burning, boundless, for a noblest godlike Form of Man, – is not that the germ of Christianity itself?" (*On Heroes, Hero-Worship, and the Heroic in History*, p. 11).

MODERN HEROES

Some heroes, or kinds of heroes, fit only certain periods. For example, it is hard to imagine an aristocratic hero like Don Juan surviving into the twentieth century. Other heroes do survive, either because their appeal continues or because they are protean enough to adapt to the times. Heracles was by no means confined to the crude image of him as Rambo-like – all brawn and no brain – but on the contrary has been depicted "in one century as the great, tragic sufferer, in another as the paragon of superhuman physical prowess and bravado, in another as the ideal nobleman and courtier, in another as the incarnation of rhetoric and intelligence and wisdom, in another as the divine mediator and a model of that way of life whose reward can only be heavenly, in another as a metaphysical struggler, and in yet another as a comic, lecherous, gluttonous monster or romantic lover, and in still another as the exemplar of virtue."[14]

In the twentieth century, as in prior centuries, not only have traditional heroes been transformed, but new heroes and new kinds of heroes have emerged. If distinctively nineteenth-century heroes were the romantic hero (Byron's Childe Harold) and the bourgeois hero (Flaubert's Emma Bovary), distinctively twentieth-century heroes include the ordinary person as hero (Miller's Willy Loman), the comic hero (Roth's Alexander Portnoy), the schlemiel as hero (Singer's Gimpel the Fool), and the absurd hero (Beckett's Vladimir and Estragon).[15] Far from divine, the contemporary hero is hopelessly human – mortal, powerless, amoral. The present-day hero is often lowly even within the human community – more the outsider than the insider, more the loser than the winner, more the villain than the savior. The contemporary hero is not a once great figure who has fallen but a figure who has never risen. Sisyphus, not Oedipus, let alone Heracles, epitomizes contemporary heroism. Yet Sisyphus is still to be commended for never giving up. Persistence replaces success, survival replaces achievement. Old-fashioned heroic virtues like courage and duty give way to new ones like irony and detachment. Because contemporary heroes scarcely reach the stature of gods, their stories fall short of myths. While this Reader includes heroes from all periods who fail in their efforts, only Sisyphus, as reinterpreted by the contemporary Albert Camus, is resigned to failure.

Yet it would surely be going much too far to argue that traditional heroism has died out. Present-day heroes in sports, entertainment, business, and politics are admired for their success, not for their perseverance, and the acclaim conferred on them reaches the same divine plateau as in times past. At most, the traditional notion of heroism as success has been supplemented, not replaced, by the notion of heroism as persistence.

MYTH AND HISTORY

The connection between myth and history is blurry. To begin with, a traditional kind of hero might have lived but be credited with exaggerated deeds or attributes. A brave soldier might become fearless; a kindly soul might become saintly. Strength typically becomes omnipotence; knowledge becomes omniscience. Indeed, mere bravery, kindliness, strength, or knowledge would not suffice. Heroic qualities must be magnified to the point of divinity.

Yet the magnifications need not be taken at face value. Americans can want to believe that George Washington was utterly truthful without fully accepting it. Brits may want very much to think that Princess Diana was wholly selfless without quite accepting the claim. Heroism permits and even requires make-believe. It may be fashionable to assert that, in the wake of the contemporary exposé of public figures, no heroes remain, but in actuality celebrities have lost little of their glitter. They remain heroes not in the face of their flaws but in defiance of their flaws, which are discounted.

Heroes can be celebrated even when their historicity is doubted. Need Jesus have performed the miracles attributed to him for his life to remain a model for Christians? Need Oedipus have even lived for him to be a tragic hero not merely for ancient Greeks but also for twentieth-century Westerners?

Indisputably fictional figures like Sherlock Holmes and James Bond are still idolized and emulated. They can even supersede historical heroes exactly because they harbor no offscreen vices that must be overlooked. They are the personification of virtues. Ironically, fictional heroes are often treated as if real: "When Conan Doyle killed Holmes off in *The Final Solution*, some London businessmen took to wearing mourning bands while, in 1954, the BBC broadcasted a special programme in honour of Holmes' hundredth birthday, featuring interviews with his old school friends, teachers, etc."[16] Holmes and Bond hold the same status for adults as fairy-tale figures do for children. They "occupy the space" between illusion and reality, between subjectivity and objectivity, between the inner world and the outer. In the phrase coined by the psychoanalyst Donald Winnicott, they act as "transitional objects," linking the one domain to the other. The need for them is never outgrown: "It is assumed here that the task of reality-acceptance is never completed, that no human being is free from the strain of relating inner and outer reality, that the relief from this strain is provided by an intermediate area of experience ... which is not challenged (arts, religion, etc.). This intermediate area is in direct continuity with the play area of the small child who is 'lost' in play."[17]

Classicist Paul Veyne begins his *Did the Greeks Believe in Their Myths?*[18] as follows: "Did the Greeks believe in their mythology? The answer is difficult, for 'believe' means so many things. Not everyone believed that Minos, after his death, continued being a judge in Hell or that Theseus fought the Minotaur, and they knew that poets [i.e., the tellers of myths] 'lie.' However, ... in the minds of the Greeks, Theseus had, nonetheless, existed. ... As for Minos, Thucydides, at the cost of prodigious mental effort, uncovers the same core at the heart of this subject: 'Of all those we know by hearsay, Minos was the earliest to have a navy'" (*Did the Greeks Believe in Their Myths?*, p. 1). Veyne shows that few Greeks rejected altogether the historicity of hero myths.

Furthermore, during the ancient period the line between the historical and the mythical kept shifting. Early on, heroes were placed in a prior, sacred, "once upon a" time – a time distinct from the present, where heroes were no longer to be found. Later, the supernatural element was removed from heroes. But heroes they remained, and the removal of the supernatural served only to bolster their historicity. Consequently, Veyne states that in the whole period from the fifth century BC to the fourth century AD, "absolutely no one, Christians included, ever expressed the slightest doubt concerning the historicity of Aeneas, Romulus, Theseus, Heracles, Achilles, or even Dionysus; rather, everyone asserted this historicity" (*Did the Greeks Believe in Their Myths?*, p. 42).

Of those who insist on a clearcut divide between history and myth, the most resolute is the folklorist Lord Raglan. His proof that heroes are mythic is that they are not historical. Pitting the biographies of indisputably historical heroes like Alexander the Great and Napoleon against the biographies of "mythic" heroes like Thesesus and King Arthur, he argues that the kinds of events that occur in the lives of mythic heroes find no counterpart in the lives of historical ones, which serve as the control group against which to test disputed cases: "Another remarkable fact is that the hero of tradition [i.e., of myth] never wins a battle. It is very rarely that he is represented as having any companions at all, and when he has he never trains them or leads them. The warrior kings of history, whether civilized or barbarian, have won their renown as leaders. When we think of them we think of serried ranks, of the Argyraspides, of the Tenth Legion, of the Guard which dies but does not surrender, and the impis which think it better to go forward and die than to go back and die. But there is nothing like that in the stories of the heroes of tradition.... All his victories, when they are actual fights and not magical contests, are single combats against other kings, or against giants, dragons, or celebrated animals."[19] Raglan concludes either that mythic heroes never lived or, at the least, that they never did the deeds for which they are extolled.

But it is not really so easy to sift out the historical from the mythical. For example, the nineteenth-century quest for the historical Jesus foundered not only because it was hard to determine which purported deeds and teachings of his were historical but also because the Gospels are a mix of would-be history and myth. As the psychologist C. G. Jung puts it, "In the gospels themselves factual reports, legends, and myths are woven into a whole. This is precisely what constitutes the meaning of the gospels, and they would immediately lose their character of wholeness if one tried to separate the individual [i.e., the historical] from the archetypal [i.e., the mythic] with a critical scalpel."[20]

Historical events as well as persons can become mythicized. In a famous work written in 1907, the classicist F. M. Cornford argued that Thucydides, commonly deemed the first scientific, realistic, secular historian, actually wrote myth. The causes of the Peloponnesian War presented by Thucydides are not the decisions of Athenian and Spartan leaders, acting on the basis of self-interest, but Fate. The *History of the Peloponnesian War* should be read as an Aeschylean tragedy, with Athens itself the tragic hero. Thucydides is not merely a moralist, exposing the effect wreaked by the competing interests between city-states and within them, but a myth maker, presenting the consequences of superhuman Fate. Thucydides may pride himself, especially *vis-à-vis* Herodotus, on writing history, but he is really writing myth – or, better, history as myth. Hence the title of Cornford's book: *Thucydides Mythistoricus*.[21] Thucydides never escapes myth.

11

THEORIES OF HERO MYTHS

The distinctiveness of *theories* of hero myths is that, as theories, they claim to know the nature of *all* hero myths. Like theories of myth generally, theories of hero myths claim to answer the main questions about the myths: what is their origin, what is their function, and what is their subject matter?

The study of hero myths goes back at least to 1871, when the Victorian anthropologist Edward Tylor argued that many of them follow a uniform plot, or pattern: the hero is exposed at birth, is saved by other humans or animals, and grows up to become a national hero.[22] Tylor did not apply to hero myths his theory of myth per se. He sought only to establish a pattern for hero myths, not to determine their origin, function, or subject matter.

In 1876 the Austrian scholar Johann Georg von Hahn used fourteen cases to argue that all "Aryan" hero tales follow an "exposure and return" formula more comprehensive than Tylor's.[23] In each case the hero is born illegitimately, out of the fear of the prophecy of his future greatness is abandoned by his father, is saved by animals and raised by a lowly couple, fights wars, returns home triumphant, defeats his persecutors, frees his mother, becomes king, founds a city, and dies young. Though himself a solar mythologist, von Hahn, like Tylor, tried only to establish a pattern for hero myths.[24]

Similarly, in 1928 the Russian folklorist Vladimir Propp sought to demonstrate that Russian fairy tales follow a common biographical plot, in which the hero goes off on a successful adventure and upon his return marries and gains the throne.[25] Propp's pattern skirts both the birth and the death of the hero. While himself a Marxist, Propp here, in his earlier, formalist phase, attempted no more than von Hahn and Tylor: to establish a pattern for hero stories.

Of the scholars who have not only delineated patterns but also analyzed the origin, function, and subject matter of hero myths, by far the most important have been the Viennese psychoanalyst Otto Rank (1884–1939), the American mythographer Joseph Campbell (1904–87), and the English folklorist Lord Raglan (1885–1964). Rank later broke irreparably with Sigmund Freud, but when he wrote *The Myth of the Birth of the Hero* (1909), he was a Freudian apostle.[26] In fact, Freud himself wrote the section of the work on the "family romance."[27] While Campbell was never a full-fledged Jungian, he wrote *The Hero with a Thousand Faces* (1949) as a kindred soul of C. G. Jung.[28] Raglan wrote *The Hero* (1936) as a theoretical ally of James Frazer.[29]

12

Otto Rank

The title of Rank's monograph is at once misleading and prescient. It is misleading because Rank's Freudian emphasis is not on the hero's birth but on the hero's later, Oedipal relationship to his parents – a relationship rooted in childhood, not birth. The birth is decisive not because of the hero's separation from his mother but because of the parents' attempt to fend off at birth the prophesied parricidal consequences. The title is prescient because Rank came to reject the orthodox Freudian priority of the Oedipal stage over any other. Like Sandor Ferenczi, Géza Róheim, and Melanie Klein, Rank came to view birth rather than the Oedipus complex as the key trauma and therefore the key source of neurosis.[30] While Freud, at least as early as 1909, was prepared to grant that "the act of birth is the first experience of anxiety, and thus the source and prototype of the affect of anxiety,"[31] he was never prepared to make birth the prime, let alone sole, source of anxiety and neurosis.[32] Freud refused to subordinate the Oedipus complex, which focuses on the father, to the trauma of birth, which necessarily centers on the mother.

The Myth of the Birth of the Hero reflects early psychoanalytic theory. Contemporary Freudians, spurred by the development of ego psychology, regard myth far more positively than early Rank and Freud did. Myths are today taken as solving problems rather than perpetuating them, as progressive rather than regressive, and as abetting adjustment to the world rather than flight from it. Myths do not just serve to vent bottled-up drives; they also serve to sublimate them. Myths are as different from dreams as akin to them. Finally, myths serve everyone, not just neurotics.[33] Nevertheless, Rank's monograph remains the classic Freudian analysis of hero myths.

For Rank, following Freud, heroism deals with what Jungians call the first half of life. The first half – birth, childhood, adolescence, and young adulthood – involves the establishment of oneself as an independent person in the external world. The attainment of independence expresses itself concretely in the securing of a job and a mate. The securing of either requires both separation from one's parents and mastery of one's instincts. Independence of one's parents means not the rejection of them but self-sufficiency. Likewise independence of one's instincts means not the rejection of them but control over them: it means not the denial of instincts but the rerouting of them into socially acceptable outlets. When Freud says that the test of happiness is the capacity to work and love, he is clearly referring to the goals of the first half of life, which for him apply to all of life.

Neuroses involve a lingering attachment to parents and instincts. To depend on one's parents for the satisfaction of instincts and to satisfy instincts in anti-social ways is to be stuck, or fixated, at a childish level of psychological development.

Rank's pattern, which he applies to fifteen hero myths, is limited to the first half of life. Roughly paralleling von Hahn's pattern, of which he was apparently unaware, Rank's goes from the hero's birth to his attainment of a "career":

> The hero is the child of most distinguished parents, usually the son of a king. His origin is preceded by difficulties, such as continence, or prolonged barrenness, or secret intercourse of the parents due to external prohibition or obstacles. During or before the pregnancy, there is a prophecy, in the form of a dream or oracle, cautioning against his birth, and usually threatening danger to the father (or his representative). As a rule, he is surrendered to the water, in a box. He is then saved by animals, or by lowly people (shepherds), and is suckled by a female animal or by an humble woman. After he has grown up, he finds his distinguished parents, in a highly versatile fashion. He takes his revenge on his father, on the one hand, and is acknowledged, on the other. Finally he achieves rank and honors. (*The Myth of the Birth of the Hero*, p. 57)

Literally, or consciously, the hero, who is always male, is a historical or legendary figure like Oedipus. The hero is heroic because he rises from obscurity to the throne. Literally, he is an innocent victim of either his parents or, ultimately, fate. While his parents have yearned for a child and abandon him only to save the father, they nevertheless do abandon him. The hero's revenge, if the parricide is even committed knowingly, is, then, understandable: who would not consider killing one's would-be killer?

Symbolically, or unconsciously, the hero is heroic not because he dares to win a throne but because he dares to kill his father. The killing is definitely intentional, and the cause is not revenge but sexual frustration. The father has refused to surrender his wife – the real object of the son's efforts: "the deepest, generally unconscious root of the dislike of the son for the father, or of two brothers for each other, is related to be competition for the tender devotion and love of the mother" (*The Myth of the Birth of the Hero*, p. 66). Too horrendous to face, the true meaning of the hero myth is covered up by the concocted story. Rather than the culprit, the hero becomes an innocent victim or at worst a justified avenger: "The fictitious romance [i.e., the myth] is the excuse, as it were, for the hostile feelings which the child harbors against his father, and which in this fiction are projected against the father" (*The Myth of the Birth of the Hero*, p. 63). What the hero seeks is masked as power, not incest. Most of all, who the hero is becomes some third party, a historical or legendary figure, rather than either the creator of the myth or anyone stirred by it. Identifying himself with the literal hero, the myth maker or reader vicariously revels in the hero's triumph, which in fact is his own. *He* is the real hero of the myth.

Why the literal hero is usually the son of royalty, Rank never explains. Perhaps the filial clash thereby becomes even more titanic: it is over power as well as revenge. Indeed, when, as in Oedipus' case, the hero kills his father unknowingly, the conscious motive can hardly be revenge, so that ambition or something else non-Freudian is needed as an overt motive.

Literally, the myth culminates in the hero's attainment of a throne. Symbolically, the hero gains a mate as well. One might, then, conclude that the myth fittingly expresses the Freudian goal of the first half of life. In actuality, it expresses the opposite. The wish it fulfills is not for detachment from one's parents and from one's anti-social instincts but, on the contrary, for the most intense possible relationship to one's parents and the most anti-social of urges: parricide and incest, even rape. Taking one's father's job and one's mother's hand does not quite spell independence of them.

The myth maker or reader is an adult, but the wish vented by the myth is that of a child of three to five: "Myths are, therefore, created by adults, by means of retrograde childhood fantasies, the hero being credited with the mythmaker's personal infantile history" (*The Myth of the Birth of the Hero*, p. 71). The fantasy is the fulfillment of the Oedipal wish to kill one's father in order to gain access to one's mother. The myth fulfills a wish never outgrown by the adult who either invents or uses it. That adult is psychologically an eternal child. Having never developed an ego strong enough to master his instincts, he is neurotic: "There is a certain class of persons, the so-called psychoneurotics, shown by the teachings of Freud to have remained children, in a sense, although otherwise appearing grown-up" (*The Myth of the Birth of the Hero*, p. 58). Since no mere child can overpower his father, the myth maker imagines being old enough to do so. In short, the myth fulfills not the Freudian goal of the first half of life but the fixated childhood goal that keeps one from accomplishing it.

To be sure, the Oedipal wish is fulfilled in only a limited fashion. The fulfillment is symbolic rather than literal, disguised rather than overt, unconscious rather than conscious, vicarious rather than direct, and mental rather than physical. By identifying himself with the hero, the creator or reader of the myth acts out in his mind deeds that he would not dare act out in the real world. Still, the myth does provide fulfillment of a kind and, in light of the conflict between the neurotic's impulses and the neurotic's morals, provides the best possible fulfillment.

As brilliant as it is, Rank's theory can be criticized on multiple grounds. One can grant the pattern while denying the Freudian meaning, which, after all, reverses the manifest one. Or one can deny the pattern itself. Certainly the pattern fits only those hero myths, or the portions of them, that cover heroes in the first half of life. Excluded, for example, would be the bulk of the myths of Odysseus and Aeneas, who are largely adult heroes. Rank's own examples come from Europe, the Near East, and India, and his pattern may not fit heroes from elsewhere. Excluded altogether are female heroes and nonaristocratic male ones.[34]

Rank's pattern does not even fit all of his own examples. Moses, for example, is hardly the son of Pharaoh, does not kill or seek to kill Pharaoh, and does not succeed Pharaoh. Moses is the son of lowly rather than noble parents, is exposed by his parents to save rather than to kill him, and is saved by the daughter of Pharaoh.

Yet far from oblivious to these departures from his scheme, Rank, in defense, appeals both to nonbiblical versions of the Moses saga that come closer to his pattern and, still more, to aspects of the biblical account that hint at the pattern. He appeals most of all to Pharaoh's fear of the coming generation of Israelite males and the consequent attempt to have them killed at birth. The mighty Pharaoh's terror before mere newborns parallels that of the hero's father before his infant son.

Still, why is there any disparity between the Moses story itself and the pattern it supposedly typifies? Rank would say that it is for the same reason that there is a disparity between that pattern and the Freudian meaning it supposedly harbors: even the pattern, not just the meaning of it, bears too wrenching a truth for both the creator and the user of the myth to confront consciously. At the same time the Moses story is close enough for the pattern to hold. A skeptic might contend that in Moses' case and that of others the divide between the conscious and the unconscious meaning is so wide that no hero pattern lurks beneath at all.

JOSEPH CAMPBELL

Though commonly called one, Joseph Campbell was never a straightforward "Jungian." Campbell differs most with Jung over the origin and function of myth. Where for Jung the archetypal contents of myth arise out of the unconscious, only in some works of Campbell's do they do so. Even then, sometimes the unconscious for Campbell is, as for Freud, acquired rather than, as for Jung, inherited. Other times the contents of myth emerge from the imprint of either recurrent or traumatic experiences. In all of these cases, as for Jung, each society creates its own myths – whatever the source of the material it uses. Other times, however, Campbell, in blatant contrast to Jung, is a diffusionist: myths for him originate in one society and spread elsewhere.

Where for Jung myth functions to reveal the existence of the archetypes of the unconscious and to enable humans to encounter those archetypes, for Campbell myth serves additional functions as well. Campbell comes to declare repeatedly that myth serves four distinct functions: to instill and maintain a sense of awe and mystery before the world; to provide a symbolic image for the world such as that of the Great Chain of Being; to maintain the social order by giving divine justification to social practices like the Indian caste system; and above all to harmonize human beings with the cosmos, society, and the parts of themselves. Jung, ever seeking a balance between the internal and the external worlds, would doubtless applaud many of these functions for keeping humans anchored to the outer, everyday, conscious world, but he himself is more concerned with reconnecting humans to the inner, unconscious world, with which they have invariably lost contact.[35]

Despite these conspicuous differences, Campbell stands close to Jung and stands closest in *The Hero with a Thousand Faces*, which remains the classic Jungian analysis of hero myths. Campbell himself, to be sure, states that he became even more of a Jungian *after* writing *Hero*.[36] But he is likely basing this characterization of *Hero* on his reliance on the Freudian Géza Róheim, who himself, however, strays from Freudian orthodoxy in a manner that, as will be explained, Campbell adopts and carries still further toward Jung.

Where for Freud and Rank heroism is limited to the first half of life, for Jung it involves the second half even more. For Freud and Rank, heroism involves relations with parents and instincts. For Jung, heroism in even the first half involves, in addition, relations with the unconscious. Heroism here means separation not only from parents and anti-social instincts but even more from the unconscious: every child's managing to forge consciousness is for Jung a supremely heroic feat.

For Freud, the unconscious is the product of the repression of instincts. For Jung, it is inherited rather than created and includes far more than repressed instincts. Independence of the Jungian unconscious therefore means more than independence of instincts. It means the formation of consciousness, the object of which in the first half of life is the external world.

The goal of the uniquely Jungian second half of life is likewise consciousness, but now consciousness of the Jungian unconscious rather than of the external world. One must return to the unconscious, from which one has invariably become severed. But the aim is not thereby to sever one's ties to the external world. On the contrary, the aim is still to return to the external world. The ideal is a balance between consciousness of the external world and consciousness of the unconscious. The aim of the second half of life is to supplement, not abandon, the achievements of the first half.

Just as classic Freudian problems involve the failure to establish oneself in the outer world, in the form of working and loving, so distinctively Jungian problems involve the failure to reestablish oneself in the inner world, in relation to the unconscious. Freudian problems stem from excessive attachment to the world of childhood; Jungian problems, from excessive attachment to the world one enters upon breaking free of the childhood world: the external world. To be severed from the internal world is to feel empty and lost.

Jung himself allows for heroism in both halves of life, but Campbell does not.[37] Just as Rank confines heroism to the first half of life, so Campbell restricts it to the second half. Rank's scheme begins with the hero's birth; Campbell's, with the hero's adventure. Where Rank's scheme ends, Campbell's begins: with the adult hero ensconced at home. Rank's hero must be young enough for his father and in some cases even his grandfather still to be reigning. Campbell does not specify the age of his hero, but the hero must be no younger than the age at which Rank's hero myth therefore ends: young adulthood. While some of Campbell's own examples are of child heroes, they violate his scheme, according to which heroes must be willing to leave behind all that they have accomplished at home. Child heroes violate even more his Jungian meaning, according to which heroes must at the outset be fully developed egos ready to encounter the unconscious from which they have become severed. Campbell's heroes should, then, be in the second half of life. Campbell does acknowledge heroism in the first half of life and even cites Rank's monograph, but he demotes this youthful heroism to mere preparation for adult heroism. He calls it the "childhood of the human hero."[38]

Rank's heroes must be the sons of royal or at least distinguished parents. Campbell's need not be, though often they are. Where Rank's heroes must be male, Campbell's can be female as well, though Campbell inconsistently describes the hero's initiation from an exclusively male point of view.[39] Finally, Campbell's scheme dictates human heroes, even though many of his examples of heroes are divine. Rank's pattern, by contrast, allows for divine as well as human heroes.

Where Rank's hero returns to his birthplace, Campbell's marches forth to a strange, new world, which the hero has never visited or even known existed: "destiny has summoned the hero and transferred his spiritual center of gravity from within the pale of his society to a zone unknown. This fateful region of both treasure and danger may be variously represented: as a distant land, a forest, a kingdom underground, beneath the waves, or above the sky, a secret island, lofty mountaintop, or profound dream state" (*The Hero with a Thousand Faces*, p. 58). This extraordinary world is the world of the gods, and the hero must hail from the human world precisely to be awed by the divine one.

In this exotic, supernatural world the hero encounters above all a supreme female god and a supreme male god. The maternal goddess is loving and caring: "She is the paragon of all paragons of beauty, the reply to all desire, the bliss-bestowing goal of every hero's earthly and unearthly quest" (*The Hero with a Thousand Faces*, pp. 110–11). By contrast, the male god is tyrannical and merciless – an "ogre" (*The Hero with a Thousand Faces*, p. 126). The hero has sex with the goddess and marries her – the reason the hero must here be male. He competes with the male god and then kills him – the reason the hero must here be male. Yet with both gods, not just the goddess, he becomes mystically one and thereby becomes divine himself.

Where Rank's hero *returns* home to encounter his father and mother, Campbell's hero *leaves* home to encounter a male and a female god, who are neither his parents nor a couple. Yet the two heroes' encounters are remarkably akin: just as Rank's hero kills his father and, if usually only latently, marries his mother, so Campbell's hero, in reverse order, first marries the goddess and then kills the god. The differences, however, are even more significant. Because the goddess is not the hero's mother, sex with her does not constitute incest. Moreover, the two not only marry but also become mystically one.

Despite appearances, the hero's relationship to the male god is for Campbell no less positive and so no less non-Freudian. Seemingly, the relationship is blatantly Oedipal. Campbell even cites Róheim's analysis of aboriginal myths and rituals of initiation, which evince the son's fear of castration by his father and the father's prior fear of death at the hands of his son: "The native Australian mythologies teach that the first initiation rites were carried out in such a way that all the young men were killed. The ritual is thus shown to be, among other things, a dramatized expression of the Oedipal [counter-]aggression of the elder generation; and the circumcision, a mitigated castration. But the rites provide also for the cannibal, patricidal impulse of the younger, rising group of males" (*The Hero with a Thousand Faces*, p. 139).

Róheim, however, departs from a strictly Freudian interpretation.[40] The sons seek not sex with their mothers but *reunion* with them. They

19

seek to fulfill not their Oedipal desires but their even earlier, infantile ones. Their fathers oppose those desires not because they want to keep their wives for themselves but because they want to break their sons' prenatal ties to their mothers. If the fathers try to break those ties by threatening their sons with castration, they also try to break the ties by offering themselves as substitutes for their wives. The fathers selflessly nourish their sons with their own blood, occasionally dying in the process.

Campbell adopts Róheim's more harmonious interpretation of the clash between sons and fathers and carries it even further. Since Campbell's hero is in the second half of life, he is not, like Róheim's initiates, seeking separation from his mother – for Róheim, as for the renegade Rank, the central experience of life. He is seeking reintegration with her. Furthermore, he is seeking reintegration with his father as well. Indeed, he is not really fighting with his father over his mother. For again, the two gods are neither his parents nor a couple. The hero is seeking from the god the same love that he has just won from the goddess. To secure it he need not give up the goddess but need only trust in the god, who is symbolized by the father: "One must have a faith that the father is merciful, and then a reliance on that mercy" (*The Hero with a Thousand Faces*, p. 130). The father sacrifices himself to his son.

When Campbell says that initiation rituals and myths "reveal the benign self-giving aspect of the *archetypal* father," he is using the term in its Jungian sense (*The Hero with a Thousand Faces*, pp. 139–40). For Freudians, gods symbolize parents. For Jungians, parents symbolize gods, who in turn symbolize father and mother archetypes, which are components of the hero's unconscious personality. The hero's relationship to these gods symbolizes not, as for Freud, Rank, and Róheim, a son's relationship to other persons – his parents – but the relationship of one side of a male's personality – his ego – to another side – his unconscious. The father and the mother are but two of the archetypes of which the Jungian, or collective, unconscious is composed. Archetypes are unconscious not because they have been repressed but because they have never been conscious. For Jung and Campbell, myth originates and functions not, as for Freud and Rank, to satisfy neurotic urges that cannot be manifested openly but to express normal sides of the personality that have not yet had a chance at realization.

By identifying himself with the hero of a myth, Rank's myth maker or reader vicariously lives out in his mind an adventure that, if ever directly fulfilled, would be acted out on his parents themselves. While also identifying himself – or herself – with the hero of a myth, Campbell's myth maker or reader vicariously lives out in the mind an adventure that even when directly fulfilled would still be taking place in the mind. For parts of the unconscious are what the myth maker or reader is really encountering.

Having managed to break free of the secure, everyday world and go off to a dangerous new one, Campbell's hero, to complete the journey, must in turn break free of the new world, in which the hero has by now become ensconced, and return to the everyday one. So enticing is the new world that leaving it proves harder than leaving home ever was. The Lotus Eaters, Circe, and the Sirens thus tempt Odysseus with a blissful, carefree life, and Calypso tempts him with immortality.

Though often misconstrued, Jung no less than Freud opposes a state of sheer unconsciousness. Both strive to make the unconscious conscious. While they differ over the origin of the unconscious and over its capacity to become conscious, the ideal for both remains consciousness. Jung opposes the rejection of ordinary, or ego, consciousness for unconsciousness as vigorously as he opposes the rejection of unconsciousness for ego consciousness. He seeks a balance between ego consciousness and the unconscious, between consciousness of the external world and consciousness of the unconscious. For Jung, the hero's failure to return to the everyday world would spell his failure to resist the allure of the unconscious.

By contrast to Jung, Campbell seeks a state of pure unconsciousness. Campbell's hero never returns to the everyday world but instead surrenders to the unconscious. Yet Campbell himself demands the hero's return to the everyday world, so how can his hero really be spurning it? The answer is that the world to which Campbell's hero returns is not really the everyday world. It is the strange, new world, which turns out to pervade the everyday one. No separate everyday world exists. The everyday world and the new world are really one: "The two worlds, the divine [i.e., new] and the human [i.e., everyday], can be pictured only as distinct from each other – different as life and death, as day and night.... Nevertheless – and here is a great key to the understanding of myth and symbol – the two kingdoms are actually one. The realm of the gods is a forgotten dimension of the world we know.... The values and distinctions that in normal life seem important disappear with the terrifying assimilation of [what is now] the self into what formerly was [to the ego] only otherness" (*The Hero with a Thousand Faces*, p. 217). The hero need never have left home after all: "Hence separateness, withdrawal, is no longer necessary. Wherever the hero may wander, whatever he may do, he is ever in the presence of his own essence – for he has the perfected eye to see. There is no separateness" (*The Hero with a Thousand Faces*, p. 386).

To say that the everyday world and the new world are one is to say that no distinctive everyday world exists. Campbell thus dismisses as illusory the "values and distinctions" of the everyday world. If no everyday world exists, then the hero's apparent return to it is a sham. If no everyday world exists, then the ego, which provides consciousness of it, is itself a sham as well. Strictly, Campbell is not reducing the everyday world to the new one. He is identifying the two. Even so, no separate everyday world remains.

By contrast to Campbell, Jung never denies the existence of the everyday world and therefore of the ego. He rejects the everyday world, the object of ego consciousness, as the *sole* reality, not as *a* reality. While he seeks to integrate the everyday world with the new one, ego consciousness with the unconscious, he denies that it is possible to fuse them. Any attempt to do so would result in the dissolution of both the everyday world and the ego itself.

Campbell's hero returns home only to save others: "The full round, the norm of the monomyth, requires that the hero shall now begin the labor of bringing the runes of wisdom, the Golden Fleece, or his sleeping princess, back into the kingdom of humanity, where the boon may redound to the renewing of the community, the nation, the planet, or the ten thousand worlds" (*The Hero with a Thousand Faces*, p. 193). Whatever the literal "boon," the symbolic one brought back by the hero is knowledge of the status of the everyday world. The hero is a seer.

Like Rank's theory, Campbell's can be faulted on various grounds. As with Rank's theory, one might grant the pattern but deny the meaning. Or one might question the pattern itself. Since it obviously applies only to myths about heroes in the second half of life, it excludes all of Rank's hero myths, or at least all of Rank's portions of them. And, as noted, it partly excludes female heroes. Whether the pattern even fits Campbell's own examples it is not easy to tell, for Campbell, unlike either Rank or Raglan, provides no set of hero myths to accompany the whole of his pattern. While he continually cites scores of hero myths to illustrate individual parts of his pattern, he does not apply his full pattern to even one myth.

One might question even so seemingly transparent a confirmation of Campbell's pattern as the myth of Aeneas, which Campbell names as an example of his pattern (see *The Hero with a Thousand Faces*, p. 30). Aeneas' descent to Hades and return does fit Campbell's scheme snugly, but Aeneas' larger itinerary does not. Rather than returning home to Troy upon completion of his journey, he proceeds to Italy to found a new civilization. Similarly, Odysseus' descent to the underworld fits Campbell's pattern, but his larger journey, which Campbell cites (see *The Hero with a Thousand Faces*, p. 58), does not. Odysseus, unlike Aeneas, does return home, but also unlike Aeneas, he arrives with no boon in hand. His return is an entirely personal triumph. Since Campbell distinguishes a myth from a fairy tale on exactly the grounds that the triumph of a mythic hero is more than personal (see *The Hero with a Thousand Faces*, pp. 37–8), Odysseus' story would thereby fail to qualify as a myth.[41]

LORD RAGLAN

Neither Rank nor Campbell focuses on the relationship between myth and ritual. Campbell would doubtless assume that every ritual has an accompanying myth, but neither he nor Rank assumes that every myth has an accompanying ritual. It is Lord Raglan who ties hero myths to rituals. He is a "myth-ritualist."[42]

Raglan's brand of myth-ritualism derives ultimately from the anthropologist James Frazer and the biblicist S. H. Hooke: myth provides the script for ritual. The specific ritual involves the king, but Frazer and, following him, Hooke in fact conflate two forms of the ritual.[43] In one form the king is a mere human being and simply plays the role of the god. The dramatic enactment of the death and rebirth of the god, who is the god of vegetation, magically causes the rebirth of the presently dead god and in turn of the presently dead vegetation. The ritual is performed annually at the end – the would-be end – of winter. In the other form of the ritual the king is himself divine – with the god of vegetation residing in him – and is actually killed and replaced. The soul of the god is thereby transferred to the new king. The killing of the king does not magically induce the killing of the god but instead simply preserves the health of the god, for the king is killed at the first sign of weakness or at the end of a fixed term so short as to minimize the chance of illness or death in office. The state of the king determines the state of the god of vegetation and in turn the state of vegetation.

Raglan adopts this second version of the ritual.[44] He attributes it to Hooke rather than to Frazer, but Hooke himself takes it from Frazer. Here the king *is* the god of vegetation rather than plays the part of the god. Consequently, the killing and replacement of the king, which initially is literal but later merely symbolic, does not magically cause the death and rebirth of the god but *is* the death and rebirth – better, the weakening and reinvigoration – of that god and therefore of vegetation.[45] For Raglan, as for Frazer and Hooke, the myth describes the life of the figure and the ritual enacts it. The function of the ritual, which is performed either at the end of the king's fixed term or upon his weakening, is, as for Frazer and Hooke, to aid the community. Besides the fertility of the earth, that aid can take the form of success in war, good health, or human fertility.

23

Venturing beyond both Frazer and Hooke, Raglan equates the king with the hero. For Frazer and Hooke, the king may in effect be a hero to his community, but only Raglan labels him one. It is Raglan who turns a theory of myth in general into a theory of hero myths in particular. Moreover, Raglan introduces his own detailed hero pattern, which he applies to twenty-one myths. That pattern extends all the way from the hero's conception to his death. In contrast to Rank's and Campbell's patterns, it therefore covers both halves of life:

1   The hero's mother is a royal virgin;
2   His father is a king, and
3   Often a near relative of his mother, but
4   The circumstances of his conception are unusual, and
5   He is also reputed to be the son of a god.
6   At birth an attempt is made, usually by his father or his maternal grandfather, to kill him, but
7   He is spirited away, and
8   Reared by foster-parents in a far country.
9   We are told nothing of his childhood, but
10   On reaching manhood he returns or goes to his future kingdom.
11   After a victory over the king and/or a giant, dragon, or wild beast,
12   He marries a princess, often the daughter of his predecessor, and
13   Becomes king.
14   For a time he reigns uneventfully, and
15   Prescribes laws, but
16   Later he loses favour with the gods and/or his subjects, and
17   Is driven from the throne and city, after which
18   He meets with a mysterious death,
19   Often at the top of a hill.
20   His children, if any, do not succeed him.
21   His body is not buried, but nevertheless
22   He has one or more holy sepulchres. (*The Hero*, p. 138)

Clearly, parts one to thirteen correspond roughly to Rank's entire scheme, though Raglan himself never read Rank.[46] Six of Raglan's cases duplicate Rank's, and the anti-Freudian Raglan nevertheless also takes the case of Oedipus as his standard.[47] The victory that gives the hero the throne is not, however, Oedipal, for the vanquished is not necessarily his father, even if, as for Rank, the father is usually the one who had sought his son's death at birth. Parts fourteen to twenty-two do not correspond at all to Campbell's scheme. The hero's exile is loosely akin to the hero's journey, but for Raglan there is no return. The hero's sepulchres do serve

24

as a kind of boon, but not for his native community. For Rank, the heart of the hero pattern is gaining kingship – or other title. For Raglan, the heart is losing kingship. Wherever Campbell's heroes are kings, the heart is their journey while king.

Rank's hero triumphs at the expense of everyone else; Lord Raglan's, like Campbell's, saves everyone else. Campbell's saving hero does not die; Raglan's must. Campbell's hero undertakes a dangerous journey to aid the community; Raglan's hero in the myth is driven from the community and, in the accompanying ritual, is sacrificed by the community. Campbell's hero can be any adult; Raglan's must be not only a male[48] but also a king. Campbell's hero must – or should – be human; Raglan's can be either divine or human.

For all Raglan's touting of the symbiosis of myth and ritual, his myth and ritual seem incongruously out of sync with each other. In the myth the protagonist is usually human. In the ritual the protagonist is always divine. The myth runs from the birth of the protagonist to his mysterious death. The ritual enacts only the portion of the myth that corresponds to the replacement of the king: the exile of the incumbent. Raglan nevertheless equates the hero of the myth with the god of the ritual: "The conclusion that suggests itself is that the god is the hero as he appears in ritual, and the hero is the god as he appears in myth; in other words, the hero and the god are two different aspects of the same superhuman being" (*The Hero*, p. 162). But how can a god lose power, let alone die? Raglan's answer is that it is the hero, not the god, who loses power and then dies – even though the hero and the god are identical!

Still, how can the myth that purportedly provides the script for the ritual be so at odds with it? Raglan's rejoinder is that the myth and the ritual are not so far apart. In both, the central figure is the king. Moreover, many of the events in the life of the hero are supernatural, so that the hero must in fact be a god himself. Above all, what Raglan considers the core of the myth – the toppling of the king – corresponds to the undeniable core of the ritual – the killing of the king when he either weakens or finishes his term. Strictly, the myth, which describes the life of a past hero, is less the script than the inspiration for the ritual, which involves the killing of the present king. The myth is intended to spur the king to submit to the ritual and thereby be a hero to his subjects.

Whether as the influence of Frazer and Hooke or as a reflection of his own nobility, Raglan is preoccupied with kingship. For him, kingship ties the hero to the god: heroes are kings, and kings are gods. True, the hero must die and must therefore be literally a mere mortal, but the hero's death accomplishes a superhuman feat: it ensures the revival of vegetation and thereby the survival of the kingdom. Raglan's heroes have the power to affect the physical world, even if only by dying. They are the saviors of their subjects.

For Rank, heroes are heroic because they dare to serve themselves. For both Campbell and Raglan, heroes are heroic because they willingly or unwillingly serve their communities. For Raglan, heroes in myth serve their communities by their victories over those who threaten their peoples' physical welfare. Hence Oedipus defeats the Sphinx, who is starving Thebes. Heroes in ritual serve their communities by their sacrificial deaths. In both myths and rituals, heroes are really ideal kings. For Campbell, heroes in myth serve their communities by their return home with a boon, typically secured only by defeating or at least taming supernatural entities. Where the boon bestowed by Raglan's hero is entirely material, that bestowed by Campbell's is wisdom. Without Raglan's hero the community would die; without Campbell's, it would remain benighted.

Like Rank's and Campbell's theories, Raglan's can be questioned on various counts. One might grant the mythic pattern but deny a connection to ritual. Or one might grant some connection but deny that, in the light of the disparity between the myth and the ritual, the connection takes Raglan's form. Or one might deny the pattern itself – denying either that it applies worldwide[49] or that it even applies substantially to Raglan's own cases. By Raglan's own tally, none of his examples scores all twenty-two points, and one scores only nine. What of hero myths in which the hero, rather than seeking or becoming king, remains the outsider in conflict with the established king – for example, the conflict in the *Iliad* between Achilles and Agamemnon?[50] Rank can at least assert that hero myths which stray from his scheme are distortions created to keep the true pattern hidden. Raglan can use no comparable ploy: there is nothing in his pattern to be kept a secret. Why, then, one might ask, do not any of his hero myths, if not all hero myths, attain perfect scores?[51]

RENÉ GIRARD

In *Violence and the Sacred* (1972) and many subsequent works, the contemporary French literary critic René Girard offers a twist to the theory of Raglan, himself never cited by Girard.[52] Where Raglan's hero is heroic because he is willing to die for the sake of the community, Girard's hero is killed or exiled for having caused the present ills of the community. Indeed, the "hero" is initially considered a criminal who deserves to die. Only subsequently is the villain turned into a hero, who, as for Raglan, dies selflessly on behalf of the community. For

Girard, the transformation of Oedipus from reviled exile in Sophocles' *Oedipus the King* to revered benefactor in Sophocles' *Oedipus at Colonus* evinces the transformation of an outcast into a saint.

The change from criminal to hero is for Girard only the second half of the process. Originally, violence erupts in the community. The cause is the inclination, innate in human nature, to imitate others and thereby to desire the same objects as those of the imitated. Imitation leads to rivalry, which leads to violence. Desperate to end the violence, the community selects an innocent member to blame for the turmoil. This "scapegoat," who is usually killed, can range from the most helpless member of society to the most elevated, including the king or queen. Where for Raglan myth directs or inspires the killing of the hero, for Girard myth is created after the killing to hide it. The myth first turns the scapegoat into a criminal who deserved to die but then turns the criminal into a hero, who has died willingly for the good of the community. The scapegoat can even become a criminal and a hero simultaneously. For the figure blamed for the turmoil is also credited with ending it, albeit by death or exile. But the criminal can also become even more of a hero thereafter.

Like both Rank and Raglan, Girard cites the case of Oedipus as a grand example of his theory. Far from causing the plague besetting Thebes during his reign as King, Oedipus, according to Girard, is in fact an innocent victim. Either there never was a plague, or the plague was not the cause of the upheaval. Alternatively, the plague is a metaphor for violence, which has spread across society like a contagion. The violence among Thebans is evinced in the tension among the principals of Sophocles' play: Oedipus, Creon, and Teiresias. The only way to end the violence and thereby preserve society is by making a scapegoat of a vulnerable member of society. Even though he is a reigning king, Oedipus is doubly stigmatized and thereby doubly vulnerable. First, he is an outsider: he is not yet known to be a Theban and has won the throne not by heredity but by the toppling of the Sphinx. Second, he is a cripple – the result of the piercing of his tendons at birth. The myth, created after the events, serves to absolve the community of responsibility for Oedipus' downfall by blaming Oedipus. He has killed his father and married his mother, and it is for his parricide and his incest that Thebes now endures plague. Oedipus deserves to be punished, and his punishment is not even death but mere exile. Myth as a cover up for the truth echoes the Freudian Rank.

For Girard, the cause of the travail is not parricide or incest but violence. Sophocles' Teiresias thus cites the parricide and the incest only as an excuse to make Oedipus the scapegoat: "If we take Tiresias's reply literally, the terrible charges of patricide and incest that he he has just leveled at Oedipus did not stem from any supernatural source of information [and so do not represent the 'truth']. The accusation is simply an act of reprisal arising from the hostile exchange of a tragic debate. Oedipus unintentionally initiates the process by forcing Tiresias to speak. He accuses Tiresias of having had a part in the murder of [Oedipus' father] Laius; he prods Tiresias into reprisal, into hurling the accusation back at him.... [For each] to accuse the other of Laius's murder is to attribute to him sole responsibility for the sacrificial crisis; but as we have seen, everybody shares equal responsibility, because everybody participates in the destruction of a cultural order" (*Violence and the Sacred*, p. 71). The Thebans decide to accept Teiresias' and Creon's views rather than Oedipus' on responsibility for the breakdown in society, and the myth then turns their opinions into the truth: "The Thebans – religious believers – sought a cure for their ills in a formal acceptance of the myth, in making it the indisputable version of the events that had recently convulsed the city and in making it the charter for a new cultural order – by convincing themselves, in short, that all their miseries were due exclusively to the plague. Such an attitude requires absolute faith in the guilt of the surrogate victim" (*Violence and the Sacred*, p. 83).

That Oedipus is not the cause of the problem and that the problem is not the plague are borne out by subsequent events. True, the plague ends, but it is soon followed by a fight for the throne among Creon, Oedipus' son Polyneices, and his other son, Eteocles. Read carefully, Sophocles challenges the myth, but never explicitly, so that the play can be taken, as it has regularly been taken, as the dramatized version of the myth rather than as, for Girard, a challenge to the myth. For Girard, the play undermines the myth in the course of presenting it.

But Sophocles' presentation of the myth, which continues with *Oedipus at Colonus*, does more than blame Oedipus for Theban woes. It proceeds to turn him into a hero. Even as king, Oedipus is heroic in deeming it his duty to end the plague that has befallen his subjects, in vowing to discover who the culprit is, and in insisting on being banished once he discovers that he himself is the culprit. Yet for Girard it is not the fallen, self-sacrificing Oedipus, as for Raglan, but the elevated one who is the real hero. Even as culprit, Oedipus has the power to save Thebes: just as his presence caused the plague, so his departure ends it. He is a hero even while a criminal. He already has the divine-like power both to bring plague and to end it. But by the time of *Oedipus at Colonus* his stature has grown. Having arrived, after years of wandering, at Colonus, near Athens, he is now beckoned to return to Thebes. Just as the welfare of Thebes once depended on Oedipus' exile, so now it depends on his return. Oedipus refuses, for we learn that Oedipus had wanted to remain at Thebes following the events in *Oedipus the King* but had been forcibly exiled by Creon and others. Now Creon is prepared to seize him and bring him back to Thebes. King Theseus offers Oedipus asylum and protection. In return, Oedipus declares that his burial spot in Athens will protect Athens against Thebes. In short, Oedipus, having in *Oedipus The King* begun as an almost divine King of Thebes, in *Oedipus at Colonus* ends as the would-be benefactor of Thebes and as almost the divine benefactor of Athens. Where for Raglan the figure killed is, as king, simultaneously a hero and a god, and is both from the start, for Girard the king is first a scapegoat – contrary to the myth – and only then a criminal and only thereafter a hero and a virtual god.

While Girard never cites Raglan, he does regularly cite Frazer, praising him for recognizing the key primitive ritual of sacrificing the king but berating him for missing the real reason for the sacrifice. Frazer, according to Girard, makes sacrifice the innocent application of a benighted, pre-scientific explanation of the world: the king is killed and replaced so that the soul of the god of vegetation, who resides in the incumbent, will stay healthy. The function of the sacrifice is wholly agricultural. There is no hatred of the victim, who simply fulfills his duty as king and is celebrated for so doing at the time of his death. Girard notes that Frazer's disciples, notably the Cambridge Ritualists (Jane Harrison, Gilbert Murray, and F. M. Cornford), link the ritual, deemed historical, to myth and in turn to tragedy, but he faults them for domesticating the link: for the Ritualists, the myth merely describes, not covers up, the deed, and the tragedy merely dramatizes, not uncovers, the deed. Indeed, tragedy turns the deed into mere metaphor: "The connection between the drama and the major mythological themes is undeniable, but in order to grasp its full significance we must transcend the approach that limits itself to thematic analysis and renounce those prejudices that might lead us to portray the 'scapegoat' purely as a product of blind superstition, a nonfunctional device bereft of any operative value" (*Violence and the Sacred*, p. 96).[53] The Ritualists use the version of Frazer's myth-ritualism in which the king is not killed but merely plays the part of the dead (not necessarily killed) god of vegetation. Girard, unaware of the differing versions of Frazer's scheme, clearly has in mind the other version, in which the king is outright killed, for the sacrifice of the king is what spurs Girard's attack on Frazer.[54]

ACKNOWLEDGMENT

For their helpful comments on the Introduction, I want to thank Steven Walker and Dean Miller. An earlier version of pp. 12–26 appeared as the introduction to

Otto Rank, Lord Raglan, and Alan Dundes, *In Quest of the Hero* (Princeton: Princeton University Press, 1990), vii–xli, and is reprinted here with permission.

NOTES

1 Thomas Carlyle, *On Heroes, Hero-Worship, and the Heroic in History*, Centenary Edition of the Works of Thomas Carlyle, ed. Henry Duff Traill, vol. 5 (London: Chapman and Hall, 1897 [1841]).

2 Thomas Carlyle, *The French Revolution*, 2 vols. (1857 edn.) in 1 (Oxford: Oxford University Press, 1989 [1837]).

3 For this corrective of the stereotypical view of Carlyle, see Philip Rosenberg, *The Seventh Hero* (Cambridge, MA: Harvard University Press, 1974), 188–93; Michael K. Goldberg, introduction to Carlyle, *On Heroes, Hero-Worship, and the Heroic in History*, Strouse Edition of the Writings of Thomas Carlyle (Berkeley: University of California Press, 1993), lviii–lx.

4 Carlyle's concern with outward accomplishment sharply distinguishes his conception of heroism from that of Friedrich Nietzsche. The achievement of Nietzsche's *übermensch*, or "overman," is personal, not societal. Rather than praising the *übermensch* for changing his society, Nietzsche praises the society that produces him. See Nietzsche, *Thus Spoke Zarathustra*, tr. Walter Kaufmann (New York: Viking Press, 1966 [1954]), esp. pt. 1.

5 See Walter E. Hougton, *The Victorian Frame of Mind 1830–1870* (New Haven: Yale University Press, 1957), ch. 12.

6 See Herbert Spencer, *The Study of Sociology* (New York: Appleton, 1874 [1873]), esp. 30–37; "The Social Organism" (1860), reprinted in his *Essays: Scientific, Political, and Speculative*, vol. I (London: Williams and Norgate, 1883 [1857]), esp. 388–92.

7 G. W. F. Hegel, *The Philosophy of History* (1837), Introduction, reprinted as *Reason in History*, tr. Robert S. Hartman, Liberal of Liberal Arts (Indiana-polis: Bobbs-Merrill, 1953), 39–40. On the compatibility of great men with laws of history, which means the compatibility of free will with laws of social progress, see, classically, John Stuart Mill, *A System of Logic*, 8th edn. (1872, 1st edn. 1843), Bk. VI, ch. 11, sections 3–4, reprinted in Mill, *The Logic of the Moral Sciences* (LaSalle, IL: Open Court, 1988), 126–33.

8 For the classic twentieth-century critique of heroism, see Eric Bentley, *A Century of Hero-Worship*, 2nd edn. (Boston: Beacon, 1957 [1944]). Bentley attacks what he calls "heroic vitalism" for its anti-democratic outlook. For a standard attack on Carlyle for promoting fascism, see also H. J. C. Grierson, *Carlyle and Hitler* (Cambridge: Cambridge University Press, 1933). For a standard defense of Carlyle against the charge, see Ernst Cassirer, *The Myth of the State* (New Haven: Yale University Press, 1946), 190–1, 216–23. On the association of Carlyle with leftwing as well as rightwing political senti-ments, see Goldberg, lxv–lxxxvi.

9 Sidney Hook, *The Hero in History* (Boston: Beacon Press, 1955 [1943]).

10 According to this distinction, myths take place in a primordial past and describe the creation of the physical world by gods, animals, or "culture heroes." Legends take place in a less distant past, within the present physical world, and "tell of migrations, wars and victories, deeds of past heroes, chiefs, and kings, and succession in ruling dynasties" (William Bascom, "The Forms of Folkore: Prose Narratives," *Journal of American Folklore* 78 [1965], 4). See also Alan Dundes, "On the Psychology of Legend," in his *Analytic Essays in Folklore*, Studies in Folklore, no. 2 (The Hague: Mouton, 1975), 164–5.

11 See Lewis Richard Farnell, *Greek Hero Cults and Ideas of Immortality* (Oxford: Clarendon, 1921); Jennifer Larson, *Greek Heroine Cults* (Madison: University of Wisconsin Press, 1995).

12 On the changing conceptions of Jesus, see Jaroslav Pelikan, *Jesus through the Centuries* (New Haven: Yale University Press, 1985), and, classically, Albert Schweitzer, *The Quest of the Historical Jesus*, tr. William Montgomery (New York: Macmillan, 1961 [1910]).

13 By contrast, classicist Cedric H. Whitman, limiting himself to ancient Greek heroes, maintains that they embodied "the heroic paradox" of seeking divinity, specifically immortality, yet accepting their human mortality: "to return to the motivation of the heroic: we mentioned as one element the urge toward divinity, a kind of wish to be a god or to be godlike.... On the other hand, there is also a passionate knowledge, a desperate self-knowledge, among all these heroes, that they are mortal and that they are destined to die" (*The Heroic Paradox*, ed. Charles Segal [Ithaca: Cornell University Press, 1982], 21–2).

14 G. Karl Galinsky, *The Herakles Theme* (Oxford: Blackwell, 1972), 1–2.

15 On the romantic hero, see, for example, Walter L. Reed, *Meditations on the Hero* (New Haven: Yale University Press, 1974). On the bourgeois hero, see Raymond Giraud, *The Unheroic Hero in the Novels of Stendahl, Balzac and Flaubert* (New York: Octagon Books, 1979 [1957]). On the ordinary person as hero, see Arthur Miller, "Tragedy and the Common Man," *New York Times*, February 27, 1949, II, 1, 3; reprinted, among other places, in *Arthur Miller, Death of a Salesman: Text and Criticism*, ed. Gerald Weales, Viking Critical Library (New York: Viking, 1967), 143–7. On the comic hero, see Stan Smith, *A Sadly Contracted Hero*, BAAS Pamphlets in American Studies, no. 5 (South Shields: British Association for American Studies, 1981). On the schlemeil as hero, see Ruth R. Wisse, *The Schlemiel as Modern Hero* (Chicago: University of Chicago Press, 1971). On the absurd hero, see, for example, David D. Galloway, *The Absurd Hero in American Fiction*, rev. edn. (Austin: University of Texas Press, 1970 [1966]). On the difficulty of heroism in the modern world, see, for example, Harry Levin, "From Priam to Birotteau," *Yale French Studies* 6 (1950), 75–82; Sean O'Faolain, *The Vanishing Hero* (London: Eyre & Spottiswoode, 1956). In response, see Edith Kern, "The Modern Hero: Phoenix or Ashes?" *Comparative Literature* 10 (1958), 325–34.

16   Tony Bennett and Janet Woollacott, *Bond and Beyond* (Basingstoke: Macmillan Education, 1987), 14.

17   D. W. Winnicott, "Transitional Objects and Transitional Phenomena" (1953), reprinted in his *Playing and Reality* (London and New York: Routledge, 1991 [1971]), 13. For a broader analysis of play, which, rather than segregating play from reality, seeks the "play element" in culture, including myth, see Johan Huizinga's classic, *Homo Ludens*, tr. not given (London: Routledge & Kegan Paul, 1949), esp. chs. 7–8.

18   See Paul Veyne, *Did the Greeks Believe in Their Myths?*, tr. Paula Wissing (Chicago: University of Chicago Press, 1988).

19   Lord Raglan, *The Hero* (London: Methuen, 1936), 194.

20   C. G. Jung, "Psychology and Religion," in *Psychology and Religion: West and East, The Collected Works of C. G. Jung*, eds. Sir Herbert Read et al., trs. R. F. C. Hull et al., vol. XI, 2nd edn. (Princeton: Princeton University Press, 1969 [1958]), 88.

21   F. M. Cornford, *Thucydides Mythistoricus* (London: Arnold, 1907).

22   See E. B. Tylor, *Primitive Culture*, 1st edn. (London: Murray, 1871), vol. I, 254–5. In an earlier essay Tylor amasses stories of children raised by beasts, but only in passing does he connect them to myths of future heroes: see "Wild Men and Beast-Children," *Anthropological Review* 1 (1863), 21–32. For a superb overview of the history of hero patterns, beginning with Tylor's, see Alan Dundes, *The Hero Pattern and the Life of Jesus* (Berkeley: The Center for Hermeneutical Studies in Hellenistic and Modern Culture, 1977); reprinted in Dundes, *Interpreting Folklore* (Bloomington: Indiana University Press, 1980), 223–61; reprinted in Otto Rank, Lord Raglan, and Alan Dundes, *In Quest of the Hero* (Princeton: Princeton University Press, 1990), 179–223. Citations are to the reprint in *In Quest of the Hero*.

23   See Johann Georg von Hahn, *Sagwissenschaftliche Studien* (Jena: Mauke, 1876), 340. Tr. Henry Wilson in John C. Dunlop, *History of Prose Fiction*, rev. Wilson (London: Bell, 1888), in an unnumbered attachment to the last page of vol. I.

24   For an application of von Hahn's otherwise neglected pattern, see Alfred Nutt, "The Aryan Expulsion-and-Return-Formula in the Folk and Hero Tales of the Celts," *Folk-lore Record* 4 (1881), 1–44.

25   See Vladimir Propp, *Morphology of the Folktale*, tr. Laurence Scott, 2nd edn., rev. and ed. Louis A. Wagner, Publications of the American Folklore Society Bibliographical and Special Series, vol. IX; Indiana University Research Center in Anthropology, Folklore, and Linguistics Publication 10 (Austin: University of Texas Press, 1968 [1958]).

26   Otto Rank, *The Myth of the Birth of the Hero*, 1st edn., trs. F. Robbins and Smith Ely Jelliffe, Nervous and Mental Disease Monograph Series, no. 18 (New York: Journal of Nervous and Mental Disease Publishing, 1914); reprinted (New York: Brunner, 1952); reprinted in Rank, *The Myth of the Birth of the Hero and Other Writings*, ed. Philip Freund (New York: Vintage Books, 1959), 3–96; reprinted in Rank et al., *In Quest of the Hero*, 3–86.

Citations are to the reprint in *In Quest of the Hero*. The second, enlarged, 1922 edition of *Der Mythus von der Geburt des Helden* has never been translated into English.

27 See Rank, *The Myth of the Birth of the Hero*, 59–62; Sigmund Freud, "Family Romances" (1909), in *The Standard Edition of the Complete Psychological Works of Sigmund Freud*, trs. James Strachey et al., vol. IX (London: Hogarth, 1959), 237–41.

28 Joseph Campbell, *The Hero with a Thousand Faces* (New York: Pantheon Books, 1949); 2nd edn. (Princeton: Princeton University Press, 1972); reprinted Mythos Series (Princeton: Princeton University Press, 1990). Citations are to the second edition.

29 Lord Raglan, *The Hero* (London: Methuen, 1936); reprinted (London: Watts, 1949); reprinted (New York: Vintage Books, 1956); reprinted (New York: Meridian Books, 1979). Part 2, which is on myth, is reprinted in Rank et al., *In Quest of the Hero*, 89–175. Citations are to the reprint in *In Quest of the Hero*. Chs. 16–17 of *The Hero* were originally published, with minor differences, as "The Hero of Tradition," *Folk-Lore* 45 (1934), 212–31.

30 See Otto Rank, *The Trauma of Birth*, tr. not given (London: Kegan Paul; New York: Harcourt, Brace, 1929).

31 Sigmund Freud, *The Interpretation of Dreams*, tr. James Strachey (New York: Avon Books, 1965 [1953]), 436 n. 2.

32 For Freud's view of the significance of birth in the wake of the break with Rank, see his *The Problem of Anxiety*, tr. Henry Alden Bunker (New York: Psychoanalytic Press and Norton, 1936), chs. 8–10; *New Introductory Lectures on Psychoanalysis*, tr. James Strachey (New York: Norton, 1965 [1933]), 87–8, 143–4. Still, Freud employs Rank's analysis of hero myths as late as his *Moses and Monotheism* (tr. Katherine James [New York: Vintage Books, 1965 (1939)], pt. 1).

33 For contemporary Freudian approaches to myth, see Jacob A. Arlow, "Ego Psychology and the Study of Mythology," *Journal of the American Psychoanalytic Association* 9 (1961), 371–93; Sidney Tarachow et al., "Mythology and Ego Psychology," *The Psychoanalytic Study of Society* 3 (1964), 9–97; Martin S. Bergman, "The Impact of Ego Psychology on the Study of the Myth," *American Imago* 23 (1966), 257–64. See also my "Fairy Tales Sí, Myths No: Bruno Bettelheim's Antithesis," *The Psychoanalytic Study of Society* 18 (1993), 381–90; reprinted in my *Theorizing about Myth* (Amherst: University of Massachusetts Press, 1999), ch. 5.

34 On Rank's theory of hero myths, see William Bascom, "The Myth-Ritual Theory," *Journal of American Folklore* 70 (1957), 109–12; Melville J. and Frances S. Herskovits, *Dahomean Narrative*, Northwestern University African Studies, no. 1 (Evanston, IL: Northwestern University Press, 1958), 85–95; Clyde Kluckhohn, "Recurrent Themes in Myths and Mythmaking," in *Myth and Mythmaking*, ed. Henry A. Murray (New York: Braziller, 1960), 53–8; Archer Taylor, "The Biographical Pattern in Traditional Narrative," *Journal of the Folklore Institute* 1 (1964), 117, 128–9; Dundes, "The Hero

Pattern and the Life of Jesus," 186, 187–90, 194–200; *Interpreting Folklore*, 51–2. On Rank's overall psychology, see esp. E. James Lieberman, *Acts of Will* (Amherst: University of Massachusetts Press, 1993 [1985]).

35 For other differences between Campbell and Jung, see my *Joseph Campbell: An Introduction*, rev. edn. (New York: Penguin/New American Library, 1990 [1987]; reprinted New York: Penguin/Meridian Books, 1997), ch. 12.

36 See Joseph Campbell, *An Open Life*, with Michael Toms, eds. John M. Maher and Dennie Briggs (Burdett, NY: Larson, 1988), 121.

37 For Jung's interpretation of heroism in both halves of life, see C. G. Jung, "The Psychology of the Child Archetype," in *The Archetypes and the Collective Unconscious, Collected Works*, vol. IX, pt. 1, 2nd edn. (Princeton: Princeton University Press, 1968 [1959]), 151–81; *Symbols of Transformation, Collected Works*, vol. V, 2nd edn. (Princeton: Princeton University Press, 1967 [1956]), 171–444; *Psychology and Alchemy, Collected Works*, vol. XII, 2nd edn. (Princeton: Princeton University Press, 1968 [1953]), 333–9; "The Tavistock Lectures" [*Analytical Psychology: Its Theory and Practice*], *Collected Works*, vol. XVIII (Princeton: Princeton University Press, 1976), 105–10. For the classic Jungian analysis of myths of the first half of life, see Erich Neumann, *The Origins and History of Consciousness*, tr. R. F. C. Hull (Princeton: Princeton University Press, 1970 [1954]), 131–256; *The Great Mother*, tr. Ralph Manheim, 2nd edn. (Princeton: Princeton University Press, 1972 [1955]), 203–8. On Jung's theory of myth, see my introduction to *Jung on Mythology* (Princeton: Princeton University Press; London: Routledge, 1998), 3–45; reprinted in my *Theorizing about Myth*, ch. 6.

38 See Campbell, *The Hero with a Thousand Faces*, 318–34. On Rank's view of heroism, see as well Campbell, *The Masks of God: Occidental Mythology* (New York: Viking, 1964), 73–4, 77; *The Power of Myth*, with Bill Moyers, ed. Betty Sue Flowers (New York: Doubleday, 1988), 124–5.

39 On females as heroes, see Campbell, *The Power of Myth*, 125. Assuming that Campbell's pattern applies only to males, Carol Pearson and Katherine Pope propose a variation in *The Female Hero* (New York: Bowker, 1981). Pearson proposes a further variation in *The Hero Within*, expanded edn. (San Francisco: HarperSanFrancisco, 1989 [1986]). On female Jungian heroes, see Coline Covington, "In Search of the Heroine," *Journal of Analytical Psychology* 34 (1989), 243–54.

40 See Géza Róheim, *The Origin and Function of Culture*, Nervous and Mental Disease Monograph Series, no. 69 (Journal of Nervous and Mental Disease Publishing, 1943); *The Eternal Ones of the Dream* (New York: International Universities Press, 1945); *Psychoanalysis and Anthropology* (New York: International Universities Press, 1950); Campbell, "Bios and Mythos: Prolegomena to a Science of Mythology," in *Psychoanalysis and Culture: Essays in Honor of Géza Róheim*, eds. George B. Wilbur and Warner Muensterberger (New York: International Universities Press, 1951), 329–43.

41 On Campbell's theory of hero myths, see Dundes, "The Hero Pattern and the Life of Jesus," 187–8; my *Joseph Campbell*, chs. 2–3; Taylor, "The Biographical Pattern in Traditional Narrative," 119–21, 128–9; Jean Dalby Clift and Wallace B. Clift, *The Hero's Journey in Dreams* (New York: Crossroad, 1988), chs. 2–3. On Campbell's theory of myth as a whole, see, in addition to my *Joseph Campbell*, *Paths to the Power of Myth*, ed. Daniel C. Noel (New York: Crossroad, 1990); *Uses of Comparative Mythology*, ed. Kenneth L. Golden (New York: Garland Publishing, 1992).

42 On the myth-ritualist theory, see my introduction to *The Myth and Ritual Theory* (Oxford and Malden, MA: Blackwell, 1998), 1–13; reprinted in my *Theorizing about Myth*, ch. 3.

43 See J. G. Frazer, *The Golden Bough*, 3rd edn., 12 vols. (London: Macmillan, 1911–15); abridged edn. (London: Macmillan, 1922); S. H. Hooke, "The Myth and Ritual Pattern of the Ancient East" and "Traces of the Myth and Ritual Pattern in Canaan," in *Myth and Ritual*, ed. Hooke (London: Oxford University Press, 1933), chs. 1, 4; Introduction and "The Myth and Ritual Pattern in Jewish and Christian Apocalyptic," in *The Labyrinth*, ed. Hooke (London: SPCK; New York: Macmillan, 1935), v–x and ch. 6; *The Origins of Early Semitic Ritual*, Schweich Lectures 1935 (London: Oxford University Press, 1938); "Myth, Ritual and History" and "Myth and Ritual Reconsidered," in his *The Siege Perilous* (London: SCM Press, 1956), chs. 3, 12; "Myth and Ritual: Past and Present," in *Myth, Ritual, and Kingship*, ed. Hooke, ch. 1. On the different versions of the ritual presented in Frazer and Hooke, see my introduction to *The Myth and Ritual Theory*, 4–6.

44 See Raglan, *The Hero*, 89–136; *Death and Rebirth* (London: Watts, 1945); *The Origins of Religion* (London: Watts, 1949), esp. chs. 9–10.

45 Strictly speaking, the chief god for Raglan is of the sky rather than, as for Frazer and Hooke, of vegetation.

46 See Raglan, "Notes and Queries," *Journal of American Folklore* 70 (1957), 359. Elsewhere Raglan ironically scorns what he assumes to be "the Freudian explanation" as "to say the least inadequate, since it only takes into account two incidents out of at least [Raglan's] twenty-two and we find that the rest of the story is the same whether the hero marries his mother, his sister or his first cousin" ("The Hero of Tradition," 230 – not included in *The Hero*). Raglan disdains psychological analyses of all stripes: in response to the Jungian H. G. Baynes, "On the Psychological Origins of Divine Kingship," *Folk-Lore* 47 (1936), 74–104, see his "Psychology and the Divine Kingship," *Folk-Lore* 47 (1936), 340–4.

47 For Raglan's own ritualist analysis of the Oedipus myth, see his *Jocasta's Crime* (London: Methuen, 1933), esp. ch. 26.

48 But see Mary Ann Jezewski, "Traits of the Female Hero: The Application of Raglan's Concept of Hero Trait Patterning," *New York Folklore* 10 (1984), 55–73.

49 See Victor Cook, "Lord Raglan's Hero – A Cross Cultural Critique," *Florida Anthropologist* 18 (1965), 147–54.

50 See W. T. H. Jackson, *The Hero and the King* (New York: Columbia University Press, 1982).

51 On Raglan's theory of hero myths and of myths as a whole, see, in addition to Cook, Dundes, "The Hero Pattern and the Life of Jesus," 179–80, 187–91; Dundes' headnote to Raglan, "The Hero of Tradition," in *The Study of Folklore*, ed. Dundes (Englewood Cliffs, NJ: Prentice-Hall, 1965), 142–4; Joseph Fontenrose, *The Ritual Theory of Myth*, Folklore Studies, no. 18 (Berkeley: University of California Press, 1966), ch. 1; Bascom, "The Myth-Ritual Theory," 103–14; "Notes and Queries," *Journal of American Folklore* 71 (1958), 79–80; Stanley Edgar Hyman, "Notes and Queries," *Journal of American Folklore* 71 (1958), 152–5; Bascom, "Notes and Queries," *Journal of American Folklore* 71 (1958), 155–6; Kluckhohn, "Recurrent Themes in Myths and Mythmaking," 53–8; Herskovitses, *Dahomean Narrative*, 104–5, 111–16; Taylor, "The Biographical Pattern in Traditional Narrative," 118–19, 128–9; Francis Lee Utley, *Lincoln Wasn't There, or Lord Raglan's Hero*, CEA Chap Book (Washington, DC: College English Association, 1965). For an application of Raglan's pattern, see, in addition to the already cited Jezewski, Alwyn D. Rees, "The Divine Hero in Celtic Hagiology," *Folk-Lore* 47 (1936), 30–41.

52 René Girard, *Violence and the Sacred*, tr. Patrick Gregory (London: Athlone Press; Baltimore: Johns Hopkins University Press, 1977). See also his *Deceit, Desire, and the Novel*, tr. Yvonne Freccero (Baltimore: Johns Hopkins University Press, 1966); *"To double business bound"* (London: Athlone Press; Baltimore: Johns Hopkins University Press, 1978); *The Scapegoat*, tr. Yvonne Freccero (London: Athlone Press; Baltimore: Johns Hopkins University Press, 1986); *Things Hidden since the Foundation of the World*, trs. Stephen Bann and Michael Metteer (London: Athlone Press; Stanford: Stanford University Press, 1987); *Job, the Victim of his People*, tr. Yvonne Freccero (London: Athlone Press; Baltimore: Johns Hopkins University Press, 1987); "Generative Scapegoating," in *Violent Origins*, ed. Robert G. Hamerton-Kelly (Stanford: Stanford University Press, 1987), 73–105; *A Theater of Envy* (New York: Oxford University Press, 1991); *The Girard Reader*, ed. James G. Williams (New York: Crossroad, 1996).

53 On the linkage of myth to tragedy, see Gilbert Murray, "Excursus on the Ritual Forms Preserved in Greek Tragedy," in Jane Harrison, *Themis*, 1st edn. (Cambridge: Cambridge University Press, 1912), 341–63. On the linkage of myth to comedy, see F. M. Cornford, *The Origin of Attic Comedy* (London: Arnold, 1914).

54 On Girard's theory of hero myths, see the special issue of Girard in *Diacritics* 8 (Spring 1978); *René Girard et le problème du mal*, eds. Michel Deguy and Jean-Pierre Dupuy (Paris: Grasset, 1982); "René Girard and Biblical Criticism," *Semeia*, no. 33 (1985); "To Honor René Girard," *Stanford French Review* 10 (1986); *Violence and Truth*, ed. Paul Dumouchel (London: Athlone Press; Stanford: Stanford University Press, 1988); James G. Williams, *The Bible, Violence, and the Sacred* (San Francisco: HarperSanFrancisco,

1991); Richard J. Golsan, *René Girard and Myth* (New York: Garland Publishing, 1993); Cesáreo Bandera, *The Sacred Game* (University Park: Pennsylvania State University Press, 1994); "Christianity: a Sacrificial or Nonsacrificial Religion?" *Religion* 27 (1997), 219–54.

THE READINGS

CHAPTER 1

SIGURD (ICELANDIC/ NORSE): HERO AS WARRIOR

INTRODUCTION

The central figure in the *Saga of the Volsungs*, the thirteenth-century Icelandic prose epic, is Sigurd. In the German, poetic version of this epic, *Das Nibelungenlied*, Sigurd is Siegfried, best known as the chief figure in Wagner's operatic cycle, the *Ring of the Nibelungen*. Sigurd is human, though descended from the god Odin. His most famous deed is the slaying of the dragon Fafnir. Sigurd is spurred by his foster father, the blacksmith Regin, who is the brother of Fafnir, and uses his sword, named Gram. His motive is crass: to get the hoard of gold guarded by Fafnir. As Fafnir dies, he prophesies that the gold will one day cause the death of Sigurd, as it does when he is betrayed by one of his wives, herself after the gold. Sigurd eats the heart of the slain dragon and is thereby able to learn the language of the birds. They warn him to kill Regin, who has been plotting to take the gold for himself. The hoard includes a magic ring, which Sigurd puts on, not knowing it harbors a curse. All of these supernatural adventures occur in the first half of the story. The second half, which ends tragically, is more human. On Sigurd, see Jesse Byock's introduction to his translation of the Saga, from which the following excerpt on Sigurd's killing of Fafnir and Regin is taken. Both Otto Rank and Lord Raglan include Sigurd or Siegfried as one of their heroes.

Original publication: *The Saga of the Volsungs*, tr. Jesse L. Byock (Berkeley: University of California Press, 1990), pp. 63–6.

THE SAGA OF THE VOLSUNGS: THE NORSE EPIC OF SIGURD THE DRAGON SLAYER

Translated by Jesse L. Byock

Now Sigurd and Regin rode up onto the heath and onto the track along which Fafnir was accustomed to crawl when he went to drink. And it is said that this cliff was thirty fathoms high at the spot where Fafnir lay to get water. Then Sigurd said: "You told me, Regin, that this dragon was no larger than a serpent, but his tracks seem excessively large to me." Regin said: "Dig a ditch and sit in it, and then, when the serpent crawls to the water, pierce him in the heart and thus cause his death. You will win great renown from such a deed." Sigurd asked: "But what will happen, if I get in the way of the dragon's blood?" "No one can advise you, if you are afraid of everything. You are not like your kin in courage," replied Regin.

Now Sigurd rode onto the heath, and Regin ran off in fear. Sigurd dug a ditch. And while he was working on it, an old man with a long beard came to him and asked what he was doing. Sigurd told him. Then the old man responded: "That is ill-advised. Dig several ditches for the blood to run into; then you sit in one of them and thrust at the heart of the worm." Then this man disappeared. And Sigurd dug the ditches in the manner described to him.

When the worm crawled to the water the earth quaked mightily, so that all the ground nearby shook. He blew poison over all the path before him, but Sigurd was neither afraid of nor concerned by the din. And when the serpent crawled over the pit, Sigurd plunged the sword up under the left shoulder, so that it sank to the hilt. Then Sigurd leapt up out of the ditch, and drew the sword out of the serpent. His arms were all bloody to the shoulder. And when the huge worm felt his mortal wound he thrashed his head and his tail, destroying everything that got in his way.

And when Fafnir received his death wound, he asked: "Who are you, or who is your father, or who is your family, you who are so impudent that you dare to bear weapons against me?" Sigurd replied: "My family is unknown to men. I am called the noble beast. I have neither father nor mother, and I have traveled alone." Fafnir answered: "If you have neither father nor mother, from what wonder were you born? And although you

42

will not tell me your name on my dying day, you know that you are lying." He answered: "My name is Sigurd and my father is Sigmund."

Fafnir then asked: "Who urged you on to this deed, and why did you let yourself be persuaded? Have you not heard that all people are afraid of me and my helm of terror? Boy with the sharp eyes, you had a keen father." Sigurd said: "A hard mind whetted me for this deed and I was supported in it by this strong hand and this sharp sword, which you are now familiar with. Few are bold in old age who are cowardly in childhood."

Fafnir said: "I know that if you had grown up with your kinsmen you would know how to fight when angered. But it is yet stranger that a prisoner taken in war should have dared to fight me, because few captives are valiant in a fight." Sigurd spoke: "You revile me for being removed from my kinsmen. Even though I was taken in war, I was not bound, and you have discovered that I was free." Fafnir answered: "You take everything I say as spoken with malice. But this gold that was mine will be your death." Sigurd replied: "Everyone wants to have wealth until that one day, but everyone must die sometime." Fafnir said: "You do not want to heed my advice, but you will drown if you voyage unwarily by sea. Remain instead on land until it is calm."

Sigurd said: "Tell me, Fafnir, if you are so wise, who are the Norns, who separate sons from their mothers?" Fafnir replied: "They are many and sundry. Some are of the race of Æsir, some are of the race of elves, and some are of the daughters of Dvalin." Sigurd said: "What is the name of that island where Surt and the Æsir will mix together their blood?" Fafnir answered: "It is called Oskapt, the uncreated."

And again Fafnir spoke: "My brother Regin caused my death, but it gladdens me that he will also cause your death. And it will go as he wishes." Again Fafnir spoke: "I have borne a helm of terror over all people since I lay on my brother's inheritance. And I blew poison in all directions around me, so that none dared come near me, and I feared no weapon. I never found so many men before me that I did not think myself much stronger, and everyone was afraid of me." Sigurd said: "This helm of terror you speak of gives victory to few, because each man who finds himself in company with many others must at one time discover that no one is the boldest of all."

Fafnir answered: "I suggest you take your horse and ride away as fast as you can, because it often happens that he who receives a mortal wound avenges himself." Sigurd said: "That is your advice, but I will do otherwise. I will ride to your den and there take the massive hoard of gold which your kin possessed." Fafnir replied: "You will ride there, where you will find so much gold that it will be plentiful for the rest of your days. And that same gold will be your death, as it will be the death of all who possess it." Sigurd stood up and said: "I would ride home, even though it would mean losing this great treasure, if I knew that I would never die. But every brave man wants to be wealthy until that one day. And you, Fafnir, lie in your death throes until Hel has you." Then Fafnir died.

After Fafnir died Regin came to Sigurd and said: "Hail, my lord. You have won a great victory, as you have killed Fafnir. None before were so bold as to dare to sit in his path. And this glorious feat will live on while the world remains." Regin stood and looked down at the ground for a long time. Then afterward he said with much emotion: "You have killed my brother, but I am hardly blameless in this deed."

Sigurd took his sword Gram, dried it off on the grass, and said to Regin: "You went quite far away when I performed this deed. I tested this sharp sword with my own hand, pitting my strength against the serpent's might, while you lay in a heather bush confused, not knowing whether it was heaven or earth." Regin answered: "That serpent might have lain a long time in his den, if you had not enjoyed the sword I made for you with my own hands. Neither you nor anyone else would yet have accomplished this deed." Sigurd replied: "When men come to battle, a fearless heart serves a man better than a sharp sword." Then out of deep sorrow Regin repeated to Sigurd: "You have killed my brother and I can hardly be considered blameless in this deed."

Then Sigurd cut the heart out of the serpent with the sword called Ridill. Regin drank Fafnir's blood and said: "Grant me one request, a trifle for you. Go to the fire with the heart, roast it, and give it to me to eat." Sigurd went and roasted Fafnir's heart on a spit. And when the juice foamed out he tested it with his finger to see whether it was done. He stuck his finger in his mouth. And when the blood from the serpent's heart touched his tongue, he could understand the speech of birds. He heard the nuthatches chirping in the brush near him.

"There sits Sigurd, roasting Fafnir's heart. Better he should eat it himself," said a bird. "Then he would be wiser than any man." Another said: "There lies Regin, who wants to betray the one who trusts him." Then a third spoke: "He should strike Regin's head off; then he alone would control the huge store of gold." Then a fourth spoke: "Sigurd would be wise to follow their advice. Afterward he should ride to Fafnir's den and take the magnificent hoard of gold which is there, and then ride up to Hindarfell, where Brynhild sleeps. There he will find great wisdom. He would be wise to take your advice and consider his own needs. I suspect a wolf where I see a wolf's ears." Then a fifth said: "He is not as wise as I thought if he spares Regin after having killed his brother." Then a sixth spoke: "It would be a wise course if Sigurd killed Regin and took the treasure for himself."

Then Sigurd said: "It will not be my ill fate that Regin shall be my death. Rather, both brothers should go the same way." He now drew the sword Gram and cut off Regin's head. After that he ate some of the serpent's heart and kept some. He then leapt onto his horse and rode along Fafnir's trail until he came to the lair, which he found open. All the doors were made of iron, as were all their fastenings. All the posts in the house were also of iron, and they had been sunk into the earth. There Sigurd found an enormous store of gold, as well as the sword Hrotti. He took from there the helm of terror, the golden coat of chain mail, and many other precious things. He found so much gold that he expected it to be more than two or even three horses could carry. He took all the gold and put it into two large chests and then took Grani by the bridle. The horse would not budge and whipping was useless. Sigurd now discovered what the horse wanted. He leapt onto his back and put spurs to him and the horse ran as if unencumbered.

Chapter 2

JOHN HENRY (AMERICAN): HERO OF STRENGTH

Introduction

According to legend, John Henry weighed forty-four pounds at birth, already spoke, already walked, immediately demanded a huge meal, and promptly left home for good. The key story told is that, as an adult working on tunnel building for the railroad, he agrees to compete with the company's steam drill to see who can drive steel faster into the rocks to bore the holes in which explosives will be placed. In the most popular known version of the story, John Henry, using a hammer, beats the machine – but then dies, from exhaustion or a stroke. Other versions place his death later, but still while working as a steel driver. John Henry is akin to the lumberjack Paul Bunyan but is a more complicated figure. His feat involves the conquest not of nature but of the machine. He represents opposition to industrialization, epitomized by the railroad. The machine he defeats threatens the livelihoods of manual laborers. Furthermore, John Henry is black, and a former slave still living in the South. His character plays on stereotypes, positive and negative alike, of blacks in post-Civil War America. While his willingness to compete evinces persistence and dignity in his work, his willingness to die for his job smacks of servility. He is at once a martyr and a slave. On John Henry, see Brett Williams, *John Henry*, from which the following selection is taken. Williams puts the myth in the likeliest historical setting, without concluding that John Henry ever lived or that the event ever occurred.

Original publication: Brett Williams, *John Henry* (Westport, CT: Greenwood Press, 1983) ch. 1 (pp. 3–13).

John Henry: A Bio-Bibliography

Brett Williams

Even among heroes John Henry is extraordinary, for his fame rests on a single epic moment when he raced and defeated a steam drill destined to take away his job. That moment has captured the imagination of balladeers and storytellers for the last century, and in their songs and tales they have woven for John Henry a whole life: an infant's prophecy, a woman he loves, a heroic test, a martyr's victory. Although this heroic tradition tells us much about John Henry's appeal, it tells us little about his real and probably rather ordinary life. Reconstructing his biography is complicated further by the problem that his is the sort of life often lost to history: as a southern black laborer born a slave and most likely dead before the nineteenth century closed, his experience would not have been chronicled in official accounts. Oral tradition offers the biographer clues to John Henry's life; from there one must look to history for evidence that such a man might have lived such a life and that he might have had the opportunity to seize a heroic moment. Ultimately, to believe that John Henry actually lived is an act of faith [. . .] In this chapter I join the clues of oral tradition to a nineteenth-century southern setting in suggesting a life for John Henry.

Regrettably, we do not even know what to make of his name. John Henry would have lived at the most complicated time possible for discovering who he was. Because he was born a slave, some plantations might have recorded his birth. Those records that survive indicate that John and Henry were the two most common names for nineteenth-century male slaves. These records generally list only one name for each person, supporting assumptions that Henry was a surname, perhaps a slave family surname, linked ultimately to a white man such as the owner of the large and populous Henry plantation of Winchester, Virginia. In the 1920s Guy Johnson found further evidence that Henry might have been a surname: in researching Carter Woodson's *Free Negro Heads of Families, 1830*, Johnson found eleven John Henrys and believed that the actual number of men with that name would have been many more.

But it seems just as plausible to assume that John Henry was a first and middle name, especially when we consider the complexity of slave-naming customs, the likelihood that plantation birth records would have ignored that complexity, and finally, the fact that many ex-slaves

47

transformed their old names once free. Slave parents, or often grand-parents, generally named children for kin as a way of rooting them in extended, though often dispersed, families. Naming was crucial in linking generations of blood kin, so that they might stand as a family although they could not share a household. Because naming was symbolically so significant, John Henry, like many others, quite possibly bore the names of two male relatives. Further, some slaves took unofficial nicknames as well as surnames other than their owners', probably to assert their sepa-rate social identities. After Emancipation, those former slaves who so desired often transformed their names, relinquishing a master's name or adding double names, perhaps to dramatize their new status. That double names were common among southern blacks once they were free is indicated by the testimony of those volunteering information on John Henry in the 1920s: all assumed that he had yet another surname. Finally, among black Americans today, John Henry is most often a double name.

However, the very ordinariness of John Henry's name makes him not only impossible to trace but perhaps suspect as well. It symbolizes his heroic role as a sort of Everyman and also links him to traditional slave heroes such as John the Conqueror or the slave John of the John and Master story cycle.

In any event, John Henry would have been born a slave in the 1830s or 1840s. Although every southern state has at some time claimed him as a native son, we cannot be sure where he was born. Most evidence seems to point to either North Carolina or Virginia. As a slave in either of these upper South states, he would have grown up in a community woven together by the kin ties of extended families who struggled to bind kin in spite of the terrible obstacles slavery imposed on family life. He would have participated in a society unique to that time and place, rooted in the Afro-American experience, joining African, American, and slave traditions to carve out in juxtaposition to the institution of slavery a culture rich in ritual, music, stories, and heroic lore. This heritage is crucial in understanding the heroic tradition, especially the poignant ballad that it produced to commemorate John Henry and the type of hero it celebrated.

In either North Carolina or Virgina, John Henry may have participated in, and surely witnessed, the great migration of slaves out of the upper South between 1815 and 1860, as the export shipping trade shifted to the less depleted and more prosperous plantations of the deep South. Only one of many practices that ripped apart slave families and disrupted slave communities, it was an especially dramatic one. One of every ten people experienced forced separation from kin: most typically this person was a single male between the ages of fifteen and twenty-nine. Everyone who witnessed it must have been struck by the arbitrary power of their owners to toy with human life.

Finally, in either North Carolina or Virginia, John Henry may have participated in, and again surely witnessed, the industrial slavery common to both states. Throughout the South owners leased out their slaves to work on railroad, canal, and levee construction or in textile factories, and in the upper South to work in ironworks and coal mines (for labor not unlike that John Henry would do as a free man). Coal mining was a particularly hazardous endeavor: plagued with accidents from rock falls, fires, and explosions, the mines had such a bad reputation that many owners sent their slaves there as punishment. Others sought insurance on their slaves, but found that by the 1850s most insurance companies were too wary of the hazards of mining to grant it. Industrial slavery was another business venture that ruptured family life; often slaves refused to go to the mines or, once there, ran away. Like the great migration, industrial slavery testified to the abandonment of human priorities to economic goals. John Henry must have come to freedom with these lessons well in mind. His heroic act, appropriately, was addressed to just this conflict.

Once free, a few former slaves found skilled jobs as blacksmiths, carpenters, or shoemakers; many more remained in farm labor, often as sharecroppers; and still others, like John Henry, joined a virtual army of inexpensive workers to build and rebuild the industrializing South. Because there were so many workers with so little bargaining power, they faced conditions in factories, on steamboats, railroads, and cattle ranges, in lumbering and turpentine camps, and in coal mines that were often terribly exploitative. Some employers still thought black laborers were little better than brute animals and worked them from sunup to sundown for wages as low as one dollar a day and punished them harshly if they performed poorly.

In many cases those supposed to be free actually worked under debt peonage, either as sharecroppers so indebted to landowners that their share of the crop could never repay the debt, as convicts on hire, or as laborers under contract to men functioning much like today's agricultural crew leaders. A great deal of migration characterized this labor force, as much of the construction work available was large scale and short term. Workers sometimes moved to the North or the Midwest seeking better positions or from one site to another at the behest of labor contractors to whom they were sometimes also in debt.

Someone who might have provided us with information about John Henry was Captain W. R. Johnson. He died in 1911, leaving no accessible records; and because he became a father only late in life (at the age of

49

fifty), he did not have the opportunity to tell his children and grand-children stories they might have been able to pass on.

Captain Johnson was a contractor who moved his force to various sites around West Virginia. He would have been John Henry's employer at the Big Bend Tunnel, one of many projects contracted out by the C & O Railroad on its way from Washington, D. C., to Cincinnati, in the hope of linking the shipping lanes of the Chesapeake Bay to the fertile Ohio Valley. Halfway there, engineers following the Greenbrier River through Summers County, West Virginia, met Big Bend Mountain. To tunnel through meant driving a mile and a quarter in treacherous red shale, but the expensive alternative was laying track along the river's great southerly loop, which after meandering for about ten miles returned to within about a mile from where it had begun. Choosing to save miles of track, the C & O hired Captain Johnson, who brought some one thousand men and boys, mostly blacks, to build Big Bend Tunnel between 1870 and 1872. It may be no reflection on Captain Johnson that *The Richmond Dispatch* reported of such laborers during those years: " . . . the majority are negroes. (They are preferred) because you can cuss a negro but whenever an attempt is made to abuse a white, there is a row."

The closest towns were Hinton, nine miles to the east, and Talcott, one mile to the west. Both were railroad towns, incorporated at the insistence of C & O officials, sustained by freight that travelled through, and by the employment opportunities offered in the rail yards, the mailroom, and on the trains. At the time of Big Bend tunnel construction, the area was a wild and desolate frontier wilderness, and the tunnel itself was not only remote from but possibly closed to the public press.

We can realistically assume, however, that the C & O's decision to tunnel through the mountain probably cost hundreds of lives. Tunneling is arduous, hazardous, and extremely intensive labor. America's longest tunnel at the time, Big Bend was much too deadly for the technology available to cope with it; and safety measures do not seem to have been a priority for railroading and contracting officials concerned with wresting the greatest possible profits from their endeavors. Many tunnel workers died from tunnel sickness (also called miner's consumption or silicosis) inflicted by the horrible foul air and smothering heat encountered in the poorly ventilated underground. The thick stone dust, the noxious blasting fumes from the 833 pounds of nitroglycerin used daily, and the smoke from the lard and blackstrap oil which fueled each day's 115 pounds of candles, were nearly intolerable.

Workers also suffered frequent accidents from bungled blasting or crashing rocks. As evidence of Big Bend's treacherous formation, Assistant Engineer James Nelson reported in 1870: "The rock formation is very hard, but disintegrates under the weather, so much so that at the time of construction of the brick arch, large cavities, sometimes fifty feet deep, were found above the timber arch." The *Railroad Gazette* noted one slide of eight thousand cubic yards at the west portal: "In fact the side of the mountain 'let go' and came down into the cut."

Most often the dead were simply buried in the big rock fill near the east portal, their deaths unreported. Chappel claims that the press reported that Negroes who died at Big Bend "hailed from nowhere and had not been christened," a telling remark which helps to explain a seemingly unfathomable lack of concern for working conditions at the tunnel. Most likely the work force was kept quite separate from the townspeople, whose race relations were problematic at best. (The county historian reported a bloody race riot in tiny Hinton several years later.)

The most dangerous tunnel work is at the heading, which is a tube-like horizontal cross section initially cut through the mountain so that the tunnel can be completed by drilling shafts downward from the tube and then blasting out the mountain's lower parts. Heading work is especially hazardous because workers must drill at a horizontal angle under a fragile, unsupported roof. Most witnesses agreed that John Henry worked at the heading near Big Bend's east portal, with other workers boring simultaneously from the west end and then through three vertical shafts as the headings progressed.

John Henry was a driver or hammer man, which meant that he spent his days driving steel drills into Big Bend's red shale in order to bore holes in which to place explosives. The drills were one-and-a-half inches in diameter and varied in length from two to fourteen feet. When a steel driver first opened a hole, he used a shorter drill, substituting longer and longer ones as he bored deeper. He worked with a partner, a shaker or turner, whose unenviable job it was to shake the drill after each blow to rotate the cutting edge and prevent rock dust from impacting around the point. Depending on whether the driver was hammering up, down, or sideways, the shaker might lie flat on his back, holding the drill between his legs, or plaster himself against the rock face with the drill crooked in his arm or close to his chest. Shakers needed very steady nerves and profound faith to steady the drills as hammers flashed by them in the tunnel's dim light: if they slipped or the drivers missed they might easily find their flesh mangled or their bones crushed.

Every few minutes the drill dulled – drivers used thousands each day – and the shaker had to exchange it for a fresh one without breaking the driver's pace. He reached out blindly to hand the old drill to blacksmiths stationed at the portals for resharpening. Once the holes had reached a depth of about fourteen feet and were ready for blasting, the powder men inserted shots of black powder or nitroglycerin. Great buckets powered by steam engines hopefully hoisted the workers high enough up the shaft to be safe from the blast. Because the equipment was primitive and the timing close, they didn't always get clear. Many accidents occurred at this point. After the rock was blown free, workers mucked it out by hand to be hauled away from the tunnel in mule-driven carts. This work was not only labor intensive but also very slow: six steel drivers working twelve-hour shifts needed a full day to bore the holes for just one blast, which advanced the heading only ten feet.

To proceed relatively quickly with the deadly and monotonous work, drivers needed to find and keep a steady pace. (In this way, steel-driving is similar to the work of a lumberjack or the effort of a long-distance runner.) Workers found that, as had been true on the plantation as well, music helped them find the necessary rhythm. Writing on railroad songs in 1899, William Barton eloquently described the tunnel work song:

> To hear these songs, not all of which are religious, at their best, one needs to hear them in a rock tunnel. The men are hurried in after an explosion to drill with speed for another double row of blasts. They work two and two, one holding and turning the drill, the other striking it with a sledge. The sledges descend in unison as the long low chant gives the time. I wonder if the reader can imagine the effect of it all, the powder smoke filling the place, the darkness made barely visible by the little lights on the hats of the men, the echoing sounds of men and mules toward the outlet loading and carting away the rock thrown out by the last blast, and the men at the heading droning their low chant to the chink! chink! of the steel. A single musical phrase or a succession of a half dozen notes caught on a visit to such a place sticks in one's mind forever. Even as I write I seem to be in a tunnel of this description and to hear the sharp metallic stroke and syncopated chant.

Thus singing was important for setting a rhythm and a pace as well as for amusement in the foul and dreary tunnel. Some witnesses and most song writers and storytellers remember John Henry as a wonderful, enthusiastic singer of these songs. Certainly his destiny has been interwoven with song; it seems likely that the first commemoration of his contest with the steam drill was through workers' hammer songs, perhaps composed and improvised by drivers and shakers moved to incorporate his heroic act into the music of the work place.

Thus far, although we cannot prove that John Henry worked in Big Bend Tunnel, we can easily demonstrate that many men like him did. His heroic contest with the steam drill is more problematic and perhaps less likely. No records exist. All we can show is that there might have been a steam drill at Big Bend, there might have been a contest, and John Henry might have won it. In the following pages I discuss each issue in turn.

Although hand laborers drove Big Bend Tunnel through, Captain Johnson might well have experimented with a steam drill there. He used other kinds of steam machinery to hoist men up through the shafts and to drill wells. Moreover, the latter nineteenth century witnessed many technological innovations in railroading, such as the introduction of the air brake and the automatic coupler to replace hand operations. Tunneling too was revolutionized during that time by the introduction of modern explosives (already in use at Big Bend) and by mechanical rock drills.

As early as 1813, well before the great rock tunnels in Europe and the United States were built, inventors were experimenting with increasingly successful drills. Tunneling projects seem to have inspired even further innovation, perhaps because hand drilling was so tedious, expensive, and slow; or perhaps because contractors, hoping to finish their projects as quickly as possible to make their bids and increase their profits, were especially energetic hustlers. Rock drill technology progressed rapidly during the fifty years of great railroad tunneling and expansion, with numerous classic Yankee innovators tinkering with the first 1849 patents of Couch and Fowle until by the 1870s and 1880s they had refined drills which could be used successfully in certain kinds of rock.

Fowle's drill, hurled like a lance into the rock face against the motion of a hollow piston, was especially influential. It inspired the clumsy 240-pound Brooks, Gates, and Burleigh drill and later the much improved Burleigh drill of 1865. Also clumsy at 372 pounds but robust enough to withstand much of the punishment in tunnel work (in which the drill's tendency is to pound itself to pieces), the Burleigh drill was a spectacular success at Massachusetts' Hoosac Tunnel. Pioneering contractors imported it there to replace the Brooks, Gates, and Burleigh which, priced at four hundred dollars, was too expensive for them to tolerate its constant breakdown.

Hoosac engineers used Burleigh drills from 1866 until they had completed the tunnel, and although they had to ship out approximately 250 machines a month for repairs, they were nonetheless pleased with the Burleigh's effectiveness. Before 1865 engineers had found hand labor at Hoosac terribly slow: they estimated that they had required fifty days' man labor to advance the tunnel a single foot. Each man had been able to bore only about nineteen inches of holes for explosives a day. Contractor Shanley compiled an extensive report comparing the cost of power drilling to the expense of hand labor during the years 1869–1874. At the tunnel's east heading, Shanley estimated that power drilling had cost four cents per inch, and hand labor nine and one-third cents per inch; in the harder rock at the west heading, machine work had cost seven and one-tenth cents per inch as opposed to thirteen cents for hand labor. On the average Shanley found he needed five and one-eighth feet of holes to remove one cubic yard of rock. Converting his estimates on the comparative cost of labor to cubic yards, he estimated that the Burleigh drill cost him 75.2 cents per cubic yard, while hand drilling required $2.9640. (Shanley's calculations include the expense of mining labor, mechanical labor, blacksmith work, iron, steel, oil, coal, interest, and depreciation. He does not indicate if he took repair costs into account, but I believe that he must have.)

Shanley's glowing report concluded that hand labor would have involved an additional twelve years and three times the expense to complete the Hoosac Tunnel. (This latter estimate was based on tests which showed that in the Hoosac micha-schist machines progressed 167 feet for every 40 feet by hand.) Similar claims from Pennsylvania's Nesquehoning Tunnel that explicitly include running and repair costs confirm his estimates. Nesquehoning engineers concluded that hand drilling cost 26.2 cents per foot, while machines required only 14.1 cents per foot. The Burleigh drill also was used successfully at Nevada's Sutro Tunnel and throughout the western mining region in 1875.

Although the Burleigh was an influential and popular innovation, it was not without its problems in certain kinds of rock and certainly not without serious rivals. American inventors patented 110 rock drills between 1850 and 1875; Europeans patented 86. Some of the best drills emerged during the years of Big Bend construction, and although most scholars have assumed that John Henry must have raced the Burleigh, his opponent might well have been one of these newer inventions. For example, the Ingersoll drill was patented in 1871 by Ingersoll Rand, which eventually merged with the Burleigh Company to produce a very highly regarded rock drill used successfully at Musconetcong Tunnel in New Jersey from 1872 to 1875. Perhaps Johnson experimented with an early Ingersoll model at Big Bend.

Another possibility would have been the American Diamond Drill Company's black diamond drill. Praised by *Scientific American* in 1871, the black diamond model sounds well equipped to meet the challenge of Big Bend. It was much simpler and more portable than earlier models and designed to drill in any position or direction (a considerable asset in tunnel work). The drill's most exciting feature was its ability to adjust to the varying hardness of different kinds of rock, although in doing so it ran erratically at vastly varying speeds. The diamond drill could bore through eleven inches of brittle sandstone in just fifty-five seconds, while four inches of much harder blue limestone required three minutes. Although its hard black diamond drill bits were too brittle to stand percussion for long, the drill's flexibility was appealing to contractors.

Throughout the 1870s rock drill technology continued to improve, with an impressive innovation in the middle of the decade: new hammer drills which ironically imitated more closely the movements of a man and thus avoided the Fowle drill's costly, stressful reciprocating motion between drill and piston, a feature that also was characteristic of its imitators.

At the C & O's Lewis Tunnel, the contractor tried the Burleigh drill for perhaps as long as nine months. Several separate reports established its presence there during part of 1870 and most of 1871, although these reports might have referred to distinct instances and several different drills. Big Bend was only forty-three miles away, but 2,046 feet longer and composed of brittle shale much more likely to clog and choke the steam drill than the sandstone at Lewis. C & O engineers interviewed during the 1920s did not recall the steam drill in use at Big Bend. But the C & O was in difficult straits during the early 1870s, overextended and overcapitalized, facing court orders to repay back taxes it had dodged, and anxious to complete the route and recover its investment. For his part, Captain Johnson wanted to finish the tunnel quickly, and he lived at an historic moment when many possibilities presented themselves for expediting the work. Manufacturers were aggressively marketing the new drills; engineering and scientific journals exulted in the time and money they could save. It seems impossible that Johnson would not have tested the Burleigh, Ingersoll, or Black Diamond drill. The affair might have been brief and unofficial; perhaps it occurred at the prompting of a salesman who had brought the drill to the tunnel for a promotional trial. Most likely there was no sale, but just a test – or a contest – between Johnson's star driver, John Henry, and the steam drill.

Contests between two steel drivers were quite common on tunneling and mining projects – perhaps to provide amusement or build morale, perhaps to encourage free overtime. Festivity sometimes surrounded the race in the form of drinking, wagers, and prize money. Since contests were commonplace, that some of the witnesses at Big Bend do not particularly recall John Henry's particular test is not especially surprising. It is also possible that this was one race his supervisors did not want publicized: the steam drill might have distracted and angered the workers, and John Henry's victory certainly would have impressed them with their employer's dependence on manual labor. Moreover, Big Bend was a mile and a quarter long, worked at five different points by one thousand laborers.

55

Some might easily have missed an isolated race in such a mammoth project.

Those who did recall the contest placed it at a logical time and place, just a few months after Johnson had assumed the tunnel contract (during the summer or fall of 1870) and at the east heading, completed in November of 1870 and closest to the Greenbrier River – the only convenient source of water to power the steam drill. Because this also was the first point to be drilled, the place witnesses named was consistent with the time; and it also seems probable that Johnson would have tested the steam drill soon after starting tunnel construction.

We must turn to the ballad for speculation on why John Henry might have agreed to a contest; Big Bend witnesses volunteered no motive. Some versions of the ballad label the hero a hammerin' fool, while others suggest that just five years out of slavery and with no place much to go, he purposefully took a stand to save his job. Perhaps his captain offered him a share of a wager, or perhaps he acted out of personal loyalty to his captain or his fellow employees. We cannot demonstrate that he raced the steam drill, but only that he might have, that history supports the claims of the ballad and the testimony of those who remember him. Re-arching of Big Bend's east portal in the 1880s concealed the holes allegedly left by the contest.

Could John Henry have won? This is perhaps the murkiest matter. We do not know how long the contest lasted or how far the contestants drove. Claims concerning the contest's duration range from thirty-five minutes to two days.

Once again we can look to recorded history for clues. A series of Massachusetts tests in 1865 using six different drills concluded that on the average they could drive 2.01 inches a minute. This particular rate would not be impossible for a man to outspeed; if we look at contest records, they vary from William Shea's 25.31 inches through Rocky Mountain granite in fifteen minutes in 1892 to the Tarr Brothers' all-time double-jack record – again through granite – of 59.5 inches in fifteen minutes (set in 1912 in Butte). Since Shea drove one and two-thirds inches a minute and the Tarr Brothers almost four inches, we can assume that John Henry could have driven over two inches, especially if he were using two hammers. Of course, an 1871 drill would have been faster than those of 1865, but if the Burleigh Drill were used, it would have had difficulty getting through the brittle shale at Big Bend. As many versions of the ballad taunt: "Your hole's done choke and your drill's done broke." The Burleigh would likely have hung up in cracks and clogged with dust. This musical detail is so consistent with what engineers claimed was the Burleigh's chief flaw that it seems more

56

plausible as an eyewitness report than merely as the product of a balladeer's imagination.

The outcome may have depended on how long the contest lasted, although it is difficult to say which contestant would have profited from a longer race. John Henry would have tired, and the drill might have required numerous repairs or even broken down completely. Often ballads claim that John Henry drove fourteen feet, and the steam drill drove only nine feet. If, as many contests did, this one lasted thirty-five minutes, we can check John Henry's distance against the Tarr Brothers' record of 59.5 inches in fifteen minutes. Given twenty more minutes at the same pace, they would have bored eleven and one-half feet. If John Henry, wielding two hammers through less resistant rock, drove fourteen feet in the same amount of time, his feat would have been heroic indeed, but just within the realm of human possibility.

Often the ballad claims that John Henry died as a result of the race, from a rollin' or a roarin' in his head (which might refer to a stroke), or because he busted his "intrels" out or simply hammered himself to death. Several witnesses believed, however, that he died later in the tunnel, possibly during a rock fall, or from a fever. Especially because he worked in the tunnel's most dangerous place, and especially because the longer the shale was exposed the more likely it was to crumble, John Henry might well have died later on. Residents of Hinton and Talcott and laborers in the tunnel ever since have firmly believed his ghost haunts Big Bend.

Tales of death have surrounded Big Bend Tunnel for many years. Although local lore for the most part ignored its black builders, many of whom must have died there, white passengers and workers who were killed later provoked the resentment and ire of area townspeople. Nineteenth-century railroading was a hazardous business generally, and the C & O was no exception. The Summers County historian notes many deaths in the rail yards at Hinton, and several local disasters, including one especially tragic event when the Big Creek trestle, flimsily built from wood, collapsed and burned along with the freight train crossing it at the time. Big Bend, also carelessly constructed, was particularly deadly. The fumes that once had suffocated its workers continued to plague those riding through. One engineer died of suffocation by smoke when his train was forced to stop in the tunnel for several minutes, and eventually public outcry over such tragedies as his death and also Big Bend's generally hazardous and unpleasant conditions forced the C & O to install fans. Throughout the 1870s the tunnel's roof was crumbling as well; one particularly scandalous accident occurred when a freight train met a mass of debris crashing down from the roof, killing the fireman and burying the engineer, who survived, however, to be killed twenty years later in the Hinton yards. Finally in 1883, Big Bend virtually caved in, killing several people and forcing the surviving passengers to take a long hike around the mountain. At this point, Hinton's District Attorney courageously took the C & O to court, where the tunnel was condemned, forcing the railroad to spend a great deal of money and ten years' time rearching it in brick. Residents, however, continued to associate it with death: a favorite tale recounted in the 1920s portrayed two brothers – Irishmen – who, finished with their work there and preparing to leave, decided to walk through one last time for sentiment's sake. As the story goes, Big Bend crashed in on them and they met an ironic death.

But most of those who died at Big Bend remain relatively anonymous. It is John Henry's death that popular culture commemorates, his ghost that workers and residents believe haunts the tunnel most vividly. We shall never know what actually became of him, but chances were probably less than even that he would have left Big Bend alive. His might have been just another unsung death; instead the heroic tradition surrounding the moment that he may have chosen to die encourages us to build a life for him. I like to envision some anonymous worker, inspired by John Henry's heroic act to weave his death into a hammer song, pacing his own toil to the life affirming refrain: "This ol' hammer, That killed John Henry, won't kill me." Through song drivers and shakers could comment discreetly and indirectly on working conditions and consequences which they were not allowed to discuss. They could also defy death. And that death which they both commemorated and defied has inspired those of us who will never face such grinding, hazardous toil to explore and appreciate the lives of those who did, as personalized in their hero, John Henry.

CHAPTER 3

FINN (IRISH/CELTIC): NATIONAL HERO

INTRODUCTION

Fi(o)nn mac Cumhaill, or Finn mac Cool, is the central character in the Fenian, or Ossianic, Cycle, one of the four main cycles of ancient Irish sagas. Finn is the chief hero among the Gaelic peoples of both Ireland and Scotland. Whether Finn was a historical character of the third century AD is still debated. Even if he was, the stories about him are clearly fictional. There are many supernatural elements. His life is predestined. In some versions he is descended from a god. His father was killed before his birth, and he is fostered by a druid. While cooking a salmon for the druid, he burns his thumb in the pan and, upon sucking his thumb to ease the pain, secures the gift of prophecy. As a mere youth, he becomes the leader of the warriors known as Fiana. His prowess at hunting is superhuman, as is his prowess at fighting. With his unerring sword he defeats all the enemies of the King of Ireland and also rids Ireland of many monsters. Yet the heart of his story is closer to the stories of Tristan and Isolde and of Lancelot and Guenivere, with Finn the counterpart to Mark or Arthur. As an ageing widower, he is betrothed – not yet, like Mark or Arthur, married – to a much younger Grainne, who falls magically in love with the equally young Diarmaid, Finn's lieutenant. The couple elope and are pursued for sixteen years by Finn, with whom they are eventually reconciled. The following selection covers most of Finn's life, ending with his final treachery against Diarmaid and his hesitation to save Diarmaid's life with his divine gift of healing. Some say that Finn, like King Arthur, is still alive, sleeping underground and waiting to return when needed. On Finn and other Irish and Celtic heroes, see Thomas F. O'Rahilly, *Early Irish History and Mythology* (Dublin: Dublin Institute for Advanced Studies, 1946);

Original publication: Lindsay Clarke, *Essential Celtic Mythology* (London: Thorsons [HarperCollins], 1997), pp. 72–8, 89–93.

Miranda Jane Green, *Celtic Myths*, Legendary Past Series (Austin: University of Texas Press, 1993); and Daragh Smyth, *A Guide to Irish Mythology*, 2nd edn. (Dublin: Irish Academic Press, 1996 [1st edn. 1988]).

ESSENTIAL CELTIC MYTHOLOGY: STORIES THAT CHANGE THE WORLD

Retold by Lindsay Clarke

There was a great marvel that lay at the root of Finn's wisdom, and it came from the time when he was raised as a youth in the mountains of Slieve Bloom. The boy's father had been killed before his birth in a bitter battle between two rival clans. Finn's own people were scattered in that war and he was raised by his mother secretly in the wild so that their enemies should not find and kill him. The youth, who was called Deimne at that time, became a fine athlete and hunter, whom all thought fair to look upon. He came one day to the banks of the Boyne where he was taken as servant by a reclusive man of knowledge called Finn the Seer. For the length of seven years that hermit had been waiting to catch the Salmon of Knowledge in the deep pool near Slane because it had been foretold that the salmon would yield up its gift of universal wisdom to a man called Finn when he caught and ate it.

Shortly after Deimne came to him, the hermit caught the salmon and gave it to his servant to cook, warning him to eat no morsel of its flesh. But sensing a strangeness about the youth when he returned with the cooked fish the Seer asked if he had eaten any part of it. "I did not," Deimne replied, "but as I turned the salmon I burned my thumb and a blister rose there, so I put it to my mouth to ease the pain of it."

"You told me your name was Deimne," said his master in sudden, dreadful suspicion. "Do you have any other name?"

"I do," the youth answered, and it was true because as he had grown towards manhood so many people had asked to know who that "fair" one was that he had been given the word for his second name. "The name I have taken," he said, "is Deimne Finn."

"Then it was for you this salmon was destined," said Finn the Seer sadly. "Now you must eat it all."

When the young Finn did as he was bidden the gift of wisdom came on him. In later life, whenever he stood in need of counsel he need only suck

60

on his thumb of knowledge and he would know at once all things that he needed to know.

The story goes on to tell how Finn wisely used his magical gift to confound his father's enemies and persuade them to join with his own people so that the two clans became one, the Fianna, over which Finn wisely ruled. As his powers grew, this most just and gifted of men took tribute from all the Kings of Ireland and put his independent strength at their service in many brave and marvellous exploits. It was the Fianna who rid their lands of every kind of giant, dragon and monster that came to trouble them. Yet if Finn was a seer and a poet and a mighty warrior, perhaps his greatest joy lay in the hunt.

The Fianna were all fine hunting men and many of their greatest adventures began with a chase through the forest that would lead them into magical enchantments and end in bloodshed. Yet because of their truthfulness and the power of their hands, they emerged victorious from all such dangers.

Finn himself had two fine hunting hounds, Bran and Sceolan, who were magical creatures, close as kin to him, and were in fact his own nephews born of Finn's sister when she was transformed into a bitch by sorcery. Finn's love of the hunt was reflected in the names given to his son, Oisin, which means "a fawn", and to his grandson, Oscar, which means "one who loves the deer."

By following an enchanted fawn into the forest, Finn, Oisin and Oscar were drawn into an alliance with the fairy gods of the *sidh* against a great host that had come to attack them; and the tale of The Chase of the Enchanted Pigs of Aengus tells how a heated rivalry between Finn and the god Aengus, as to whether Finn's hounds were stronger than the god's swine, might have led to a disastrous war between gods and heroes had not Finn wisely decided to opt for peace. Yet the most powerful tale of Finn as a hunting-man tells not about the enchanted chasing after a deer or a boar, but of the doom laden pursuit of a woman and the man she loved, and this is the way of that sad story.

It was in the time when the years were making an old man of Finn, and good sleep had not come to him often since the death of his wife. Longing for a companion in his old age, he sent word to Cormac mac Art, the High King at Tara, that he wished to wed his daughter, Grainne. Now there could be no nobler match for a king's daughter than to be wedded to Finn, the hero of all Ireland, but things had not always been easy between Cormac and Finn, and Grainne was known to have refused the hand of every man that asked for it. So it was a matter of relief to all, that when Cormac asked Grainne whether she would consent to the wedding, she answered that if Finn was a fitting son-in-law for her father, then why should he not be a fitting husband for her.

So Finn was invited to claim his bride at a great wedding feast to be held at the king's high seat. Accompanied by his chosen men, Finn came to Tara in great state and was warmly welcomed by Cormac the King. Yet Grainne herself took less pleasure in Finn's arrival, for though she had heard much of his great deeds, and her passionate heart had quickened at those tales, she had never set eyes on Finn before. She was dismayed now to find that the man to whom she was betrothed was already older than her own father.

"It is a great wonder, that Finn did not seek me out in marriage for his son, Oisin, rather than for himself," she thought, "for the match would have been more fitting." Yet Finn found Grainne as fair as he had dreamed, and as they sat together he sought to charm his betrothed by letting her display her powers of quick speech in answer to his riddles.

"What is whiter than the snow?" he asked.

"The truth," she said at once.

"And what is sharper than a sword?"

"The wit of a woman between two men."

"And what is quicker than the wind?" asked Finn.

"A woman's mind," Grainne answered, and in all her answers she uttered no word of a lie; but the truth was, she had no love for Finn; and at the wedding feast as the food was served, and the songs were sung, and all the noble company made good cheer, her eager eyes were everywhere but on the man to whom she was betrothed.

Finn's druid sat beside her at the table, and Grainne asked him the names of all the company who had accompanied Finn to the feast. One by one the druid named the heroes of the Fianna until lastly she asked, "And who is that fair-speaking man who sits at Oisin's left hand?"

"That is Diarmaid, son of Duibhne," the druid answered, "third man of the Fianna, after only Finn himself and Finn's son, Oisin, and the best lover of women in the wide world."

And while Grainne gazed on the handsome face of that dark haired man who wore a cap dashingly pulled down across his brow, there was a loud commotion among the dogs fighting for scraps beneath the table. As Diarmaid rose to part them, the cap covering part of his temple fell from his head, and at the sight of the love-spot suddenly revealed there, Grainne felt her heart ravished by ungovernable love for the man.

With flame rising at her throat, she called to her serving-maid, telling her to bring from the sun-room the great golden drinking cup that would hold wine enough for almost all that company. When the cup was brought, Grainne secretly drugged the wine that was in it, and with her own hand carried it to Finn, bidding him drink deep. Then she passed on round the tables so that no man could refuse her until the cup was empty, and all had drunk from it except Diarmaid himself along with Finn's son, Oisin, his grandson, Oscar, and the Druid who sat at Grainne's side.

It was not long before all who had drunk from the cup fell into deep slumber. Then Grainne rose from her place and with the breath taut at her throat stood before Diarmaid, saying, "I am asking that you take my love, Diarmaid, son of Duibhne, and that you bring me out of this house tonight."

Astonished by her words, Diarmaid swore that he would have no secret dealings with a woman who was already promised to his lord. "It is a great wonder that you give your love to me, daughter of Cormac, and not to Finn," he protested, "for there is no greater lover of woman in the land than he."

Then Grainne told the bewildered man how she had been gazing on his face when the cap fell from his brow, revealing the love-spot there, and how her heart had instantly filled with a love so powerful that she could not live long if it remained unanswered.

Now Diarmaid knew the power of the love-spot that had been put on his brow by the god Aengus, and it was for that very reason he had striven to keep it concealed. Lamenting the unhappy chance that had let Grainne's gaze fall on it, he strove now to resist the claims of her love, saying that even if he wished to betray his loyalty to Finn, he dare not do it.

"Yet is it not said of the Fianna both that they are fearless and that they must never give offence to womankind?" said Grainne.

"It is," Diarmaid admitted.

"Then do I put you under bonds not to refuse me now," she cried, and saw Diarmaid blanch at the conflict opened in his mind by the power of her invocation. "I shall wait for you by the walls of Tara," she said, leaving him then, "and if you are a true man you will carry me away from this place tonight before Finn and the King my father wake from their sleep."

Trapped between loyalty to his lord and a bond that no man could honourably break, Diarmaid turned in hot confusion of mind to those of his friends who were still awake, telling them what had happened and asking their advice.

"Though I am my father's son," Oisin answered, "I tell you that if the woman has laid her bonds on you, no guilt can fall to you in going with her." And Oscar, Finn's grandson, added further that there could be no greater shame for a man than to break the sacred bonds laid on him by a woman.

Still agonized by the conflict, Diarmaid turned at last to Finn's druid for his counsel. Shaking his head, the druid answered, "I too tell you to go with Grainne, though it is in my mind that you will get your death by it."

So gathering up his weapons, and grievously bidding his friends farewell, Diarmaid left that hall of sleepers, and found Grainne waiting for him in the night. Together they climbed out of Tara by the spears he fixed in the outer wall, and when they were on the other side, Diarmaid said, "This is an evil journey you are come on, Grainne, for I know no corner of Ireland that will hide the two of us. It were better for us now that we turn back before Finn wakes." But Grainne answered him that she herself would never turn back, nor would she ever be parted from him unless it was death itself that parted them.

Then, murmuring with a heavy heart that he would nevertheless keep faith with Finn, Diarmaid led Grainne off into the night. They travelled far, crossing the River Shannon at Athlone, until they came at last to the place called the Wood of the Two Huts. It was there, in the middle of the wood, that Diarmaid made a dwelling for Grainne, with a fence woven out of willow wands and so built that it had seven doors by which they might escape from it.

When Finn woke from his drugged sleep and learned of the flight of Diarmaid and Grainne, he was consumed by a rage so dark that his friends feared for his wits and felt more sympathy for Diarmaid than for their jealous lord. [...]

Then it was agreed that, for the sake of peace, those conditions would be granted, and after their sixteen hard years of wandering, Diarmaid and Grainne were allowed to settle far away from Finn and Tara, in a fair place that was called Rath Grainne. Four sons and a daughter were born to them there, and for a long time they lived in such peace that men would say there was no richer man in Ireland, nor one more filled with content than Diarmaid, who had been a wandering outcast once.

As part of the peace settlement a new marriage was arranged between Finn and another of Cormac's daughters, but ever afterwards a residue of bitterness burned in his heart for the shame that Diarmaid had brought on him. Nor was Grainne herself wholly content, for she thought it a shame on the honour of her house that neither the High King her father, nor Finn the first man of the Fianna, ever came there to grace it with their presence.

One day she complained of this to her husband and Diarmaid asked why she would want them to come when she knew the enmity they still bore towards him in their hearts. But how was it ever to be ended, Grainne protested, if no generous or fond-hearted word ever passed between them? "It is my wish that we give them a great feast here at our home," she said, "and that way you will again win their affection."

So Diarmaid consented to it, and Finn came with all the host of the Fianna to Rath Grainne; and Cormac mac Art, High King of Ireland, came with all his retinue, and a great feasting was made that lasted from night to night throughout the space of a whole year.

On the last night of that festive year Diarmaid heard the voices of hounds at chase sounding through his sleep. When he asked Grainne if she heard the noise, she said that it was only a dream laid on him by the *Tuatha de Danaan*, and he should shake it from him. But on the next morning, Diarmaid rode out to see who it was that hunted on his land. At the crest of Ben Gulbainn he found Finn alone but for his great hound, Bran. Angrily Diarmaid demanded if it was he who had hunted there that night in breach of their agreement. But Finn denied that he had been hunting, saying only that when he had been out exercising his hounds, one of them had lit on the scent of a wild boar. It was a dangerous beast that the Fianna had failed to hunt down many times, and had already killed thirty of his men. Then Finn looked out across the hill and saw where the boar was thundering towards them, driven on by the huntsmen of the Fianna. "There is danger to you in confronting that boar, Diarmaid," he said. "We should leave the hill to him."

Stung by Finn's condescension, Diarmaid declared that he was not afraid to face a charging boar, and knew no reason that he should not do so.

"Do you not know," Finn answered him, "that it was your own father who killed the son of a steward once, and that the steward used his magic power to turn his son's remains into that earless Green Boar, vowing that one day your father's son would die on its tusks?"

"I know nothing of that," said Diarmaid, "nor will I quit my own hill because of a boar. Lend me your hound Bran and I will put an end to the beast."

But Finn would not lend him the hound, saying that Bran had often faced this boar before and could do nothing against it. Then Diarmaid looked Finn long in the eye and said, "It is in my mind that you made this hunt to find my death, Finn."

"And if that were so," Finn answered, "did you not give me good cause to wish your death when you shamed me before all the Fianna in Tara's hall?"

"And do you still blame me for that, Finn," said Diarmaid, "when in all my life I never did anything against you but that one thing? And even that I did only because Grainne put her bonds on me, and I would not fail in my bonds for all the good there might be in the world." And when Finn did not answer him, he sighed and added, "Yet if my death is waiting for me here, then there is no use in my fleeing from it."

So Diarmaid balanced his javelin in his hand, saying, "It is an unwise thing not to follow the counsel of a good woman, for Grainne bade me bring my great sword, the *Moralltach*, with me this morning, and I did not heed her." Then he turned away from Finn and advanced across the hill to face the charge of the boar that the huntsmen of the Fianna drove towards him. And when the boar was close upon him he took straight aim and hurled it with all his strength so that the point hit the beast squarely in its tusked face. Yet the spear glanced off that massive head, leaving its bristled hide unscratched, and still it came on at him. So Diarmaid drew the short sword at his side and brought it down over the boar as it reached him; but the blade broke across its back, and the tusks of the boar tore into him as it threw him from his feet, and gored and trampled him so that his bowels were out where he lay on the ground of Ben Gulbain.

With the last of his strength, Diarmaid turned as the force of the boar carried its hot bulk past, and lifting the hilt of the sword that was still in his hand, he hurled it with such despairing fury that it crashed into the back of the boar's skull and smashed its brains. Then Diarmaid lay back in his blood under the heavy sky.

When Finn came up to him, the dying hero said, "And will you not save me, Finn, for it is well known that water brought in your hands has the power to heal any man not yet dead?"

"I know of no spring on this hill," Finn answered.

"Not nine steps from where you stand," Diarmaid gasped, "is the best spring in all Ireland."

By this time the huntsmen of the Fianna had come up, with Finn's grandson, Oscar, at their head; and when Oscar heard this and saw that Finn still did not move he urged him to bring the water to his dying friend without delay. So Finn went to the spring and gathered water in his cupped hands, but as he stared into the little pool his thoughts darkened and by the time he came back to where Diarmaid lay, all the water had slipped away between his fingers.

With the blood already at his mouth, Diarmaid said, "Is your heart still so hard against me, Finn? Will you not bring me some water now?"

So Finn returned to the spring and filled his hands again, but again the thought of Grainne darkened his mind, and his hands were empty on his return. A piteous sigh broke from Diarmaid's throat then, and Oscar stood before Finn saying, "I beg you to bring him some water, Finn, for if you do not, I vow that one or other of us will die beside him on this hill."

Finn hastened back to the spring then; and when he returned the cup of his healing hands was filled, but even as he knelt beside the man who had been both his enemy and his friend, the breath passed out of Diarmaid, and all the men of the Fianna gave out three shouts for the grievous pity of that death.

CHAPTER 4

DUKE OF WELLINGTON (ENGLISH): NATIONAL HERO

INTRODUCTION

National heroes are as old as nations. Abraham, Moses, and David are heroes of ancient Israel; Aeneas, Romulus, and Numa, heroes of ancient Rome. Sir Arthur Wellesley (1769–1852), the first Duke of Wellington, was a statesman, including Prime Minister, but he was above all a general, and was most acclaimed for his defeat of Napoleon at Waterloo in 1815, sending Napoleon into his second and permanent exile. The veneration accorded Wellington bordered on worship. In the following selection Iain Pears shows how he came to symbolize the English char-acter and how his success was seen as the inevitable triumph of the English character over any other – with the French character symbolized by Napoleon himself. Wellington's heroism lay in his gentlemanly quali-ties: his modesty, his steadfastness, his self-discipline, his common sense. He was imagined to embody the aristocratic qualities that England would need in fending off the continuing threat posed by France. That threat was not merely of renewed war but also of French-like revolution at home. Of the thousands of biographies of Wellington, see, for example, Elizabeth Longford, *Wellington*, 2 vols. (London: Weidenfeld & Nicol-son, 1969 and 1972); and Neville Thompson, *Wellington after Waterloo* (London: Routledge & Kegan Paul, 1986). On national myths, see *Myths and Nationhood*, eds. Geoffrey Hosking and George Schöpflin (London: Hurst, 1997).

Original publication: Iain Pears, "The Gentleman and the Hero: Wellington and Napoleon in the Nineteenth Century," in *Myths of the English*, ed. Roy Porter (Cam-bridge: Polity Press, 1992), ch. 9 (pp. 216–36).

THE GENTLEMAN AND THE HERO

Iain Pedrs

Since the earliest guidebooks in the sixteenth century, the English view of the foreigner has changed remarkably little. Despite the rise and fall of several empires, the alliances with and wars against virtually every country on the Eurasian continent, the English have been able to comfort themselves with the view that foreign character is pretty much stable. From the Tudors if not earlier, Germans have been seen as obedient but unimaginative gluttons; Italians as greasy and dishonest; Spaniards as cold and sinister; the French as dandies and egotists; the Dutch as worthy but dull. All, it went without saying, were untrustworthy, most were dishonest and none could match an Englishman.

The constancy of these stereotypes is strange, considering that Englishmen's views of themselves – and hence of the qualities which they considered worthy – have undergone remarkable transformations in the same period. In the sixteenth century, Erasmus commented on their openness, and proneness to kissing everyone. In the seventeenth century, they went through a dour and serious phase before national frivolity broke out once more. While supposedly possessing Bottom, that great ability to endure suffering without complaint, the eighteenth-century English were very much proud of their emotions, which supposedly led them to burst into tears on any occasion, commit suicide with frequency, become melancholy, get drunk and fall in love with noisy panache.

The arrival of the Victorian worship of self-discipline – again in myth if not necessarily in reality – represented an enormous swing of self-perception that was accompanied by the rise of the Great Man cult. The nineteenth century saw the production of innumerable biographies, portraits and statues to give examples of true merit. This was not, of course, an entirely new phenomenon; a "temple of British Worthies" had been constructed at Stowe in the 1740s and in the early eighteenth century "heads of eminent men" were displayed to inspire the owners with thoughts of greatness. The difference was that the eighteenth-century hero tended to be long dead, the representative of abstract ideals – courage, patriotism, learning and so on; the nineteenth century revered more recent heroes, frequently ones who were still alive, presenting their lives in close detail through the medium of the well-researched, authoritative and often polemical biography, and stressing the qualities of their personality as much as their deeds.

69

The visions of the foreigner and the Englishman were embedded in stereotypical characters for simplicity's sake, with the creation of a gallery of stock characters – the mynheer, the bürgermeister, the courtly fop, the bravo, the inquisitorial priest – which served to encapsulate each nation and was contrasted with an equally stereotypical Englishman – the squire, John Bull, or whoever. Such characters popped up in cartoons, on the stage and in literature from the sixteenth century to the nineteenth. At the same time, and on a slightly more intellectual level, real characters from history or the recent past could be brought into close proximity, one of the classic combinations being the trio of Henry VIII, Francis I and Charles V: bluff and hearty, frivolous and artistic, serious and pious. Other conjunctions – Elizabeth and Philip, Marlborough and Louis XIV, Buckingham and Richelieu – could all be compressed through the medium of history or biography in a way which illuminated, reinforced and, in some measure, created differences in national character.

Of all the nineteenth century's modern heroes, the Duke of Wellington was by far the most eminent, and the contrast between him and Napoleon Bonaparte was an enduring element in contemporary literature. The importance of this conjunction is no longer obvious; Napoleon is still a perennial topic for biography and continues to exert a fascination, but the reputation of Wellington has faded somewhat. Children are no longer taught about Vittoria, Salamanca or the Talavera, let alone Assaye; his tomb draws only a fraction of the visitors who go to the Invalides. This personal eclipse, however, partly masks the permanent impact Wellington exercised in the way his character, and the qualities he came to symbolize, became built into the national consciousness as part of the essential fabric of Englishness. This is not to assert that Wellington created a new image of what it was to be English; rather, he encapsulated a newly-forming vision of national type which, through his personal success and the way he could be opposed to the personification of foreign threat, provided a form of shorthand by which this notion could be disseminated.

In this essay I will try to lay out the salient elements of Wellingtonian Englishness, and to argue that he represented the prototype of a new model gentleman, fine-tuned to suit the requirements of an industrial but hierarchic society still deeply alarmed at the implications of France's revolutionary legacy. Particularly after his withdrawal from active politics and especially after his death, Wellington-worship was a curious amalgam of diverse elements – xenophobia, modernism, chivalry, patriotism, individualism, classicism. Equally, it was a reasonable reflection of the Duke himself, for he imprinted his character on the English self-image at the same time as he was a vehicle for national aspiration and moulded himself to fit the requirements of others. As he himself said: "I am the Duke of Wellington, and must do as the Duke of Wellington doth."

For several hundred years the English had, against all contrary evidence, loudly asserted their superiority over – and to – all comers. It was disconcerting when Waterloo suggested this boasting might be true after all. Being the richest and most powerful nation in Europe was dangerous unless reasons could be found to explain it; unless the sources of superiority could be isolated, they could not be reproduced, and if they were not reproduced England's dominance would prove illegitimate and perhaps also short-lived. Modern scholarship would maintain that the explanation which found favour – one based essentially on an account of character – was entirely erroneous. None the less, it was still strongly held and found its most perfect embodiment in the victor of Waterloo. "In all that has singled out England from the nations, and given her the front place in the history of the world, the Duke of Wellington was emphatically an Englishman."

Perhaps one of the highest points of extreme "Wellingtonism" came on the 18 November 1852, when he was given the last heraldic funeral in England. The emphasis on elements of chivalry was unusual; as a writer to the *Gentleman's Magazine* noted, heraldic devices were now rare: "In the ordinary modern funeral, even of persons of the highest rank, all these various modes of heraldic display are now obsolete." However much the code of chivalry was attracting renewed attention, Wellington's funeral was unique in being awash with Pennons, Guidons and Banners, Trophies, Atchievements and Bannerols. Similarly, enormous play was made in almost every newspaper and magazine which wrote on the event (and they all did) of the extraordinary list of honours the Duke racked up over his long life, this being read out in full by a herald over his coffin and reprinted almost obsessively by biographers for the next two decades.

Alongside this clear reference to English hierarchy and tradition, however, the funeral also stressed classical parallels and more modern elements of British history. The funeral car itself was a direct allusion to the long line of British worthies who had been similarly honoured – including Cromwell (1658), Marlborough (1722) and Nelson (1806) – but also to the common ancestor of them all, the wagon which had borne Alexander the Great to Alexandria. At the same time, and showing the distinct footprints of Prince Albert, instructions were issued that the car "should...do credit to the taste of the artists of England". More than this, it was to "afford an instance of the remarkable rapidity with which the most elaborate works can be manufactured in the gigantic establishments of Sheffield and Birmingham".

71

The funeral ceremony itself was also an exemplar of modernism, a state affair which built on the experience of the Great Exhibition the previous year, and had some of the same objects in view. For contemporary commentators, the significance of both was proven by the sheer quantity of people who attended, the mobilization of a mass audience serving as a demonstration of national solidarity and unity. At both, the huge numbers were brought in by rail, with the rail companies organizing special funeral excursions for the latter occasion. Equally, recent practice in handling large numbers of people – the police were organized by the man who had directed crowd control at the Exhibition – enabled the authorities to ensure a dignified ceremony by concentrating forces in the places where experience suggested they might most be needed.

But why was such an enormous effort made to honour Wellington? He was, certainly, England's most distinguished military commander since Marlborough, but it was none the less the case that no general had ever been praised, in life or in death, with the extraordinary generosity he received. Part of the explanation lay not merely in his role in recent events but also in the way in which much of the history of Europe was reconstructed by English writers around the middle of the century. Just as the Whig historians had tended to present a spectacle of progress towards the triumph of constitutional liberty, so now the international past was recast as an inexorable rise towards national hegemony. Sir Edward Creasy's *Fifteen Decisive Battles of the World*, for example, presented a logical progression from Marathon to Waterloo, with the last campaign ushering in an era of universal peace, freedom and prosperity. Wellington was portrayed, therefore, not merely as a successful general, but rather as the culmination of two millennia of strife, and as the man who finally produced the peace of nations under the benevolence of English supremacy. A further stimulus, of course, was the more immediate fear that this happy state might prove short-lived without the sturdy resistance which he represented; his funeral took place less than a year after the *coup d'état* which brought Napoleon III to the French throne, and authors of all stripes linked the death of the English hero and the resurrection of the French one through his nephew as a possibly ominous sign for the future.

More overtly, however, the event was also shaped as an answer to a similar funeral which took place in Paris some twelve years previously, with the "retour des cendres" and the ceremonial burying of Napoleon Bonaparte's mortal remains under the dome of Les Invalides. From the beginning, comparisons were made with this earlier ceremony. While the French funeral had been sneered at for the gimcrack nature of its decorations, and the flimsy, temporary style of its furniture, the organizers of the Duke's farewell set out to ensure that it contained "nothing mean, tawdry, theatrical, inappropriate". While Napoleon's funeral car was of "pine and papier-maché", Wellington's was of bronze and oak. The funeral was to emphasize substance rather than style, and provide a material contrast between English solidity and the French preference for flashy but empty display.

None the less, caution was required. The English liked to see themselves as a nation pre-eminently able to produce heroes, but peculiarly resistant to the fawning displays of devotion to them that was so dangerous an element of the French character. As the *Illustrated London News* explained, "The English are said to be a people who do not understand shows and celebrations... unlike the French and other nations of the continent, they have no real taste for ceremonial. There is, doubtless, some truth in this. We are a practical people." The funeral of the Duke was thus not an adulatory farewell for a Great Man, but rather a demonstration that the English could excel even at things for which they had no natural affinity: "What Englishmen resolve to do, they always do well;... this event shall be solemnised as becomes the mightiest nation in the world." Equally, the Wellington who was entombed in St Paul's had not aroused such emotions when he was Prime Minister in the 1830s; his direct political involvement rather tended to be written off as something of an aberration by authors more concerned with delineating the greatness of his character and concentrating on the magnitude of his military achievements.

Just as Wellington's funeral took place in the shadow of Napoleon's and was in a sense an answer to it, so the depiction of the Duke's character was marked throughout all the biographies by the presence of his great adversary. This was inevitable; Wellington's entire career depended on Napoleon, and the parallels between the two men – born in the same year, educated in French military academies, rising through their abilities, leading their countries' armies, and meeting once in a final showdown – were too obvious and appealing to be resisted. "There does not exist an epic, the foundations of which are better suited for artistic purposes than the story of Wellington's struggle with Napoleon's power."

Carefully interpreted, the quarter century of fighting involving the whole of Europe could be reduced to a more simple collision between two countries and two sets of ideas as represented by two men. That they were portrayed in highly different fashions goes without saying, but nothing could be further from the truth than the comment of a French journalist that "France and England will never agree on the manner of judging Napoleon and the Duke of Wellington". In fact, French and English commentators agreed almost entirely; it was the meaning read into the judgements which often differed radically.

From the beginning, the biographical approaches to the two men have differed markedly. It is, for example, remarkable how Wellington's *personal* reputation is jealously guarded. While Napoleon's memory has been subjected to innumerable accounts of his somewhat dull love life, the state of his haemorrhoids examined in medical treatises, his relationship with his mother and his marshals scrutinized for the slightest sign of homosexuality, his death analysed for evidence of murder, the personal activities of Wellington – who had as many, if not more, affairs and whose attitude to such matters was much more open than the somewhat prim Bonaparte's – have been treated with the most extreme delicacy.

To a considerable extent, the pair were responsible for their later reputations; certainly few men in the period devoted as much time to the attempt to fine-tune their images. Napoleon laboured away on St Helena writing his memoirs to boost the idea of the peaceful law-giver; Wellington carefully had others edit vast volumes of his dispatches to strengthen the image of "a chief, distant, Olympian, severe". Thus, he was described as being disdainful of honours and titles, despite the enormous collection he acquired, some of which he solicited; mindful only of his duty, despite the vast financial rewards he accumulated; too direct and honest to be a politician, despite three years as Prime Minister and nearly two decades of dominance in the back rooms of power. His military reputation was scarcely touched by the fact that his role in baulking reforms led to disaster in Crimea, his reputation as a defender of liberty unmarked by his willingness to turn out the troops to block reform movements in England.

To list these factors is not to say that Wellington was in fact reprehensible; rather, I merely wish to note that abundant material existed for an unfavourable portrait at the time of his death or afterwards, had anyone wanted to make use of it. It is similarly notable that, however much his memory might have faded in recent decades, his reputation has not changed a great deal. On most important points, the portrait painted in Elizabeth Longford's biography of 1969 is the same as that offered by Brialmont in 1852, or Guedalla in 1931. Biographers create their subjects through the material they choose to use; with Wellington the concern was to present a picture of almost unalloyed virtue embodied in a particular character and outlook. As with many other heroes, too, memorialists were not always content to stay firmly with the record, but were often happy to invent anecdotes to fit the point being made. Some at least of the Duke's reputation for the terse but pungent *bon mot* depends on statements he never actually made or which were improved on afterwards.

For all that many admired him, most French commentators assigned Wellington a very secondary place in the universal pantheon of Great

Men. John Lemoinne maintained that "it will not be said that Wellington was of the true race of Heroes". Biographies of Napoleon habitually compare the Emperor with the likes of Alexander, Caesar and Charlemagne, that is, with soldier–rulers, rather than with mere generals. Rarely do his admirers even bother to mention the man who beat him at Waterloo. Indeed, they implied that Wellington did not defeat Napoleon; only God was mighty enough to bring him down: "To the question, was it possible for Napoleon to win this battle, our answer is, No. Because of Wellington? Because of Blucher? No. Because of God... Napoleon had been impeached in heaven and his fall decreed; he was troublesome to God." For admirers of Napoleon, French or English, the Emperor bestrode the continent like a colossus, while Wellington was a mere theatre commander. Any comparison between the two could only reduce the Emperor and, according to one French author, the Duke was almost unknown in France by the time of his death. In contrast, writers on Wellington rarely adopted the tactic of trying to diminish Napoleon's ability – "Let him be exalted, on the contrary, for it suffices to have conquered and dethroned him" – rather laying out a series of parallel but opposite qualities possessed by their chosen champion. Waterloo was sufficient demonstration of their superiority.

So what lessons did admirers of Wellington draw from the perusal of the two careers? In the stampede of biographies that followed his death, the contest between the two men was elevated to a battle of giants, a personalized clash in which two opposing forces – good and bad, Frenchness and Englishness struggled against each other. Generally speaking, there was agreement that, if seen in strictly personal terms, Napoleon was infinitely superior as both man and hero: "It may be conceded that the schemes of the French emperor were more comprehensive, his genius more dazzling, and his imagination more vivid...". In comparison, his opponent was a plodder: most commentators were willing to agree, more or less, with Hugo's statement that "Wellington was the technician of war, Napoleon was its Michelangelo." This, of course, meant that Waterloo needed to be explained. None of the constituent elements of Wellington's success was flashy, none would ever excite any but the most diligently patriotic poets to launch into verse. But, demonstrably, they won, and it was in Wellington's very mundaneness, the almost dull doggedness that eschewed personal extravagance, that the source of true greatness was found.

So, in contrast to his opponent's fire and brilliance, Wellington possessed "patience in action", or "simplicity sublime". As the *Times* obituary put it, allying his achievements with the fundamental nature of the nation, "the chief characteristic of Wellington's mind was that sterling good sense which is said to distinguish the capacities of his countrymen in general". Common sense was not important merely as a personal quality, but could be seen to have had profound political overtones. Napoleon was the upstart, the man gifted with talents so enormous that they could not be contained and which ended up being perverted and used for personal gain, Wellington was forever the loyal servant, acting for the best of his King and country at all times:

> "From the instant I gained a superiority, I have recognised neither master nor laws" – was the confession of Napoleon.

> "I am the Prince Regent's servant; and will do whatever he and his government pleases" – was the language of Wellington.

Napoleon was the creation of the revolution, and ended by bringing his country and cause to ruin and defeat. Wellington, the product of Burkean conservatism, boosted his to world dominance and utter security. In the political and social turmoil of the period of reform and Chartism, their careers were also a lesson in the virtues of English political stability:

> With a nation like the French, fond of glory, enamoured more of equality than of liberty, a general like Bonaparte must of necessity arrive at dictatorial power, and next, at the crown. But with a nation like the English, a man of Wellington's mould could aspire but to constitutional and regular greatness. On both sides, men and countries were admirably adapted to each other.

The self-characterization of Wellington as "nimmukwallah", a man who had "eaten the King's salt" and was bound to obey him forever, was perhaps the most constant theme referred to throughout biographies, and was again a characteristic accepted as perfectly English by domestic and foreign commentators.

Allied to this theme of service to the state was a contest to gain the moral high ground of classical precedent. On both sides of the channel, Roman memory was important; Napoleon's eagles, legion of honour and triumphal arches are an easy demonstration of French awareness. But whereas admirers of Napoleon preferred to concentrate on the soldier, laying stress on the period before the Imperial adventure, supporters of Wellington concentrated on Napoleon as Emperor: for them, the Englishman was the representative of Roman republican values, with Napoleonic egotism and self-aggrandizement embodying the excesses of Roman decline. Wellington is compared to the likes of Fabius, Scipio and other loyal servants of the ancient Republic – "In all he seemed the Roman of old, save in pomp." Equally, ever more stress is laid on Spartan simplicity, again in a fashion which erases something of the true picture. Thus the youthful dandy, or the Wellington of Apsley House and Stratfield Saye, vanishes in favour of the "abstemious, active, self-denying man" who never tasted wine or spirits, rose at dawn and slept on a couch with a pillow stuffed with horsehair. Moreover, there were few who omitted to draw the appropriate moral lesson that the revolutionary who grabbed for personal supremacy brought the world down on his head, while the loyal servant ended up as Prime Minister, loaded with riches and honours, and died universally admired and loved:

> The emperor fell, the scaffolding crumbled away and he who raised it with heroic temerity only survived his irreparable shipwreck for a few years in exile. His fortunate rival...saw open before him another career...is not such a lesson a striking proof of the final ascendency of reason and of good sense over all the boldness and all the flights of imagination and of genius?

In military ability also, biographers almost deliberately stressed different aspects of the two men's respective abilities, so that Napoleon appeared a more exciting leader and Wellington a less. While the Emperor's strategic skills and vision in command were constantly referred to – the lightning dashes across half a continent, the tactical flair and imaginative grasp of strategic possibilities – Wellington was singled out for his logistical skills, his caution and his humanity. Such an opposition is forced; Napoleon's success lay above all in his organizational abilities and Wellington was capable of rapid and imaginative moves. The way such a contrast was built up through selection of evidence again illuminates the method by which the Englishman was shown to be superior. Wellington relied little on providence and more on forward planning. Napoleon, beloved of fate, was supported by fortune in the manner of a Greek hero, and when fortune abandoned him he fell. Much of his success, therefore, was owed less to his inherent abilities than to plain good luck:

> Napoleon might be said to have been one of those brilliant, but wild batsmen who with luck in their favour can hit up a century in record time. In his first innings sixes and boundaries flowed from his bat, but with catches dropped all over the field... His luck held for a long time...but he never attempted to play for his side and in other features of his game he was quite useless. His second innings was short and ignominious, though the bowling against him was easy and his opponents an unpractised and hastily got together team.

English accounts refer frequently to the rapacity of French troops but stress Wellington's attempts to keep his under control. Once again, the contrast is forced. The sack of Badajoz was as violent as anything performed by the Grand Army, and the death of more than 100,000 Portuguese as a result of the Torres Vedras campaign generally fails to be mentioned even in a footnote. Such omissions were virtually compelled by the idealized opposition created between Napoleon the egotist and destroyer, and Wellington the selfless protector:

> [Napoleon] marshalled on his side licence, cupidity and expediency and transfigured them with a bright haze of glory. Wellington headed the protest of law against licence, of conscience against cupidity, of justice against expediency, and walked in the plain light of duty... In Napoleon's case, living men became dead corpses merely to prop his throne; in Wellington's they were sacrificed that mankind might be delivered from an intolerable yoke.

Thus, the juxtaposition of the two men, and the aspects of their careers singled out for emphasis, were essential for the task of transforming Wellington – the man who restored the Bourbons in Spain and France, who opposed the Reform Act and deployed thousands of troops to protect London against the Chartists – into the champion of liberty: "The sword of Wellington was never drawn to enslave, but to liberate. He was never the oppressor, but always the friend of the nations among whom he appeared."

For all that Wellington was presented as a saviour, however, the picture presented was not one of a typical hero; rather, biographers were at pains to leave such characteristics to the Emperor and define their subject almost in deliberate opposition to them. However electric and fascinating, heroes were dangerous people to have around in a quiet, peaceful, law-abiding country. Heroes, especially romantic ones, had particular qualities that enabled them to be recognized. Above all there was the notion of destiny, of being touched by God and preordained for great things. While biographers of Napoleon successfully isolated incidents from his youth which presage the actions of the man – for example his leading a snowball fight at school – writers on Wellington gave up and confessed that he was not a "heaven-born general". Quite the opposite, in fact; in his youth, even his mother remarked that "anyone can see he has not the cut of a soldier". Wellington's achievements came from hard work, study and practice. While he earned greatness, Napoleon did not, in the sense that the Frenchman had no option but to be great – the implication being that Wellington was in some way more meritorious and industrious.

A second aspect of heroes is that they leave everything changed after them, their presence in the world pushing it in a new direction. The hero is a man who upsets the status quo. Wellington's impact was less dramatic; Napoleon tore the world to pieces, and Wellington's task was merely to put it back together again:

> Having battled for the established order as a soldier, he fought a rearguard action against change as a politician. Calculating and grudging retreat was scarcely the stuff of the hero; Wellington and his ilk were not creators, inventors, parents of ideas. The world cannot live upon negations; it requires faith, as lungs require air. Man must love liberty as an absolute good, not submit to it as a necessary evil.

A third characteristic is that heroes have, to use the modern term, charisma; their uniqueness is instantly sensible to those who come into contact with them. Again, Napoleon, portrayed as Jove, the man who struck like a thunderbolt, had this quality and he "dazzled the world". Wellington's personality never dazzled anyone; Nelson took him for some junior officer until told who he was. At the opposite end of his life he was accosted in the street by someone who thought he was "Mr Smith". The anecdotes themselves would be trivial, but for the fact that they were repeated countless times by biographers who sensed in them something characteristic of a man who, although inordinately vain about his position, liked to present himself as ordinary. The image also comes through in art: Ingres showed Napoleon as Jupiter or touching soldiers for scrofula; David's portrayal of Napoleon crossing the Alps shows an elemental hero. The parallel depiction of Wellington crossing the Pyrenees looks more like an English gentleman out for an afternoon's exercise in Kent. In his life and in the way he was represented, Wellington was portrayed in a consciously unheroic fashion.

Similarly, heroes inspire enormous love and loyalty in those who will pick themselves up and follow. Napoleon was said to have generated enormous passion among his army and among the French, driving his hungry and ill-equipped soldiers in Italy on to ever greater deeds through his personality, oratory and example. The image of the *petit caporal* was carefully preserved throughout the period of Empire, as one of the few remnants of revolutionary fraternalism. Wellington inspired little devotion in those who served him. While Napoleon talked to his soldiers in the familiar *tu*, Wellington pointed at his with a cane and called them scum. Napoleon liked to give his troops a fraternal embrace, Wellington recommended flogging them. "He was not a loveable character," said one historian, while another noted that he acquired a reputation for being unsympathetic, ungenerous and ungrateful to his subordinates. He never spoke of glory to his army, and took no interest in soldiers once his task was done; the army was packed up "like a machine", and unlike other generals Wellington associated afterwards only with his old officers. Again this was taken as a reflection of national character:

> The English soldier does not like to feed upon imagination, and with empty stomach he would not care much about being contemplated by forty centuries. But with such high-sounding words as those you will make the French soldier go on to the end of the world...it is quite enough to talk to him of victory and glory; he will readily die for the sake of a rhyme.

A further element of nineteenth-century heroism was individualism, and the way biographers treated both men in this respect presents one of the most intricate tinkerings with conventions in the portraits. Napoleon's genius marked him as an individual *par excellence*; Wellington's contentment with serving militated against such isolation. But from another perspective there was an attempt to reverse the picture: Napoleon's achievement was seen as the result of the mass mobilization of an entire country, and indeed an entire continent; his victories were ascribed to the vast resources he had at his disposal and represented as the ultimate expression of French centralism. Wellington, on the other hand, was presented as the lone voice in the wilderness, fighting almost forgotten in the Peninsula, the only person who could see that victory was possible and having to defeat not only the French but also the British government in order to achieve his ends. His triumph was the embodiment of the confused and ramshackle approach in which the English have always taken such inordinate pride. Again this point was raised almost to a key tenet of military theory to explain his victory. Wellington's professionalism was downplayed in favour of pragmatic improvisation so that it could be contrasted with the rigidities of a Cartesian devotion to grand plans: "They planned their campaigns just as you might make a splendid piece of harness. It looks very well; and answers very well; until it gets broken; and then you are done for. Now I made my campaigns of ropes. If anything went wrong, I tied a knot; and went on." Wellington himself stressed his indispensability: "I am obliged to be everywhere and if absent from any operation something goes wrong." Later authors also concentrated on the idea that the British government was more of an obstacle than a help to his progress. "Napoleon was never...so harassed by the French, as Wellington was by the English, Spanish and Portuguese governments." The point was of some importance, and it was the only one in which French and English biographers differed, each trying to demonstrate that their hero was the more personally responsible for his achievements. Hugo maintained that the victory of Waterloo was the victory of the army, not of the general, while also implying that Napoleon's triumphs were his own. An obituary in the legitimist *L'Union* maintained that, far from the government impeding Wellington, he was merely "the instrument of British policy".

Finally, the true hero resembled a human meteor; such people "burn quickly and die young". Alexander, the greatest of them, conquered the world and died by his mid-thirties; more recently the likes of Shelley, Byron and Schubert, romantic artists all, died before middle age. Nelson, the opposite of Wellington in many ways, and Wolfe, died at the point of ultimate victory. Wellington neither burned himself out nor ended his career in exile, poverty or misunderstood disgrace. He "had none of that compulsive anxiety, or of that theatrical melancholy, which often leads heroes to private asylums". Or, it could be added, leads them to exile. While Napoleon ended as Prometheus, chained to the rock of St Helena, Wellington's iron control of his talents and passions enabled him to outlive his rival by thirty years and end his days strolling in Hyde Park surrounded by grandchildren and universal adulation. Napoleon in death was shown in apotheosis, the heavens rent by an enormous thunderstorm; the illustration of Wellington dying showed him comfortably asleep in his armchair, surrounded by friends and family, to the accompaniment of typically English drizzle. In all, one was depicted through allegory, the other was shown in comfortable, affluent domesticity.

The post-mortem contest and contrast of Napoleon and Wellington was given many meanings by those who used it. It typified the contest of order against revolution (or freedom against feudalism for the Napoleonists); of method against madness (or caution against genius); of modesty against ambition, of civilization against anarchy and even of gentlemen against players. It is notable, for example, that while English writers stressed Napoleon's professionalism to the point of describing him virtually as a mercenary, Wellington's equally professional outlook on soldiering was played down. In the context of the English tradition that very much distrusted the narrowing effects of specialization, preferring the generalist as the more appropriate embodiment of gentility, this is not, perhaps, altogether surprising, especially when combined with a long-standing suspicion of standing armies and a preference for local militias too incompetent to pose a constitutional threat. However inappropriate, the notion that Waterloo represented the triumph of the gentleman over the professional was another major element in Wellington's Englishness.

While Napoleon's genius made him an aberration who could be admired but not imitated, the qualities of a Wellington – acquired rather than innate, human rather than godlike – could serve as a useful example for others. Biographers were at pains to point out that the abilities of Wellington were such that he would have been successful at any task to which he turned his hand, great or small. The qualities of a Napoleon, in contrast, could only come through in the deeds he performed: without an entire continent at his disposal and an empire to run, he rapidly became absurd. For Wellington's biographers it was a note of praise to assert that he had many of the qualities of a good book-keeper, and to mention that his post-Waterloo career was longer than his time as a serving soldier. Napoleon could not do anything but be himself; he withered and died after power was taken from him, and his efforts to drill a couple of hundred troops on Elba, or cultivate his garden on St Helena, became a symbol of personal decline.

The elaborate construction of the two men had the strange effect of making the defender of hierarchy more of a "man of the people" than was the son of revolution. As servant of the Crown he acted more in the interests of the people than Bonaparte as the self-appointed protector of 1789. However high his achievements raised him, Wellington was merely a man and a subject, and so others could follow the path he took without endangering everyone else. His career and success were moral object lessons for those who came after him, the main point being that staying within the system was both more honourable and more rewarding than trying to change it. "Children of England, great and noble as Wellington was, here are qualities you can all imitate. This is the stuff of which heroes are made . . . This path of duty is the *Queen's* highway open to both sexes and to all ranks and conditions . . . " The difficulty was, of course, that it could have been reasonably pointed out that relatively few women, hand-loom weavers or coal miners had much of a chance of being elevated to the peerage, let alone being placed in command of an army or made Prime Minister. To counter such arguments Wellington was recast in such a way that he became both the epitome of hierarchy and an example of the new meritocracy, a mingling of two conceptions of personal value that had been effectively opposed for at least a century. In this respect his origins as a member of the somewhat lowly Irish aristocracy was useful. While his aristocratic forebears enabled genealogists to stretch his lineage back to the English warrior King Edward I, and enormous stress was placed on his place in the social hierarchy, he was also presented – indeed he developed the impression himself – as a form of self-made man, who rose through talent rather than connection: "He possessed interest enough to make merit available, but not enough to dispense with it. On a remarkable occasion in after times he spoke, in the House of Peers, of having 'raised himself' by his own exertions to the position he then filled."

Since the sixteenth century, gentility in England has been described in terms of both birth and merit. While Wellington was more than aware of the former – his tendency to prefer members of the aristocacy for officers has been widely noted – the public presentation emphasized the latter. He became the ultimate definition of gentility, of social and political position justified by merit rather than as a right, and thus helped modify the concept which, throughout the nineteenth century, was the English ideological answer to the revolutionary notion of equality. As a response to the Citizen, the English placed greater stress on the Gentleman, and found its most perfect embodiment in the man who was "far prouder of being an English gentleman than of all his honours and titles".

While in the context of English politics Wellington could be presented as a self-made man, in that of international competition, his aristocratic birth was stressed. Wellington had the balance, modesty and moderation of the true gentleman by birth; Napoleon the vulgarity, coarseness and excitability of the Mediterranean *parvenu*. Wellington's measured tone was contrasted with the egotistical propaganda of France, with authors particularly fixing on Waterloo as the ultimate example; very few fail to mention that whereas Napoleon issued a triumphant dispatch announcing victory before the battle had started, Wellington's own account was so underplayed that many thought he was announcing a defeat. Again, the evidence was stretched to make if fit the contrast between English understatement and French bombast. Wellington's army frequently complained that his dispatches failed to mention meritorious conduct and gave the impression that he alone was responsible for victory; where these complaints are referred to, his actions are explained away as arising from his belief that all had acted as a team.

National myths grow out of circumstance and survive even when a substantial body of evidence exists to suggest that they may, in fact, be erroneous. The association of character and power embodied by Wellington not only survived throughout the heyday of Empire; the type he represented may be said to have reached its apotheosis in the Second World War. Once again, the image was of an England standing alone, threatened by a foreign tyrant and nearly defeated by a larger, more aggressive foe. None the less it overcame its civilized distaste for fighting, and won through by sheer persistence when all others had given up. The public school fighter pilots were the descendants of Wellington's aristocratic officers, just as Montgomery's logistical skills and caution were considered sounder than Rommel's dash and flair. Churchill took on the previously Wellingtonian role of the lone outsider convinced that victory was possible and getting on with producing one. As with the Napoleonic wars, the verdict tends to be that England should not have won; that

83

Germany had the greater resources and the better generals and was better able to mobilize an ideologically inspired society, while all Britain had was a dogged determination to defend freedom and civilization. Ultimately, defects of character brought Hitler low, just as they had undermined Napoleon, and British moral superiority enabled the nation to keep its nerve until the foreigner made the fatal mistake which reified his faulty personality. The fact that the crucial error in both cases was to invade Russia made the parallel even more convincing.

Each age needs its myths, and the Victorian age in particular needed its great men. Where the Victorian heroes did not exist, they were invented or, as in the case of Wellington, reconstructed and modified. The picture presented to the public was not false; merely selected, simplified and overladen with authorial comment to stress comparisons and make points. Wellington was a far more complex, contradictory and interesting character than he ever admitted or Victorian adulation allowed him to be.

On his death nearly a quarter of a million people filed before his coffin, and more than that number lined the route to St Paul's on the day of the funeral. Most came from precisely those classes of people he had worked so hard to keep out of political power, and yet they came none the less and gave every indication of genuine sadness on his death. Popular admiration for Wellington existed because he represented a national self-image which was valid even for those who disagreed absolutely with the politics he espoused. For all his innumerable faults, his reputation as the man of honour, the embodiment of power without ambition, courage without ostentation, loyalty without greed, care without distasteful public shows of emotion, had become and remained the essence of how the English liked to see themselves – "In him England admires her own likeness." Rather than concentrating on diplomatic negotiations, industrial and economic resources, his victory became a triumph of national and individual personality, and established the pattern for the popular interpretation of later conflicts as well: "Wellington may have been less gifted in scope and vision than Napoleon, but he was far superior in character, and it is usually character that wins in the long run."

having realized what he had become, "Now no dray moves more readily to the thill [wagon] than I to the painter's chair."

The grounds for Washington's continued popularity were revealed in statements offered during the increasingly elaborate celebrations of his birth. An editorial in the *New York Gazette* asked: "After the Almighty Author of our existence and happiness, to whom, as a people, are we under the greatest obligation? I know you will answer 'To Washington.'" In the same issue of the *Gazette,* a poet sung: "Glorious deeds he has done, / By him our cause is won / Long live great Washington!" The apotheosis was complete. Having delivered his country from the yoke of British tyranny, Washington had become the reason for America's present well-being. He would be the reason for America's future well-being, too. Returning to public life as leader of the Federal (Constitutional) Convention in Philadelphia, he was met by the joyous chiming of bells.

Yet, the enthusiastic reaction to Washington's arrival in Philadelphia bothered many citizens. Not the man praised but the praise itself was the basis of their concern. Unchallenged, the panegyric was beginning to border on blasphemy. Many pious Philadelphians who saw the Washington cult rejuvenated at the Federal Convention must have recalled one "Mary Meanwell's" letter to the *Freeman's Journal,* written five years earlier, after the Yorktown campaign:

> Having read Mr. Bradford's paper of Nov. 21, these words struck me, "WASHINGTON, THE SAVIOUR OF HIS COUNTRY." I trembled and said, "Shall we attribute to the arm of flesh, what the Almighty has done for America? I respect our great general, but let us not make a GOD of him!" It must give him pain, and cause him to blush, when he finds that "What is due to our Creator is attributed to him."
>
> The first of the ten commands, which forbid idolatry, is now before me. For this reason, Sir, I am not ashamed to date this from the time that my Bible suggested the thought to me, when I recollected what I read in Mr. Bradford's paper and compared it with the Almighty's command.

In deification there are also political dangers. Miss Meanwell recognized this in her follow-up letter, which described the excessive praise of Washington as an offense "to every principled whig." With this assessment many readers must have agreed. If the overwhelming and seemingly unconditional praise of Washington helped to mobilize the aspirations and sentiments of the rebelling colonists, it might also allow Washington to assume power outside the law and to use that power to impose his will upon others, with the help of the army he then commanded. William Tudor had expressed this concern two years before Yorktown. Even though final victory was then far from sight, he warned of its consequences as he spoke of Washington in a public address:

> Bondage is ever to be apprehended at the close of a successful struggle for liberty, when a triumphant army, elated with victories, and headed by a popular general may become more formidable than the tyrant that has been expelled.... Witness the aspiring CROMWELL!.... A free and wise people will never suffer any citizen to become too popular – much less too powerful. A man may be formidable to the constitution even by his virtues.

Tudor's speech articulated an apprehension that had been felt by others. In late 1777, almost a year after he had warned Congress against its "superstitious veneration" of General Washington, John Adams expressed relief that the American victory at Saratoga was not masterminded by him. Adams explained: "If it had been, idolatry and adulation would have been unbounded; so excessive as to endanger our liberties, for what I know. Now, we can allow a certain citizen to be wise, virtuous and good without thinking him a deity or Savior."

In view of these anxieties, what Washington did not do during the final phase of his military career was more important than his positive accomplishments. As John W. Daniel later put it, "he left mankind bewildered with the splendid problem of whether to admire him most for what he was or what he would not be." Indeed, what Washington was, in the popular view, was shaped to a great extent by what he chose not to be. The facts of the matter were many and well known. The main point was recognized by the Marquis de Chastellux during his 1781 travels: "This is the seventh year that [Washington] has commanded the army, and that he has obeyed the Congress; more need not be said, especially in America, where they know how to appreciate all the merit contained in this simple fact." The observation was a sound one. Despite many wartime disagreements with Congress, Washington faithfully deferred to its policies and so affirmed the then cherished but not yet established principle of civilian control of the military. When given emergency dictatorial powers by Congress, he never abused them. Despite his great popularity, which could have been used as a cushion against military setbacks and a weapon against Congress, Washington made it known to Congress that he was ready to resign his command at any time. Even more, he showed himself to be a great ally when Congress was itself in need. During the Newburgh crisis, when Washington could have taken over the government by military coup, he dissuaded his unpaid officers and men from taking action against the vulnerable and financially bankrupt Congress. And not only did Washington sternly rebuke those who wished to restore the monarchy around him; he hastened to surrender his military power at war's end and returned to private life. Washington's wartime conduct stilled the fears of those who saw in his prestige the seeds of tyranny. That Washington had placed himself above suspicion, and that his reputation largely hinged on this achievement, is the key to understanding his postwar role in national affairs. [...]

No objective observer would have misunderstood the people's attitude toward their new President. When Washington left New York in 1790 for a "Northern Tour" through nearby New England, he was met with tumultuous welcomes. A year later, he was received with similar enthusiasm in the distant states of the South. Washington's reception in Charleston, the South's largest city, magnified the adulation he had received in the more than thirty other towns and villages he had visited during his "Southern Tour" – and showed not only how sincere but also how universal his veneration had become. It was a perfect reflection of how American citizens everywhere felt about him.

Thirteen neatly uniformed naval captains rowed Washington into Charleston harbor, where he was quickly surrounded by forty boats and ships, each profusely arrayed with colorful bunting, each alive with banners and streamers, each filled with noisy spectators waving welcome. A barge carrying musicians and singers pulled beside the President, and, reenacting the traditional reception for waterborne English monarchs, serenaded him on his way to shore. (That part of his welcome must have caused the guest to wince. If critics reacted so violently to his courtly, yet subdued, levees, what would they think about this bombastic reception?) As he disembarked, cannons roared and church bells rang. A committee led by the state governor and chief city magistrate greeted him and, after a round of introductions, led him to a massive parade in his honor. Through all this, "an uncommonly large concourse of citizens" (more than a majority of the city's population, according to one correspondent) "reiterated shouts of joy and satisfaction." [...]

And, detractors of Washington paid a high price for their criticism – at least those who held or aspired to public office. Personal attacks on Washington were as counterproductive in the South, where Republicanism was strong, as they were in the Federalist states of the North. While traveling in North Carolina, Robert Goodloe Harper (a South Carolinian) made this point in his letter to Alexander Hamilton:

> The old man never stood higher or firmer than he does through these states. [Absalom] Tatom, one of the North Carolina members, lost his election for speaking dis-respectfully of him..... That a man should oppose the [Jay]

treaty, [the people] could account for and bear; it was natural, they said, for men to differ in opinion on such subjects; but it was inconceivable to them that any man, without improper motives, a bad heart, or a most perverted judgement, should speak with disrespect of the old man, as they call him, or do any act which implied a want of confidence in his integrity.... The Election for Electors in this state is made by the people. While it was understood that General Washington would consent to be reelected, no man however popular, had the least chance of becoming an elector if he was understood to be opposed to the old man. Ever since he has declined, some very popular Candidates, it is thought, will be very much injured in the election, by their known dislike to him.

The attitudes that Mr. Harper described were part of a cult that had fully established itself during Washington's first presidential term. By 1791, two years after he took office, the "monarchical" and "idolatrous" celebration of his birthday had become a national custom. There was hardly a town anywhere too small to have at least one ball or banquet on that day to honor Washington. In Philadelphia, the capital, as in all large cities, the celebrations were especially elaborate:

Tuesday the 22d inst. being the anniversary of the birth of the PRESIDENT OF THE UNITED STATES, when he attained to the 59th year of his age – the same was celebrated here with every demonstration of public joy. The Artillery and Light Infantry Corps of the city were paraded and at 12 o'clock a federal salute was fired. The congratulatory compliments of the members of the Legislature of the Union – the Heads of the Departments of State – foreign Ministers, officers, Civil and Military of the state – the Reverend Clergy – and of Strangers and Citizens of distinction, were presented to the President on this auspicious occasion.

Three years later, the animosities excited by the Jay Treaty induced the Congress to drop the practice of adjourning on the President's Birthday. Nationwide, however, the birthday pageants were more glittering than ever. Not only did supporters remark on the "unusual joy and festivity" of the occasion, but also opponents, like James Madison, acknowledged an "unexampled splendor" in the public demonstrations. These exhibitions differed from those held during Washington's regional tours and other travels, when local citizens turned out to greet and honor him. Washington's Birthday involved multiple celebrations, simultaneously observed by every city and town in the country. It was a national event, equaled only by July Fourth in enthusiasm and resplendence. The birth of the nation and the birth of Washington had become commemorative touchstones for the American people.

The Federalist establishment, it is true, gloried in the Washington's Birthday celebrations, but to regard them as mere political choreography is to miss an essential feature which linked them to other forms of public ritual. By providing the members of society with a periodic occasion to reaffirm their common national sentiments, the observance of Washington's birthday took on the character of a religious rite. "There can be no society," said Durkheim, "which does not feel the need of upholding and reaffirming at regular intervals the collective sentiments and the collective ideas which make its unity and its personality." These occasions "do not differ from religious ceremonies, either in their object, the results which they produce, or the processes employed to attain these results." In both ceremonies, civil and religious, a synchronization of activities produces a synchronization of sentiments. From this unity results a more acute sense of the sacred. (A mocking newspaper reference by a Republican critic to Washington's Birthday as America's "Political Christmas" underscores the point.) Washington's Birthday was indeed a sacred day: a time for communion, a time when the sanctity of the nation, and the strength of the people's attachment to it, could be reaffirmed. The Washington's Birthday observance seemed like a religious communion because on that day "we feel our natures raised by the contemplation, and dignified by an alliance with its object." Observers noticed that the riotousness and drunkenness that marked other public gatherings during the year were on this day totally absent. Like any religious liturgy, the Birthday rites extolled good and condemned evil: They "nourished in our bosoms public spirit, disregard of unmerited opprobrium, contempt of whatever is base, and the admiration of everything which is truly great, noble, and illustrious."

The religious quality of the Birthday celebrations was also evident in the sanctity of its object. Sacred figures perform feats deserving of pious gratitude, and they enjoy immunity from criticism. Likewise, when Washington's Republican opponents disparaged the recognition of his birthday, the faithful could be assured that what they were hearing was more profane than dogs "baying the moon." Citizens everywhere beheld

with indignation the malicious attempts of a few ungrateful persons, to tarnish the glory of this justly renowned hero and republican, [but] it is highly gratifying to perceive, that the body of the people entertain that undiminished sense of his virtues, which the grateful heart, from a recollection of past services, cannot but acknowledge him to possess.

And so the communion, and the nation, was preserved. "All ranks of citizens vied with each other in mutual congratulations [to] the *Man who unites all hearts.*"

July Fourth oratory carried the same message. On this holiday, no one's name was venerated more often than Washington's, and none were condemned more violently than his detractors'. To oppose Washington, every American was told, was to be an enemy of national unity. Robert Forsyth's 1796 Princeton College speech was representative, and almost all who heard it, or read it in the newspapers, agreed with its conclusions:

> Faction! curst offspring of hell begot on mercenary interest!... [T]hou has dared to shew thy horrid visage for a moment, crawling from the infernal pit, and to spit thy venom and sulphur on the untarnished, the immortal glory of Washington! his powerful genius shall crush thy head, and plunge thee down again into the abyss from whence thou hast sprung! O Washington! whose name, on every return of this anniversary, I shall pronounce with enthusiasm along with the sacred name of *country*.

The nation's regard for Washington was attested to in other ways. It was expressed in the increasing number of counties and towns named after him, including the Territory (District) of Columbia, which had earlier been designated the nation's permanent capital. The "Washington Marches" remained a favorite of the public and were played on almost any pretext. Francis Hopkinson's "Toast" (1778) and "Seven Songs" for Washington (1788) also remained popular. Of the production of poems there was no end. Graven images abounded. The Mint Act, which forbade impressions of Washington's image on federal coins, did not stop state and local institutions from producing them or from importing them from Great Britain. With equal zeal, painters continued their work. The subject was reluctant, but the need for his likeness was too strong to be resisted. During his presidency alone Washington sat at least once, and often more than once, for no less than fifteen different artists. "No American, and few world figures before the age of photography – except, possibly, Louis XIV and Napoleon – sat for portraits as often as Washington did." Enriching the nation with up-to-date likenesses of its hero, the artists also enriched themselves. Gilbert Stuart, who sought sittings with Washington to repay his debts, found himself in April 1795 with a backlog of thirty-nine requests for copies of his portraits. These, according to his daughter, he dashed off at the rate of one every two hours. Other artists did not do quite as well, but they made more money with Washington than they would have made without him.

At the end of his second term, then, Washington remained the new nation's hero and emblem. He held a virtual monopoly on the public's affection and overshadowed anyone who stood in his presence. Even his successor to the presidency, John Adams, on his own inauguration day, complained to his wife about the wet eyes cast upon his predecessor, Washington, who sat beside him as he made his public inaugural address. When that speech was done, the multitude ran after Washington, not Adams, and gave thunderous voice to its affection for him. [...]

If George Washington had become king of America, as some of his admirers would have liked, his remaining years of life would have been spent in a placid glow of gratitude and affection. The full weight of the outrage occasioned by the new government's decisions would have fallen on the head of his prime minister. It was fortunate that this was not the case, for if the agent of those decisions were not also the man the people adored, the government might not have survived as well as it did. Yet, the price paid by Washington was most dear. Although he knew that his enemies were massively outnumbered by his friends, he was devastated by the personal insults and charges brought against him, and he left office a tired and wounded man. He was too close to the scene to know that the very attacks that so injured him personally had actually strengthened his public reputation. Those attacks had drawn attention, as perhaps nothing else could, to the suffering that Washington endured for the nation's benefit; they transformed the unselfish and trustworthy patriot into an Innocent One. His eulogists would recall that Moses, too, was reviled by those he had delivered from bondage, and that his sufferings endeared him even more to posterity. Washington's detractors thus unwittingly secured what the nation most needed: a symbol that not only made unpopular but necessary policies acceptable but also gave to the people a tangible representation of its own rising greatness.

CHAPTER 6

ROBIN HOOD (ENGLISH): CLASS HERO

INTRODUCTION

It continues to be debated whether Robin Hood lived, but his heroic status is unchallenged. In the many versions of his story, he is, variously, a yeoman, a noble who has unfairly lost his inheritance, an Englishman fighting Norman lords, and a defender of the peasantry against avaricious lords. It is as roguish class hero, which was not the original version of his life, that he is most touted. He kills the King's deer and steals from the rich to give to the poor. He invariably outfoxes the mean Sheriff of Nottingham, who serves the rich. Robin is daring, clever, and honest. His closest counterparts are Billy the Kid and Jesse James, folk heroes of the American counterpart to Sherwood Forest, the American West. None of the three is a revolutionary. All elude the law rather than change it. While Robin seems a wholly human hero, he does reside in the forest, with its supernatural associations, and his skill with the bow veers on the superhuman. In the following selection Robin bests the Sheriff's archers and dupes the Sheriff. Lord Raglan includes Robin Hood as one of his heroes. For the differing versions of Robin Hood's life, see Francis James Child, *The English and Scottish Popular Ballads*, vol. 3 (New York: Cooper Square, 1965 [1889]), ballads 117–54. On both the historical and the legendary Robin Hood, see J. C. Holt, *Robin Hood*, rev. edn. (London: Thames and Hudson, 1988 [1982]).

Original publication: Henry Gilbert, *Robin Hood* (Ware: Wordsworth, 1993 [1912]), pp. 88–100.

ROBIN HOOD

Henry Gilbert

When the meal was ended, Robin called Little John to his side and said:

"John, hath the proud potter of Wentbridge set out on his journey yet?"

"Ay, master," replied John, "he went through but yesterday, with horse and cart laden with his pots and pans. A brisk man is he, and as soon as the snows are gone he is not one to play Lob-lie-by-the-fire."

Robin asked where the potter would be lodging that night, and John told him. Then Robin called Bat and Michael to him.

"Thou didst ask for a task," he said, "and I will give thee one. It may be a hard one, but 'tis one thou must do by hook or by crook. Thou knowest well the ways of the forest from here to Mansfield, for thou hast both fled from thy lord at Warsop. Now I will that ye go to Mansfield for me this night and seek the proud potter of Wentbridge. Tell him that I crave a fellowship of him. I wish him to let me have his clothes, his pots, his cart and his horse, for I will go to Nottingham market disguised."

"This will we do right gladly, master," said Bat. "We will take our staves and our swords and bucklers and start on our way forthwith."

Little John began to laugh heartily.

"Ye speak as if thou thinkest it will be no more than to say 'bo!' to a goose," he said. "But if thou knowest not the proud potter of Wentbridge, that lacking he will soon make up in thee by the aid of his good quarterstaff."

"I know, Little John," said Bat with a laugh, "that he hath given thee that lesson."

"Ye say truly," said honest John; "evil befell me when I bade him pay toll to the outlaws last harvest time, for he gave me three strokes that I shall never forget."

"All Sherwood heard of them," said Bat; "but the proud potter is a full courteous man, as I have heard tell. Nevertheless, whether he liketh it or not, he shall yield Master Robin his wish."

"Then I will meet thee at the Forest Herne where the roads fork beyond Mansfield," said Robin, "an hour after dawn tomorrow."

"We will fail not to be there with all that thou wishest," replied Bat, and together he and Michael set out under the starlight on the way to Mansfield.

Next day, into the market-place of Nottingham drove a well-fed little brown pony, drawing a potter's cart, filled with pots and pans of good Wentbridge ware. The potter, a man stout of limb, plump of body, and red of face, wore a rusty brown tunic and cloak, patched in several places, and his hair seemed to have rare acquaintance with a comb. Robin indeed was well disguised.

Farmers, hucksters, merchants, and butchers were crowded in the market-place, some having already set up their booths or stalls, while others were busy unloading their carts or the panniers on their stout nags. The potter set his crocks beside his cart, after having given his horse oats and hay, and then began to cry his wares.

He had taken up a place not five steps from the door of the sheriff's house, which, built of wood and adorned with quaint designs, occupied a prominent place on one side of the market-place; and the potter's eyes were constantly turned on the door of the house, which now was open, and people having business with the sheriff rode or walked up and entered.

"Good pots for sale!" cried the potter. "Buy of my pots! Pots and pans! Cheap and good today. Come, wives and maidens! Set up your kitchens with my good ware!"

So lustily did he call that soon a crowd of country people who had come to the market to buy stood about him and began to chaffer with him. But he did not stay to bargain; he let each have the pot or pan at the price they offered. The noise of the cheapness of the pots soon got abroad, and very soon there were but half a dozen pots left.

"He is an ass," said one woman, "and not a potter. He may make good pots, but he knoweth naught of bargaining. He'll never thrive in his trade."

Robin called a serving-maid who came just then from the sheriff's house, and begged her to go to the sheriff's wife, with the best respects of the potter of Wentbridge, and ask whether the dame would accept his remaining pots as a gift. In a few minutes Dame Margaret herself came out.

"Gramercy for thy pots, good chapman," she said, and she had a merry eye, and spoke in a very friendly manner. "I am full fain to have them, for they be good pots and sound. When thou comest to this town again, good potter, let me know of it and I will buy of thy wares."

"Madam," said Robin, doffing his hat and bowing in a yeomanly manner, "thou shalt have of the best in my cart. I'll give thee no cracked wares, nor any with flaws in them, by the Mass, but every one shall ring with a true honest note when thou knock'st it."

The sheriff's wife thought the potter was a full courteous and bowerly man, and began to talk with him. Then a great bell rang throughout the house, and the dame said:

"Come into the house if thou wilt, good chapman. Come sit with me and the sheriff at the market table."

This was what Robin desired. He thanked the dame, and was led by her into the bower where her maidens sat at their sewing. Just then the door opened and the sheriff came in. Robin looked keenly at the man, whom he had only seen once before. He knew that the sheriff, Ralph Murdach, was a rich cordwainer who had bought his office from the grasping Bishop of Ely for a great price, and to repay himself he squeezed all he could out of the people.

"Look what this master potter hath given us," said Dame Margaret, showing the pots on a stool beside her. "Six pots of excellent ware, as good as any made in the Low Countries."

The sheriff, a tall spare man of a sour and surly look, glanced at Robin, who bowed to him.

"May the good chapman dine with us, sheriff?" asked the dame.

"He is welcome," said the sheriff crossly, for he was hungry, and had just been outwitted, moreover, in a piece of business in the market-place. "Let us wash and go to meat."

They went into the hall of the house, where some twenty men were waiting for the sheriff and his lady. Some were officers and men of the sheriff, others were rich chapmen from the market.

When the sheriff and his wife took their seats at the high table, all the company sat down, Robin being shown a seat midway down the lower table. A spoon of horn was placed on the table where each sat, and a huge slice of bread, called a trencher, but for drinking purposes there was only one pewter cup between each two neighbours. Then the scullions from the sheriff's kitchen brought in roasted meat on silver skewers, and these being handed to the various guests, each would take his knife from his girdle, rub it on his leg to clean it a little, and then cut what he wanted from the skewer, laying his portion on the thick slice of bread. Then, using his fingers as a fork, the guest would eat his dinner, cutting off and eating pieces of his trencher with his meat, or saving it till all the meat was eaten.

On the rush-covered floor of the hall dogs and cats fought for the meat or bones thrown to them, and at the door beggars looked in, crying out for alms or broken meat. Sometimes a guest at the lower end of the table would throw a bone at a beggar, intending to hit him hard, but the beggar would deftly catch it and begin gnawing it. When, as sometimes happened, the beggars became too bold and ventured almost up to the table, a serving-man would dart among them with his staff and thump and kick them pell-mell out through the door.

Suddenly, a sturdy beggar came forthright into the hall and walked up among the sprawling dogs towards the high seat. Instantly a serving-man dashed at him and caught hold of him to throw him out.

"I crave to speak with the sheriff," cried the beggar, struggling with the man. "I come with a message from a knight."

But the serving-man would not listen, and began to drag the beggar to the door. The noise of their struggle drew the attention of all the guests, and Robin, looking up, recognised the beggar. It was Sir Guy's spy, whom he had met but yesterday, and who had outwitted the two outlaws whom Robin had sent to take him – Richard Malbête, or, as the English would call him, Illbeast.

The beggar fought fiercely to free himself, but the serving-man was a powerful fellow, and Malbête's struggles were in vain. Suddenly he cried:

"A boon, Sir Sheriff! I have a message from Sir Guy of Gisborne!"

The sheriff looked up and saw the struggling pair.

"Let the rogue speak," he cried. The servitor ceased the struggle, but still held the beggar, and both men stood panting, while Richard Illbeast glared murderously at the man beside him.

"Speak, rogue, as his worship commands," said the servitor, "and cut not my throat with thy evil looks, thou scarecrow."

"I come from Sir Guy of Gisborne," said the beggar, turning to the high table, "and I have a message for thy private ear, Sir Sheriff."

The sheriff looked at him suspiciously.

"Tell me thy message, rogue," said the sheriff harshly.

The beggar looked desperately round at the faces of the guests, all of which were turned to him. Some laughed at his hesitation, others sneered.

"He hath a private message for thy ear, sheriff," cried one burly farmer with a laugh, "and light fingers for thy jewels."

"Or," added another amid the laughter, "a snickersnee [small dagger] for thyself."

"Give some proof that you bear word from him you prate of," commanded the sheriff angrily, "or I will have thee beaten from the town."

"A dozen cut-purses set upon me in the forest," said Richard Illbeast, "and robbed me of the purse in which was Sir Guy's letter to thee!"

A roar of laughter arose from all the guests. This was a likely tale, they thought, and japes and jokes were bandied about between them.

"What sent he thee to me for, knave?" shouted the sheriff. "A likely tale thou tellest."

"He sent me to aid thee in seizing that thieving outlaw, Robin Hood!" cried Richard Illbeast, beside himself with rage at the laughter and sneers of the guests, and losing his head in his anger.

Men roared and rocked with laughter as they heard him.

"Ha! ha! ha!" they cried. "This is too good! The thief-taker spoiled by thieves! The fox mobbed by the hares he would catch!"

"Thrust him forth," shouted the sheriff, red with rage. "Beat the lying knave out of the town!"

"I am no knave!" cried Richard. "I have fought in the Crusade! I have –"

But he was not suffered to say further what he had done: a dozen men-servants hurled themselves upon him. Next moment he was out in the market-place, his cloak was torn from his back and his bags ripped from him. Staves and sticks seemed to spring up on all sides, and amidst a hail of blows the wretch, whose heart was as cruel as any in that cruel time, and whose hands had been dyed by many a dreadful deed, was beaten mercilessly from the town along the road to the forest.

For a little time the guests at the sheriff's table continued to laugh over the beggar's joke, and then the talk turned on a contest which was to be held after dinner at the butts outside the town between the men who formed the officers of the sheriff, for a prize of forty shillings given by their master.

When the meal was ended, therefore, most of the guests betook themselves to the shooting, where the sheriff's men shot each in his turn. Robin, of course, was an eager onlooker at the sport; and he saw that not one of the sheriff's men could shoot nearer to the mark than by the length of half a long arrow.

"By the rood!" he said, "though I be but a potter now I was a good bowman once, and e'en now I love the twang of my string and the flight of my arrow. Will you let a stranger try a shot or two, Sir Sheriff?"

"Ay, thou mayst try," said the sheriff, "for thou seemest a stalwart and strong fellow, though by thy red face thou seemest too fond of raising thy own pots to thy lips with good liquor in them."

Robin laughed with the crowd at the joke thus made against him, and the sheriff commanded a yeoman to bring three bows. Robin chose one of these, the strongest and largest, and tried it with his hands.

"Thou'rt but poor wood, I fear," he said, as he pushed the bow from him and pulled the string to his ear. "It whineth with the strain already," he went on, "so weak is the gear."

He picked out an arrow from the quiver of one of the sheriff's men and set it on the string. Then, pulling the string to its fullest extent, he let the bolt fly. Men looked keenly forward, and a shout from the chapmen went up when they saw that his bolt was within a foot of the mark, and nearer by six inches than any of the others.

"Shoot another round," said the sheriff to his men, "and let the potter shoot with thee."

Another round was accordingly shot, and each man strove to better his previous record. But none got nearer than the potter had done, and when the last of them had shot his bolt they stood aside with glum faces, looking at the chapman as he stepped forward and notched his arrow upon the string.

He seemed to take less pains this time than before. The bolt snored away, and in the stillness with which the onlookers gazed, the thud, as it struck the broad target, two hundred yards away, was distinctly heard. For a moment men could not believe what their keen eyes told them. It had hit the centre of the bull's eye, or very close thereto.

The target-man, who stood near by the butt to report exactly on each shot, was seen to approach the target and then to start running excitedly towards the archers.

"It hath cleft the peg in three!" he shouted.

The peg was the piece of wood which stood in the very centre of the bull's eye. A great shout from all the bystanders rose up and shook the tassels on the tall poplars above their heads, and many of the chapmen gripped Robin by the hand or clapped him on the back.

"By the rood!" one said, "thou'rt a fool of a chapman, but as a bowman thou'rt as good as any forester."

"Or as Robin o' th' Hood himself, that king of archers, wolf's-head though he be," said another, a jolly miller of the town.

The sheriff's men had black looks as they realised that they had been worsted by a plump potter, but the sheriff laughed at them, and coming to Robin, said:

"Potter, thou'rt a man indeed. Thou'rt worthy to bear a bow wherever thou mayest choose to go."

"I ha' loved the bow from my toddling days," said the potter, "when I would shoot at small birds, ay, and bring them down. I ha' shot with many a good bowman, and in my cart I have a bow which I got from that rogue Robin Hood, with whom I ha' shot many a turn."

"What!" said the sheriff, and his face was hard and his eyes full of suspicion. "Thou hast shot with that false rascal? Knowest thou the place in the forest where he lurketh now, potter?"

"I think 'tis at Witch Wood," said the potter easily. "He hath wintered there, I ha' heard tell as I came down the road. But he stopped me last autumn and demanded toll of me. I told him I gave no toll on the king's highway except to the king, and I said I would e'en fight him with quarterstaff or shoot a round of twenty bolts with him to see if I were not a truer archer than he. And the rogue shot four rounds with me, and said that for my courtesy I should be free of the forest so long as my wheels went round."

100

This was indeed the fact, and it was this friendship between Robin and the proud potter which had made Bat's task of obtaining the potter's clothes and gear for Robin an easy one.

"I would give a hundred pounds, potter," said the sheriff gloomily, "that the false outlaw stood by me!"

"Well," said the potter, "if thou wilt do after my rede [advice], Sir Sheriff, and go with me in the morning, thee and thy men, I will lead thee to a place where, as I ha' heard, the rascal hath dwelled through the winter."

"By my faith," said the sheriff, "I will pay thee well if thou wilt do that. Thou art a brave man and a stalwart."

"But I must e'en tell thee, sheriff," said the potter, "that thy pay must be good, for if Robin knows I ha' led the dogs to his hole, the wolf will rend me, and it would not be with a whole skin that I should go through the forest again."

"Thou shalt be well paid," said the sheriff, "on my word as the king's officer."

But he knew, and the potter knew also, that the sheriff's promise was of little worth, for the sheriff loved his money too well. But the potter made as if he was satisfied. When the sheriff offered him the forty shillings which was the prize for winning at the shooting, the potter refused it, and so won all the hearts of the sheriff's men.

"Nay, nay," said the potter; "let him that shot the best bolt among your men have it. It may be that 'twas by a flaw of wind that my arrow struck the peg."

The potter had supper with the sheriff and his men, all of whom drank to the potter as a worthy comrade and a good fellow. A merry evening was passed, and then Robin was given a bed in a warm corner of the hall, and all retired to rest.

Next morning, before it was light, all were afoot again. A jug of ale was quaffed by each, and a manchet of rye bread eaten. Then the horses were brought round, together with the potter's pony and cart, and with the sheriff and ten of his men the potter led the way into the forest.

Deep into the heart of the greenwood the potter went, by lonely glades and narrow deer-drives by which not one of the sheriff's men had gone before. In many places where an ambuscade could easily be laid the sheriff and his men looked fearfully around them, and wondered whether they would win through that day with whole skins.

"Thou art sure thou knowest the way, potter?" said the sheriff more than once.

"Know the road, forsooth!" laughed the potter. "I ha' not wended my way up and down Sherwood these twenty years without knowing my way. Belike you think I lead you into fearsome lonely places. But do you think a rascally wolf's-head will make his lair by the highway where every lurching dog can smell him out?"

"How dost thou know that the false outlaw hath wintered in the place you named?" asked the sheriff, with suspicion in his eyes.

"So the peasants tell me in the villages I have passed on my way from Wentbridge," replied the potter. "I will take thee to within half a mile of the Witch Wood, and then thou must make thy own plans for taking the rogue."

"What manner of place is Witch Wood?" asked the sheriff.

" 'Tis a fearsome place, as I ha' heard tell," said the potter. " 'Tis the haunt of a dreadful witch, and is filled with dead men's bones. Outside 'tis fresh and fair with trees, but there are caves and cliffs within, where the witch and her evil spirits dwell among the grisly bones, and the churls say that Robin o' th' Hood is close kin to her, and that while he is in the greenwood he is within her protection and naught can harm him."

"How so?" asked the sheriff, and the ten men glanced fearfully around and closed up together.

"They say that she is the spirit of the forest, and that by her secret power she can slay any man who comes beneath the trees, or lock him up alive in a living trunk of a tree, or cast him into a wizard's sleep."

"What be those things there?" asked the sheriff, pointing in front of him. They had now come to an opening in the forest, where the trees gave way to a piece of open rising ground covered with low bushes. On a ridge in its midst was a great oak, its broad limbs covering a great space of ground, and beneath its shade were three tall upright stones, leaning towards each other as if they whispered.

" 'Tis the Three Stane Rigg," said the potter. "Men say that they be great grey stones as thou seest by daylight, but when owls hoot and the night wind stirs in the bushes, they turn into witch hags which ride about like the wind, doing the bidding of the great witch of the forest – bringing murrain or plague, cursing the standing corn, or doing other ill to men."

Men looked in each other's eyes, and then turned their heads swiftly away, for they were half ashamed to see the fear in them, and to know that dread was in their own. All men in those days believed in wizards and witches, even the king and his wisest statesmen.

"I think," said the sheriff gruffly, "thou shouldst have told us these things ere we set out, and I would have brought a priest with us. As it is –"

Shrieks of eldritch laughter rang out in the dark trees beside them. So sudden and so fearful were the cries, that the horses stopped and trembled as they stood, while their riders crossed themselves and looked peeringly into the gloom of the forest. "Let us ride back!" cried some, while one or two turned their horses in the narrow path and began to retreat.

Again the mad laughter rang out. It seemed to come from all parts of the dark earthy wood about them. More of the men put spurs to their horses, and in spite of the cries of the sheriff bidding them to stay, all were soon riding helter-skelter away from the spot.

The potter, standing up in his cart, and the sheriff, dark of look, listened as the sound of the thudding hooves became fainter and fainter in the distance.

"The craven dolts!" cried the sheriff, grinding his teeth. Yet, for all his bravery, he himself was afraid, and kept looking this way and that into the trees.

Suddenly the potter cracked his whip. Instantly the clear notes of a horn sounded away in the open glade, and next moment there came some twenty men in brown, who seemed to rise from the ground and to issue from the trunks of the trees. Some even dropped to the ground from boughs just above where the sheriff stood.

"How now, master potter," said one tall fellow, bearded and bare-headed, "how have you fared in Nottingham? Have you sold your ware?"

"Ay, by my troth," said the potter. I have sold all, and got a great price for it. Look you, Little John, I have brought the sheriff himself for it all."

"By my faith, master, he is welcome," cried Little John, and gave a great hearty laugh, which was echoed by all the outlaws standing around when they saw the angry wonder on the sheriff's face.

"Thou false rogue!" cried he, and his face beneath his steel cap went red with shame and chagrin. "If I had but known who thou wert!"

"I thank good Mary thou didst not," said Robin, taking off the potter's cloak and then the tunic, which had been stuffed with rags to make him look the stouter.

"But now that thou art here, sheriff, thou shalt dine with us off the king's fat deer. And then, to pay thy toll, thou shalt leave thy horse and thy armour and other gear with me."

And thus was it done. The sheriff, willy-nilly, had to dine off a steak cut from a prime buck, and washed down his meal with good sack, and having been hungry, he felt the better for it.

Then, when he had left his horse and all his arms with Robin Hood, and was preparing to return home on foot, the outlaw ordered a palfrey to be led forward, and bade the sheriff mount it.

"Wend thy way home, sheriff," he said, "and greet thy wife from me. Thy dame is as courteous and kind as thou art sour and gruff. That palfrey is a present from me to thy lady wife, and I trust that she will think kindly of the potter, though I cannot hope that thou thyself wilt think well of me."

Without a word the sheriff departed. He waited till it was dark ere he rode up to the gate of Nottingham and demanded to be let in. The gateman wondered at the sheriff's strange return, riding on a lady's palfrey, without so much as a weapon in his belt or a steel cap on his head. The tale of the shamefaced men who had returned earlier had been wormed out of them by the wondering citizens, and the sheriff, hoping to creep home unobserved, was disagreeably surprised to find the streets full of gaping people. To all their questions he returned cross answers, but as he alighted at his own door he heard a laugh begin to arise, in cackling bursts, among the crowd before his house, and when he was inside he heard the full roar of laughter rise from a thousand throats.

Next day there was never a man so full of anger as Sheriff Murdach. The whole town was agrin, from the proud constable of the castle with his hundred knights, to the little horseboys in the stables – all smiled to think how the sheriff had gone with his posse to capture the outlaw Robin, led by a false potter who was the rogue Robin himself, and had been captured and spoiled.

CHAPTER 7

COYOTE (NATIVE AMERICAN): CULTURE HERO

INTRODUCTION

Coyote is a leading figure in the mythology of many North American Indian tribes. Sometimes he is a trickster, tripping up humanity. Other times he is a fool, harming himself. Still other times he is a culture hero, helping humanity. As a culture hero, he is credited with creating human beings, creating fellow animals, and even creating the physical world. He is also often credited with stealing fire, light, and water and bestowing them on humanity. His efforts as culture hero employ the same skills he uses as trickster. The following selection from the mythology of the Karok Indians of Northwest California is one version of the theft of fire by Coyote and other animals. Coyote is at once human and animal – itself a trickster quality. He is like the snake in the Garden of Eden. And like the snake, he is eventually demoted to a mere animal, though only in later myths and not as punishment. Coyote steals fire less out of revenge against its possessors or out of concern for humanity, as in the case of Prometheus, and more out of joy at outsmarting its possessors. But a hero he remains, for without him humans would be bereft of fire and thereby bereft of warmth and cooking. On North American Indian myths, all of which include tales of culture heroes, see, among the classic works, Frank Hamilton Cushing, *The Mythic World of the Zuni*, ed. Barton Wright (Albuquerque: University of New Mexico Press, 1988 [1896]); Franz Boas, *Tshimshian Mythology*, in Thirty-First Annual Report of the Bureau of American Ethnology, 1909–10, 27–1037 (Washington, DC: Government Printing Office, 1916); George Dorsey, *The Mythology of the Witchita* (Norman:

Original publication: A. L. Kroeber and E. W. Gifford, *Karok Myths*, ed. Grace Buzaljko (Berkeley: University of California Press, 1980), pp. 196–7.

University of Oklahoma Press, 1995 [1904]); Ruth Benedict, *Zuni Mythology*, 2 vols., Columbia University Contributions to Anthropology, vol. XXI (New York: Columbia University Press, 1935); Stith Thompson, *Tales of the North American Indians* (Cambridge, MA: Harvard University Press, 1929); and A. L. Kroeber, *Yurok Myths*, ed. Grace Buzaljko (Berkeley: University of California Press, 1976). More popularly, see John Bierhorst, *The Mythology of North America* (New York: Quill/William Morrow, 1985).

KAROK MYTHS

A. L. Kroeber and E. W. Gifford

HOW PEOPLE GOT FIRE

Mary Ike (1940)

There was no fire. Coyote went all over looking for fire. Coyote discovered fire in the far north. He returned and told people he had seen fire, he had found it. They talked over the means of getting the fire. They lined up with Frog next to the river. Grouse said, "I'll be on top of the mountain. I am pretty slow, but I can fly down the hill."

The Bear said he could run down the hill, so they put him on the next mountaintop.

Turtle said, "I can run down too. I'll draw in my feet and head and roll down."

Aixlechton (a bird on A'u'ich which is white below, brown above, and calls like a seagull) said, "I can travel over two mountains, two ridges."

Fox said, "I'll take a hand in it, too."

Measuring Worm said, "I can go over about ten ridges and mountains and not have to run downhill."

Coyote went up north where the fire was. The girls there were Yellow Jackets. Coyote said to them, "You all sit around and I'll make you pretty." Coyote said, "Come on, girls. We'll all go into the house."

Coyote took black oak bark and put it in (the) fire to burn. To the girls, he said, "You all close your eyes. You will not be pretty if you open your eyes." While they had their eyes shut he pulled the bark out of the fire with his heel. "Keep your eyes closed. I've got to go outside for a minute. Don't open your eyes while I am gone."

Then he ran and ran and ran with the fire. He became exhausted and passed it to Fox.

After a time the girls opened their eyes and realized Coyote was gone. They set out in pursuit and finally spied Fox with the fire.

Fox ran until he came to Measuring Worm and passed the fire on to him. Measuring Worm wriggled around, as he reached from mountain to mountain. He went a long way. Then Measuring Worm passed it to Bear. Bear ran down the mountain, but was slow in climbing up the next mountain.

Bear passed it to Grouse. Grouse went a long way with it. Grouse passed it to the bird Aixlechton. He passed it to Turtle, and Turtle rolled down the mountain to Frog, who had his mouth wide open to receive the fire.

The Yellow Jackets grabbed the Frog, but Frog jumped into the river with the fire in his mouth. The Yellow Jackets gave up. It was no use. They went back. Frog came up and spat out the fire to willow trees. Now you can get fire from willows. Willow roots are used for fire drills.

CHAPTER 8

MAUI (HAWAIIAN/ POLYNESIAN): HERO AS TRICKSTER

INTRODUCTION

The most popular hero in Polynesian mythology is Maui. Like Coyote for North American Indians, Maui for Polynesians is a trickster as well as a hero. More precisely, the heroism of both relies on trickery rather than on power. In Hawaiian mythology, where Maui is not quite so popular as elsewhere in Polynesia, he is celebrated above all for securing fire, for prolonging the summer, and for "pushing up" the heavens to provide more sky. The following selection presents several of the many Hawaiian versions of his saga. (Different islands have their own versions.) Even though Maui's genealogy makes him semi-divine, he is mortal. Still, his magical-like talents make him superhuman. Moreover, he acts as a liaison between the divine and the human worlds, enlisting the divine to abet the human. Joseph Campbell recounts one version of the story of Maui's theft of fire. The term "trickster" has come to be associated with Jung, for whom it is a prominent "archetype" – itself a term that has been co-opted by Jungians. Both terms antedate Jungian psychology, which offers one way but not the only way of analyzing the trickster figure. On the trickster, see Paul Radin, *The Trickster* (New York: Schocken, 1972 [1956]), with commentaries by C. G. Jung and Karl Kerényi; *The Zande Trickster*, ed. E. E. Evans-Pritchard, Oxford Library of African Literature (Oxford: Clarendon, 1967); and *Mythical Trickster Figures*, eds. William J. Hymes and William G. Doty (Tuscaloosa: University of Alabama Press, 1993).

Original publication: Martha Beckwith, *Hawaiian Mythology* (Honolulu: University of Hawaii Press, 1970 [1940]), pp. 229–31.

HAWAIIAN MYTHOLOGY

Martha Beckwith

East Maui versions: Birth, Finding fire, Fishing up islands, Snaring the sun. Maui is not the child of Hina by Akalana in the natural way but is begotten one day when she has a longing for seaweed, goes out to the beach at Kaanomalo to gather some, and, finding a man's loincloth on the beach, puts it on and goes to sleep. The child born from this adventure is named Maui-a-Akalana and her husband says, "We have found our lord!"

Maui's first feat is getting fire from the mud hens while they are roasting bananas. Hina teaches him to catch the littlest one. He finds them at Waianae on Oahu. Each time he approaches they scratch out the fire. When he finally succeeds in seizing the littlest mud hen she tries to put him off by naming first the taro stalk, then the ti leaf as the secret of fire. That is why these leaves have hollows today, because Maui rubbed them to try to get fire. At last the mud hen tells him that fire is in the water (wai), meaning the tree called "sacred water" (wai-mea), and shows him how to obtain it. So Maui gets fire, but he first rubs a red streak on the mud hen's head out of revenge for her trickery before letting the bird escape.

Maui's next feat is stopping the sun from moving so fast. Hina sends him to a big wiliwili tree where he finds his old blind grandmother cooking bananas and steals them one by one until she recognizes him and agrees to help him. He sits by the trunk of the tree and lassoes the sun's rays as the sun comes up. The sun pleads for life and agrees that the days shall be long in summer and short during the six winter months.

While Maui is still a child he goes fishing with his brothers and gets them to go far out to the fishing ground called Po'o directly seaward from Kipahulu and in a line with the hill called Ka-iwi-o-Pele. Here with his hook called Manai-a-ka-lani (Come from heaven) he catches the big ulua of Pimoe. For two days they pull at it before it comes to the surface and is drawn close to the canoe. The brothers are warned not to look back. They do so. The cord breaks, and the fish vanishes. That is why the islands are not united into one.

Pushing up the heavens. The sky presses down over the earth. A man "supposed to be Maui" says to a woman that if she will give him a "drink from her gourd" [a euphemistic expression] he will push up the sky for her. She complies and the man [standing on Kauiki] thrusts the sky upward. Today, although the clouds may hang low over the mountain of Halea-kala, they refrain from touching Kauiki.

West Maui versions: Birth. Maui is the son of Hina-lau-ae and Hina. The family lives at Makalia above Kahakuloa. While Maui is still unborn, some men out fishing see a handsome child diving from a high cliff into the sea, and they pursue. The child makes for home and returns to his mother's womb. Thus they know that a magician is to be born.

Lanai variant. Pu'upehe is the supernatural son of Kapoko-holua the father, Kapoiliili the mother, who live on the island of Lanai, which goes at this time by the name of Ka-ulu-laau. For thirteen months Pu'upehe lives unborn and frightens his mother by speaking to her from her womb and playing the ghost as a spirit abroad, in which form he sends fish to his father's line through his god Pua-iki and learns the arts of warfare by overhearing an expert teaching others how to kill Pu'upehe's father. He demands awa to chew and tobacco, both of which seem to be new customs to his parents. When he leaves his mother's body it becomes flat; when he returns it is again swollen.

Maori variant. Whakatau, son of Apakura, is formed by the god Rongo out of Apakura's apron when she leaves it one day on the sand. Kites are seen flying in the air but no one is visible because Whakatau is under the sea. One day he comes out on shore and is pursued, but no one can catch him but his mother Apakura.

Snaring the sun. The sun goes so fast that Hina has trouble in drying her strips of bark cloth. Maui observes the sun from Wailohi and sees where it rises. He fashions strong cord of coconut fiber from Peeloko (Paeloko) at Waihee. The sun is rendered tractable and Maui then turns to punish Moemoe, who has derided his effort. Moemoe flees until overtaken north of Lahaina, where he is transformed into the long rock beside the road today.

Maui's rescue. While Maui is away snaring the sun, his mother bears an owl-child. Maui is kind to the owl. Once he is taken prisoner and is to be offered in sacrifice at Moali'i. Hina and the owl, hearing of his danger, follow him. The owl releases him and Hina sits down, covers him with her clothing and pretends to pick fleas. Thus he is saved.

CHAPTER 9

CHRISTOPHER COLUMBUS (ITALIAN): HERO AS EXPLORER

INTRODUCTION

Christopher Columbus (1451–1506), who was Genoese, persuaded the King and Queen of Spain, Ferdinand and Isabella, to sponsor an expedition across the Atlantic to find a new, western route to India. In 1492, commanding three small ships, he in fact discovered various Caribbean islands, including Hispaniola. He made three more expeditions, discovering parts of South and Central America. Replaced as Governor of Hispaniola, brought back to Spain to chains after his third voyage, and rebuffed in his continual claims for more honors and income, Columbus died embittered and neglected. While he never reached North America, he nevertheless came to be heralded as the discoverer of America. The following selection juxtaposes the "mythic" Columbus with the historical one. The mythic Columbus is tied to the image of America as an unspoiled, bountiful, Eden-like world, one awaiting discovery, cultivation, and Christianity. Columbus here is a fearless, unswerving adventurer, concerned more with discovery than with gold. It is his rapacious underlings and his avaricious superiors who betray his idealism and exploit the native peoples. Insofar as Columbus' heroism takes the form of a dangerous journey to an unknown world, he fits snugly Campbell's concept of the hero. Insofar as Columbus is seen as the agent of God, he is superhuman. Insofar as the world he discovers is paradise-like, his conquest of it elevates him as well. The historical Columbus was less noble. He was as callous as his men toward the native Americans, was as greedy for gold as they, and corrupted more than civilized the new world. Among

Original publication: Claudia L. Bushman, *America Discovers Columbus* (Hanover, NH: University Press of New England, 1992), pp. 5–10.

the many demythicized accounts of Columbus that appeared at the time of the quincentennial of his first voyage, see Kirkpatrick Sale, *The Conquest of Paradise* (New York: Knopf, 1990). See also the debate in *Columbus: Meeting of Cultures*, ed. Mario B. Mignone, Filibrary Series, no. 4 (Stony Brook, NY: Forum Italicum, 1993).

America Discovers Columbus

Claudia L. Bushman

The Failure

Columbus was a great seaman who made a magnificent error. He did not know where he was going, and he had no reliable guidance. By the time of his first voyage, people knew that the world was round, but they had not yet set off westward into the unknown. Columbus persuaded himself that the distance between the Azores and Japan was only one-quarter of the actual mileage. This faulty image of the world prevented him from succeeding according to his plan, for his imagined earth had a circumference of just three-quarters the size of the real one. Something was across the waters, but he was wrong about what and where it was. If the New World had not been in his way, Columbus would have perished, for his ships could never have carried supplies far enough to reach the Indies. Everyone would have starved, or Columbus would have been tossed overboard so that his crews could return home. Because of his mistaken conceptions about the globe, when he arrived at the New World, he did not know where he was. He could not reconcile the new place with his expectations, but he could not accept that where he had gotten to was different from the place he had intended to go.

Columbus envisioned the New World from within his European framework. He claimed already inhabited lands for Spain, enacting European rituals. New World gold would enrich his sovereigns, and he promised them too much. In spite of his amazing results, he could not produce the riches he was eager to display. He severely punished the native population in his attempt to produce the gold and to bring the two worlds into line. Columbus, who aimed above all to please his sovereigns, alienated them. Trying to bring honor to Europe by despoiling the new land, he managed only his own disgrace. He lost the honors of the Old World as the privileges the monarchs had promised him were withdrawn.

But he never felt at home in the New World he explored. His experiences cut him off from his homeland without making a place for him in the New World. He was the first alienated American – lost and never found. Though driven to search the West, he never truly left Europe. He could not understand his mistreatment when he felt that he had behaved honorably. Often portrayed as a visionary, Columbus remained stuck fast to the past.

Columbus treasured his mistreatment. After his sovereigns, somewhat inadvertently, replaced him as the leader of his colony and brought him home from his third voyage in chains, he always carried his fetters with him and ordered them buried with him as a bitter reminder. He wore out his final years plying Ferdinand with petition after petition, demanding the punishment of his oppressors and the restitution of all the privileges bestowed upon him by the capitulation of 1492. He felt himself, a great servant of God, betrayed by enemies on all sides. Columbus died a disappointed man, once again sure that he was right and everyone else wrong.

A leader with his drama and vision should have inspired his men to follow him anywhere; they were used to taking orders and should have worshipped him. But they did not. His voyages were rife with mutinous conflict. He kept his own counsels, misleading others, sacrificing them to his cause. He was as stubborn as he was single-minded, a frightening man, driven by his demons.

He spent his life following a vision real only to him. He sailed on where others would have turned back; he sacrificed everything to his cause. In doing so, he wrested success from likely failure, and he made the impossible easy for those who came after him. His solemnity and ceremony imbued a significant event with martial pomp and religious music, suitable myth and color. His stubborn loneliness led him to actions that changed the world.

Perhaps it is unfair to require that all men who make major contributions to society be kindly and generous, that all men who accomplish heroic deeds be heroes themselves. The need to make a great man out of the person who accomplished a great deed generated much of our Columbian literature. The excessive praise made him worthy of his achievements and compensated for his mistreatment and suffering. He is at the center of every account, the good, wise, noble man badly treated by others. The very wonder and richness of the Columbus stories rests in the mystique of the humble man who could maneuver the crown, discover a world, and found a nation, and, in the end, be portrayed as a victim.

113

The Myth

According to the mythic story, Columbus discovered America. The land was pure, new, empty, pristine, virtually uninhabited. The few people who lived there were considered primitive and uncivilized, just waiting to be improved by Western culture and religion. Europeans had been led to this fresh new world by God to establish freedom and Christianity. A humble, visionary man had overcome the prejudices of wise men and the hazards of nature, following his own star to a magnificent destiny. Because of his example, we can all sail uncharted seas, bound by our dreams rather than by the experience of others.

It is the nature of critical inquiry to overthrow accepted assumptions of the past, and such has been done to the myths of Columbus. These New World myths had provided a basis for understanding the world. But we are now uncomfortable with these old assumptions, and we have turned them on their heads. Now we know that Columbus was not the first to come here and was actually more the despoiler than the discoverer, for he laid waste a country full of people living harmoniously in a highly developed culture. We lack confidence in grand solo ventures, being more comfortable with tolerance of others' views and with cooperation. We distrust divine explanations and heroes in general.

The native Americans and slavery always posed a problem in Columbian mythmaking. Since the natives were depicted originally as children of nature living in a good and golden age, it followed that their corruption occurred as a result of exposure to European civilization. The journeys of Columbus, the visionary, on the other hand, had to be part of a master plan and therefore good. To solve this difficulty, Columbus was provided with a crew of rank materialists and potential criminals who needed only the sight of innocence to unleash their limitless greed and ravening depravity. That Columbus himself was benevolent, there could be no doubt, for if God's plan was good, if the doctrine of progress was to be believed, then the instrument by which man's progress was to be worked out in the New World must also be good. In trade for this preservation of his reputation were the leadership abilities of Columbus: In order to demonstrate his essential goodness, he could have only limited power and influence over his wicked underlings. As a leader of men and a colonizer, he had to be an underachiever.

None of this explicative seems relevant any longer. Today people doubt that a plan of progress exists, or that the role of Columbus in history was inevitable and therefore good. Today's thinkers are willing to entertain the idea that the voyages of Columbus were a big mistake. He should have stayed home and left the original Americas in peace. Even this thought, however, is not a new idea. Whether or not America was a mistake was debated in the eighteenth century. The Abbé Raynal, a French cleric and man of letters who wrote a history of the New World, sponsored a contest where money prizes were awarded for essays discussing the subject. Yet the old mythic story is still told, while new myths are being created.

In the century since the Columbian Exposition, the mariner's reputation has suffered. In 1892, Columbus symbolized progress. In 1992, he symbolizes American failure. The Admiral of the Ocean Sea who gave a new world to Castile and Leon, long revered as the discoverer of America and as the person whose gift to the civilized world was second only to that of Jesus Christ, has been thrust from his position of honor. He has been found guilty of disregarding the rights of the native population of the new lands he visited and of instituting policies that led to the decimation of indigenous populations. He set in motion the relentless torrent of greedy Europeans who despoiled the pristine land, filling it with adventurers and outcasts from tired civilizations. Though still honored and praised by certain ethnic groups, he has fallen from his high position. Racial guilt and environmental devastation justify the opposition of protest groups.

In the past, the statement "Columbus discovered America" was a truism. Now that "truth" is no longer acceptable. Instead of discussing the "discovery" – for no man can claim to discover a land already inhabited – we carefully speak of the "encounter," the "enterprise," and the "exchange," guarded words that emphasize the business nature of the voyages, the greed of the explorers, and the "gift" to the New World of degenerate European culture, values, vices, and germs. These are the concerns of contemporary people. Potentially enthusiastic celebrations for America's first major quincentary are thus tempered with concern for groups wronged and with sorrow that the first relations between Europe and the American continents were lacking in sensitivity and tolerance.

In the past, Columbus was traditionally distanced from other wicked Spanish conquerors. Such protection tends now to be denied him. Times are such that discussion of his virtues will be subordinated to exposés of his avarice and cruelty.

CHAPTER 10

PENTHESILEA
(AMAZONIAN): FEMALE
HERO AS MALE

INTRODUCTION

The Amazons are mentioned briefly in the *Iliad*, where the Greek hero
Bellerophontes is expected to die at their hands but in fact manages to kill
them. Other Greek heroes, including Theseus and Heracles, are similarly
esteemed for their defeat of the Amazons. Because of Theseus' abduction of
either Hippolyte, the Amazon queen, or Antiope, her sister, the Amazons
bear a grudge against the Greeks and come to the aid of King Priam of
Troy. In one of the various epics of the Trojan War composed after the
Iliad, Achilles is credited with killing the Amazon Queen Penthesilea, but
only after she has killed many Greeks. Yet for all her ferocity, Penthesilea
is also seductive, and Achilles falls in love with her corpse. The following
selections come from the ancient mythographer Apollodorus, who
describes the Amazons' battles with Greeks, and from the ancient historian Herodotus, who describes the Amazons' rapprochement with the
Scythians. Ancients were divided over whether the Amazons were historical. Moderns have likewise been divided. The modern historicizing view
goes back to the nineteenth-century Swiss jurist and classicist J. J. Bachofen, who took their myths as evidence of a long suppressed form of
society. For Bachofen, the Amazons symbolize a universal stage of society
that antedated present-day patriarchy. In its tamer form, this matriarchal
stage was one of monogamy, with sex limited to reproduction. In its

Original publication: Apollodorus, *The Library*, ed. and tr. James George Frazer, Loeb
Classical Library (London: Heinemann; New York: Putnam's, 1921), vol. I, pp. 149–
53 (Bk. II, iii. 1–2); vol. II, pp. 143–5 (Epitome, i.16), 211–13 (Epitome, v.1–2).
Herodotus, *The Histories*, tr. Aubrey de Sélincourt, rev. A. R. Burn (Harmondsworth:
Penguin, 1972 [1954]), pp. 306–9 (iv.110–17).

extreme form, males were rejected altogether. The epitome of extreme matriarchalism was the Amazons, who mated with males once a year simply to produce more female members. The defeat of the Amazons – and for all their fierceness they are usually defeated – symbolizes for Bachofen the succession of matriarchy by the first of several stages of patriarchy, which has existed for so long ever since as to seem the natural form of society. The Amazons are heroic in their independence, their courage, and their skill. They meet males on male terms. In transcending their gender, they blur the boundary between masculine and feminine. On the Amazons, see William Blake Tyrrell, *Amazons* (Baltimore: Johns Hopkins University Press, 1984); and Mary R. Lefkowitz, *Women in Greek Myth* (Baltimore: Johns Hopkins University Press, 1984), ch. 1. See also J. J. Bachofen, *Myth, Religion, and Mother Right*, tr. Ralph Manheim (Princeton: Princeton University Press, 1967).

APOLLODORUS: THE LIBRARY

Translated by J. G. Frazer

APOLLODORUS

Bellerophon, son of Glaucus, son of Sisyphus, having accidentally killed his brother Deliades or, as some say, Piren, or, as others will have it, Alcimenes, came to Proetus and was purified. And Stheneboea fell in love with him, and sent him proposals for a meeting; and when he rejected them, she told Proetus that Bellerophon had sent her a vicious proposal. Proetus believed her, and gave him a letter to take to Iobates, in which it was written that he was to kill Bellerophon. Having read the letter, Iobates ordered him to kill the Chimera, believing that he would be destroyed by the beast, for it was more than a match for many, let alone one; it had the fore part of a lion, the tail of a dragon, and its third head, the middle one, was that of a goat, through which it belched fire. And it devastated the country and harried the cattle; for it was a single creature with the power of three beasts. It is said, too, that this Chimera was bred by Amisodarus, as Homer also affirms, and that it was begotten by Typhon on Echidna, as Hesiod relates. So Bellerophon mounted his winged steed Pegasus, offspring of Medusa and Poseidon, and soaring on high shot down the Chimera from the height. After that contest Iobates ordered him to fight the Solymi, and when he had finished that task also, he commanded him to combat the Amazons. And when he had killed them also, he picked out the reputed bravest of the Lycians and bade them lay an ambush and slay him. But when Bellerophon had killed them also to a man, Iobates, in admiration of his prowess, showed him the letter and begged him to stay with him; moreover he gave him his daughter Philonoe, and dying bequeathed to him the kingdom.[. . .]

Theseus joined Hercules in his expedition against the Amazons and carried off Antiope, or, as some say, Melanippe; but Simonides calls her Hippolyte. Wherefore the Amazons marched against Athens, and having taken up a position about the Areopagus they were vanquished by the Athenians under Theseus. [. . .]

Penthesilia, daughter of Otrere and Ares, accidentally killed Hippolyte and was purified by Priam. In battle she slew many, and amongst them Machaon, and was afterwards herself killed by Achilles, who fell in love with the Amazon after her death and slew Thersites for jeering at him.

Hippolyte was the mother of Hippolytus; she also goes by the names of Glauce and Melanippe. For when the marriage of Phaedra was being celebrated, Hippolyte appeared in arms with her Amazons, and said that she would slay the guests of Theseus. So a battle took place, and she was killed, whether involuntarily by her ally Penthesilia, or by Theseus, or because his men, seeing the threatening attitude of the Amazons, hastily closed the doors and so intercepted and slew her.

HERODOTUS: THE HISTORIES

Translated by Aubrey de Sélincourt

Revised by A. R. Burn

HERODOTUS

About the Sauromatae there is the following story. In the war between the Greeks and the Amazons, the Greeks, after their victory at the river Thermodon, sailed off in three ships with as many Amazons on board as they had succeeded in taking alive. (The Scythians call the Amazons *Oeorpata*, the equivalent of *mankillers, oeor* being the Scythian word for "man", and *pata* for "kill".) Once at sea, the women murdered their captors, but, as they had no knowledge of boats and were unable to handle either rudder or sail or oar, they soon found themselves, when the men were done for, at the mercy of wind and wave, and were blown to Cremni – the Cliffs – on Lake Maeotis, a place within the territory of the free Scythians. Here they got ashore and made their way inland to an inhabited part of the country. The first thing they fell in with was a herd of horses grazing; these they seized, and, mounting on their backs, rode off in search of loot. The Scythians could not understand what was happening and were at a loss to know where the marauders had come from, as their dress, speech, and nationality were strange to them. Thinking, however, that they were young men, they fought in defence of their property, and discovered from the bodies which came into their possession after the battle that they were women. The discovery gave a new direction to their plans; they decided to make no further attempt to kill the invaders, but to send out a detachment of their youngest men, about equal in number to the Amazons, with orders to camp near them and take their cue from whatever it was that the Amazons then did: if they pursued them, they were not to fight, but to give ground; then, when the pursuit was abandoned, they were once again to encamp within easy range. The motive behind this policy was the Scythians' desire to get children by the Amazons. The detachment of young men obeyed their orders, and the Amazons, realizing that they meant no harm, did not attempt to molest them, with the result that every day the two camps drew a little closer together. Neither party had anything but their weapons and their horses, and both lived the same sort of life, hunting and plundering.

Towards midday the Amazons used to scatter and go off to some little distance in ones and twos to ease themselves, and the Scythians, when they noticed this, followed suit; until one of them, coming upon an Amazon girl all by herself, began to make advances to her. She, nothing loth, gave him what he wanted, and then told him by signs (being unable to express her meaning in words, as neither understood the other's language) to return on the following day with a friend, making it clear that there must be two men, and that she herself would bring another girl. The young man then left her and told the others what had happened, and on the next day took a friend to the same spot, where he found his Amazon waiting for him and another one with her. Having learnt of their success, the rest of the young Scythians soon succeeded in getting the Amazons to submit to their wishes. The two camps were then united, and Amazons and Scythians lived together, every man keeping as his wife the woman whose favours he had first enjoyed. The men could not learn the women's language, but the women succeeded in picking up the men's;

so when they could understand one another, the Scythians made the following proposal: "We", they said, "have parents and property. Let us give up our present way of life and return to live with our people. We will keep you as our wives and not take any others." The Amazons replied: "We and the women of your nation could never live together; our ways are too much at variance. We are riders; our business is with the bow and the spear, and we know nothing of women's work; but in your country no woman has anything to do with such things – your women stay at home in their waggons occupied with feminine tasks, and never go out to hunt or for any other purpose. We could not possibly agree. If, however, you wish to keep us for your wives and to behave as honourable men, go and get from your parents the share of property which is due to you, and then let us go off and live by ourselves." The young men agreed to this, and when they came back, each with his portion of the family possessions, the Amazons said: "We dread the prospect of settling down here, for we have done much damage to the country by our raids, and we have robbed you of your parents. Look now – if you think fit to keep us for your wives, let us get out of the country altogether and settle somewhere on the other side of the Tanais." Once again the Scythians agreed, so they crossed the Tanais and travelled east for three days, and then north, for another three, from Lake Maeotis, until they reached the country where they are to-day, and settled down there. Ever since then the women of the Sauromatae have kept to their old ways, riding to the hunt on horseback sometimes with, sometimes without, their menfolk, taking part in war and wearing the same sort of clothes as men. The language of these people is the Scythian, but it has always been a corrupt form of it because the Amazons were never able to learn to speak it properly. They have a marriage law which forbids a girl to marry until she has killed an enemy in battle; some of their women, unable to fulfil this condition, grow old and die in spinsterhood.

CHAPTER 11

EVE (BIBLICAL): DEFIANT HERO

INTRODUCTION

Since all humanity suffers for the misdeeds of Adam and Eve, the pair might seem most unlikely candidates for heroism. But heroism can take many forms, and that of Adam and Eve involves their bold defiance of God in the quest for divinity. Eve is more heroic than Adam because she acts first. The snake shrewdly turns to her, not to Adam, even though she, in this second of the biblical creation myths, was created both after Adam and out of Adam. The couple had been prohibited by God from eating the fruit of the Tree of Knowledge in the Garden of Eden. But the talking snake tempts Eve with the prospect not merely of knowledge but, with it, of divinity. She then gives some of the fruit, itself unspecified, to Adam. The sexual self-consciousness they secure, God regards as properly restricted to the gods, and he evicts them out of fear that otherwise they will proceed to eat from the Tree of Life, which till now has been allowed them, and become fully divine. God is motivated less by justice than by concern for his "turf." The Hebrew Bible is hardly committed, the way Judaism later comes to be, either by a rigid monotheism or by a rigid divide between divinity and humanity. There are other gods beside the God who speaks ("like one of us" [Genesis 3.22]), and the possibility of humans becoming gods is taken for granted. The Bible does not itself need to endorse the actions of Adam and Eve for them to be considered heroes. On Adam and Eve, see *A Walk in the Garden*, eds. Paul Morris and Deborah Sawyer, Journal for the Study of the Old Testament Supplement Series 136 (Sheffield: Sheffield Academic Press, 1992). On changing views of Eden over the millennia, see Jean Delumeau, *History of Paradise*, tr. Matthew O'Connell (New York: Continuum, 1995).

Original publication: Book of Genesis, Revised Standard Version, chs. 2–3.

THE NEW OXFORD ANNOTATED BIBLE WITH THE APOCRYPHA

Edited by Herbert G. May and Bruce M. Metzger

2 Thus the heavens and the earth were finished, and all the host of them.[2] And on the seventh day God finished his work which he had done, and he rested on the seventh day from all his work which he had done.[3]So God blessed the seventh day and hallowed it, because on it God rested from all his work which he had done in creation.

4 These are the generations of the heavens and the earth when they were created.
In the day that the LORD God made the earth and the heavens,[5]when no plant of the field was yet in the earth and no herb of the field had yet sprung up – for the LORD God had not caused it to rain upon the earth, and there was no man to till the ground;[6]but a mist went up from the earth and watered the whole face of the ground –[7]then the LORD God formed man of dust from the ground, and breathed into his nostrils the breath of life; and man became a living being.[8] And the LORD God planted a garden in Eden, in the east; and there he put the man whom he had formed.[9]And out of the ground the LORD God made to grow every tree that is pleasant to the sight and good for food, the tree of life also in the midst of the garden, and the tree of the knowledge of good and evil.

10 A river flowed out of Eden to water the garden, and there it divided and became four rivers.[11]The name of the first is Pishon; it is the one which flows around the whole land of Hav'ilah, where there is gold;[12]and the gold of that land is good; bdellium and onyx stone are there.[13]The name of the second river is Gihon; it is the one which flows around the whole land of Cush.[14]And the name of the third river is Tigris, which flows east of Assyria. And the fourth river is the Euphra'tes.

15 The LORD God took the man and put him in the garden of Eden to till it and keep it.[16]And the LORD God commanded the man, saying, "You may freely eat of every tree of the garden;[17]but of the tree of the knowledge of good and evil you shall not eat, for in the day that you eat of it you shall die."

18 Then the LORD God said, "It is not good that the man should be alone; I will make him a helper fit for him."[19]So out of the ground the LORD God formed every beast of the field and every bird of the air, and

brought them to the man to see what he would call them; and whatever the man called every living creature, that was its name.[20]The man gave names to all cattle, and to the birds of the air, and to every beast of the field; but for the man there was not found a helper fit for him.[21]So the LORD God caused a deep sleep to fall upon the man, and while he slept took one of his ribs and closed up its place with flesh;[22]and the rib which the LORD God had taken from the man he made into a woman and brought her to the man.[23]Then the man said,

> "This at last is bone of my bones
> and flesh of my flesh;
> she shall be called Woman,
> because she was taken out of
> Man."

[24]Therefore a man leaves his father and his mother and cleaves to his wife, and they become one flesh.[25]And the man and his wife were both naked, and were not ashamed.

3 Now the serpent was more subtle than any other wild creature that the LORD God had made. He said to the woman, "Did God say, 'You shall not eat of any tree of the garden'?"[2]And the woman said to the serpent, "We may eat of the fruit of the trees of the garden;[3]but God said, 'You shall not eat of the fruit of the tree which is in the midst of the garden, neither shall you touch it, lest you die.'"[4]But the serpent said to the woman, "You will not die.[5]For God knows that when you eat of it your eyes will be opened, and you will be like God, knowing good and evil." [6]So when the woman saw that the tree was good for food, and that it was a delight to the eyes, and that the tree was to be desired to make one wise, she took of its fruit and ate; and she also gave some to her husband, and he ate.[7]Then the eyes of both were opened, and they knew that they were naked; and they sewed fig leaves together and made themselves aprons.

8 And they heard the sound of the LORD God walking in the garden in the cool of the day, and the man and his wife hid themselves from the presence of the LORD God among the trees of the garden.[9]But the LORD God called to the man, and said to him, "Where are you?"[10]And he said, "I heard the sound of thee in the garden, and I was afraid, because I was naked; and I hid myself."[11]He said, "Who told you that you were naked? Have you eaten of the tree of which I commanded you not to eat?"[12]The man said, "The woman whom thou gavest to be with me, she gave me fruit of the tree, and I ate."[13]Then the LORD God said to the woman, "What is this that you have done?" The woman said, "The serpent beguiled me, and I ate."[14]The LORD God said to the serpent,

"Because you have done this, cursed are you above all cattle, and above all wild animals; upon your belly you shall go, and dust you shall eat all the days of your life.

15 I will put enmity between you and the woman, and between your seed and her seed; he shall bruise your head, and you shall bruise his heel."

16 To the woman he said, "I will greatly multiply your pain in child-bearing; in pain you shall bring forth children, yet your desire shall be for your husband, and he shall rule over you."

17 And to Adam he said, "Because you have listened to the voice of your wife, and have eaten of the tree of which I commanded you, 'You shall not eat of it,' cursed is the ground because of you; in toil you shall eat of it all the days of your life;

18 thorns and thistles it shall bring forth to you; and you shall eat the plants of the field.

19 In the sweat of your face you shall eat bread till you return to the ground, for out of it you were taken; you are dust, and to dust you shall return."

20 The man called his wife's name Eve, because she was the mother of all living. 21 And the LORD God made for Adam and for his wife garments of skins, and clothed them.

22 Then the LORD God said, "Behold, the man has become like one of us, knowing good and evil; and now, lest he put forth his hand and take also of the tree of life, and eat, and live for ever" – 23 therefore the LORD God sent him forth from the garden of Eden, to till the ground from which he was taken. 24 He drove out the man; and at the east of the garden of Eden he placed the cherubim, and a flaming sword which turned every way, to guard the way to the tree of life.

CHAPTER 12

PROMETHEUS (ANCIENT GREEK): DEFIANT HERO

INTRODUCTION

The myth of Prometheus is the counterpart to the myth of the Garden of Eden. Both myths describe vain attempts to secure for humans attributes or possessions intended only for gods. Prometheus is the counterpart less to Eve or to Adam than to the snake, for he defies Zeus on behalf of humanity. Going further than the snake, he does not merely goad humans but himself steals fire from Zeus and gives it to humanity. At the same time his motives are more mixed than those of the snake. He is the son of a Titan, and the Titans have been toppled as rulers of the world by Zeus and the Olympians. Prometheus' defiance of Zeus therefore stems considerably from loyalty to his father. The main source of the story is Hesiod, who, in one of his epics, the *Theogony*, takes the conflict back to a stage that the other epic, the *Works and Days*, presupposes. According to the *Theogony*, from which the selection below comes, Prometheus first tries to deceive Zeus by disguising the better part of the sacrifice that humans are offering him. Prometheus assumes that Zeus will choose the portion that looks more appetizing but that in fact contains mere bones. Humans will then be left with the meat and fat hidden in the ox's stomach. While Zeus spots the trick, he nevertheless proceeds to choose the worse portion, and in retaliation for the intended deception punishes humanity by withholding fire. Like immortality in Eden, the fire would have been given humanity had no conflict with God arisen. But Prometheus then does manage to trick Zeus and steal fire for humanity. In retaliation, Zeus punishes not only Prometheus – by binding him to a rock and having his liver eaten anew each day by an eagle – but also humanity – by giving it woman, who, like the bones covered up by white

Original publication: Hesiod, *Theogony*, tr. Richmond Lattimore (Ann Arbor: University of Michigan Press, 1959), pp. 153–9 (lines 507–602).

fat, is alluring on the outside but unwholesome underneath. Humanity here means males only. For the weary farmer Hesiod, woman means endless demands and endless mouths to feed. However courageous, Prometheus' deed, like the snake's, harms rather than helps humanity. For editions of Hesiod, see *Hesiod: The Homeric Hymns and Homerica*, ed. and tr. H. G. Evelyn-White, Loeb Classical Library (Cambridge, MA: Harvard University Press; London: Heinemann, 1914); *Theogony*, ed. and tr. Norman O. Brown, Library of Liberal Arts (Indianapolis: Bobbs-Merrill, 1953); *Theogony*, ed. and tr. M. L. West (Oxford: Clarendon Press, 1966); *Works and Days*, ed. and tr. M. L. West (Oxford: Clarendon Press, 1978); and *Theogony*, ed. and tr. Richard S. Caldwell (Cambridge, MA: Focus Classical Library, 1987). See also Robert Lamberton, *Hesiod*, Hermes Books (New Haven: Yale University Press, 1988).

HESIOD

Translated by Richmond Lattimore

Iapetos took Klymene,
   the light-stepping daughter of Ocean,
to be his wife, and mounted into the same bed
   with her,
510 and she bore him a son, Atlas,
   of the powerful spirit,
and she bore him high-vaunting Menoitios,
   and Prometheus
of the intricate and twisting mind,
   and Epimetheus
the gullible, who from the beginning
   brought bad luck to men
who eat bread, for he first accepted
   from Zeus the girl Zeus fashioned
and married her.
            Menoitios was mutinous,
   and Zeus of the wide brows
515 struck him with the blazing thunderbolt
   and dropped him to Erebos
because of his too-great hardihood
   and outrageous action.

But Atlas, under strong constraint,
   at earth's uttermost
places, near the sweet-singing Hesperides,
   standing upright
props the wide sky upon his head
   and his hands never wearied,
520 for this was the doom
   which Zeus of the counsels dealt out to him.
And in ineluctable, painful bonds
   he fastened Prometheus
of the subtle mind, for he drove a stanchion
   through his middle. Also
he let loose on him the wing-spread eagle,
   and it was feeding
on his imperishable liver, which by night
   would grow back
525 to size from what the spread-winged bird
   had eaten in the daytime.
But Herakles, the powerful son
   of lightfooted Alkmene,
killed the eagle
   and drove that pestilential affliction
from Iapetos' son, and set him free
   from all his unhappiness,
not without the will of high-minded Zeus
   of Olympos
530 in order that the reputation
   of Thebes-born Herakles
might be greater even than it had been
   on the earth that feeds many.
With such thoughts in mind he honored his son
   and made him glorious,
and angry as he had been before,
   he gave up his anger;
for Prometheus once had matched wits
   against the great son of Kronos.
535 It was when gods, and mortal men,
   took their separate positions
at Mekone, and Prometheus,
   eager to try his wits, cut up
a great ox, and set it before Zeus,
   to see if he could outguess him.

127

He took the meaty parts and the inwards
　　thick with fat, and set them
before men, hiding them away
　　in an ox's stomach,
540　but the white bones of the ox he arranged,
　　with careful deception,
inside a concealing fold of white fat,
　　and set it before Zeus.
At last the father of gods
　　and men spoke to him, saying:
"Son of Iapetos, conspicuous among all Kings,
old friend, oh how prejudicially
　　you divided the portions."
545　So Zeus, who knows imperishable counsels,
　　spoke in displeasure,
but Prometheus the devious-deviser,
　　lightly smiling,
answered him again, quite well aware
　　of his artful deception:
"Zeus most high, most honored
　　among the gods everlasting,
choose whichever of these the heart within
　　you would have."
550　He spoke, with intent to deceive, and Zeus,
　　who knows imperishable
counsels, saw it, the trick
　　did not escape him, he imagined
evils for mortal men in his mind,
　　and meant to fulfil them.
In both his hands he took up the portion
　　of the white fat. Anger
rose up about his heart
　　and the spite mounted in his spirit
555　when he saw the white bones of the ox
　　in deceptive arrangement.

Ever since that time the races of mortal men
　　on earth have burned
the white bones to the immortals
　　on the smoky altars.

Then Zeus the cloud-gatherer
　　in great vexation said to him:

"Son of Iapetos, versed in planning
    beyond all others,
560 old friend, so after all you did not forget
    your treachery."
So Zeus, who knows imperishable counsels,
    spoke in his anger,
and ever remembering this deception
    thereafter, he would not
give the force of weariless fire
    to the ash-tree people,
not to people who inhabit the earth
    and are mortal,
565 no, but the strong son of Iapetos
    outwitted him
and stole the far-seen glory
    of weariless fire, hiding it
in the hollow fennel stalk;
    this bit deep into the feeling
of Zeus who thunders on high,
    and it galled the heart inside him
when he saw the far-seen glory of fire
    among mortal people,
570 and next, for the price of the fire,
    he made an evil thing for mankind.
For the renowned smith of the strong arms
    took earth, and molded it,
through Zeus's plans, into the likeness
    of a modest young girl,
and the goddess gray-eyed Athene
    dressed her and decked her
in silverish clothing, and over her head
    she held, with her hands,
575 an intricately wrought veil in place,
    a wonder to look at,
and over this on her head
    she placed a wreath of gold, one
that the very renowned smith
    of the strong arms had fashioned
580 working it out with his hands,
    as a favor to Zeus the father.
On this had been done much intricate work,
    a wonder to look at:

wild animals, such as the mainland
   and the sea also produce
in numbers, and he put many on,
   the imitations of living
things, that have voices, wonderful,
   and it flashed in its beauty.
585   But when, to replace good,
   he had made this beautiful evil
thing, he led her out
   where the rest of the gods and mortals
were, in the pride and glory
   that the gray-eyed daughter of a great
father had given; wonder
   seized both immortals and mortals
as they gazed on this sheer deception,
   more than mortals can deal with.
590 For from her originates the breed
   of female women,
and they live with mortal men,
   and are a great sorrow to them,
and hateful poverty they will not share,
   but only luxury.
As when, inside the overarching hives,
   the honeybees
595 feed their drones (and these are accomplished
   in doing no good,
while the bees, all day long
   until the sun goes down
do their daily hard work
   and set the white combs in order,
and the drones, spending their time
   inside the hollow skeps,
garner the hard work of others
   into their own bellies),
600 so Zeus of the high thunder established women,
   for mortal
men an evil thing,
   and they are accomplished in bringing
hard labors.

CHAPTER 13

OEDIPUS (ANCIENT GREEK): TRAGIC HERO

INTRODUCTION

There are various ancient versions of the story of Oedipus, and many of them antedate Sophocles' in the play *Oedipus the King*. But Sophocles' version is by far the best known. According to the classic definition of Aristotle, who cites the play as an example, tragedy involves more than disappointment or even suffering. It requires a fall, or a reversal, from high to low. Where the nontragic Odysseus suffers for twenty years but returns home to regain his throne and wife, the tragic Oedipus falls from regaled king to cursed exile, whatever reconciliation comes at the end. Tragedy also requires that the hero be the cause, not merely the victim, of the downfall. Even though Oedipus has been fated to kill his father and to have sex with his mother, his fall comes not with the commission of the deeds but, much later, with his discovery of the fact. Without the discovery, he would have lived happily ever after as the honored savior of Thebes. Even if, as King, he is obliged to end the plague that has struck Thebes, he is not obliged to end it the way he does: by consulting the Oracle to find out how to stop it himself. Even if other means of ending the plague, praying and sacrificing, have proved vain, the Oracle decrees that the murderer of Laius, Oedipus' predecessor, simply be banished, not cursed. Even if Oedipus needs to consult Teiresias to discover the murderer, he does not need to discover his relationship to Laius or to Jocasta, and Teiresias tries in vain to dissuade him from discovering that relationship. Even Teiresias' prediction that Oedipus will discover what he has done does not mean that Oedipus has been fated to discover it. The discovery depends on Oedipus' continuing arrogation to himself of the

Original publication: Sophocles, *Oedipus the King*, tr. David Grene, in *Sophocles I, The Complete Greek Tragedies* (Chicago: University of Chicago Press, 1942), pp. 11–17 (lines 1–146).

role of savior of the city. Finally, tragedy requires that the hero learn from the downfall. President Richard Nixon's fall was not tragic because he blamed only others for his forced resignation and gained no insight into himself. Oedipus comes to recognize that he is a mere mortal who had ruled over Thebes as if he were a god. His "fatal flaw," if he can be said to harbor one, is not a sin but an error, and the corrective is not repentance but a revised view of the world. Otto Rank, Joseph Campbell, Lord Raglan, and René Girard (especially in *Violence and the Sacred*, tr. Patrick Gregory [London: Athlone Press; Baltimore: Johns Hopkins University Press, 1977], chs. 3, 7) all cite Oedipus as a hero. On Oedipus as a tragic hero, see Bernard Knox, *Oedipus at Thebes* (New York: Norton, 1971 [1957]). On parallels to the Oedipus tale worldwide, see *Oedipus: A Folklore Casebook*, eds. Lowell Edmunds and Alan Dundes (Madison: University of Wisconsin Press, 1995 [1983]); and Lowell Edmunds, *Oedipus: The Ancient Legend and Its Later Analogues* (Baltimore: Johns Hopkins University Press, 1985). The following excerpt from *Oedipus the King* presents Oedipus' god-like view of himself at the outset of the play.

SOPHOCLES I: OEDIPUS THE KING

Translated by David Grene

CHARACTERS

Oedipus, King of Thebes

Jocasta, His Wife

Creon, His Brother-in-Law

Teiresias, an Old Blind Prophet

A Priest

First Messenger

Second Messenger

A Herdsman

A Chorus of Old Men of Thebes

OEDIPUS THE KING

SCENE: *In front of the palace of Oedipus at Thebes. To the right of the stage near the altar stands the Priest with a crowd of children. Oedipus emerges from the central door.*

OEDIPUS

Children, young sons and daughters of old Cadmus,
why do you sit here with your suppliant crowns?
The town is heavy with a mingled burden
of sounds and smells, of groans and hymns and incense;
I did not think it fit that I should hear   5
of this from messengers but came myself, –
I Oedipus whom all men call the Great.

                             (*He turns to the Priest.*)
You're old and they are young; come, speak for them.
What do you fear or want, that you sit here
suppliant? Indeed I'm willing to give all   10
that you may need; I would be very hard
should I not pity suppliants like these.

PRIEST

O ruler of my country, Oedipus,
you see our company around the altar;
you see our ages; some of us, like these,   15
who cannot yet fly far, and some of us
heavy with age; these children are the chosen
among the young, and I the priest of Zeus.
Within the market place sit others crowned
with suppliant garlands, at the double shrine   20
of Pallas and the temple where Ismenus
gives oracles by fire. King, you yourself
have seen our city reeling like a wreck
already; it can scarcely lift its prow
out of the depths, out of the bloody surf.   25
A blight is on the fruitful plants of the earth,
A blight is on the cattle in the fields,
a blight is on our women that no children
are born to them; a God that carries fire,
a deadly pestilence, is on our town,   30
strikes us and spares not, and the house of Cadmus
is emptied of its people while black Death

grows rich in groaning and in lamentation.
We have not come as suppliants to this altar
because we thought of you as of a God,   35
but rather judging you the first of men
in all the chances of this life and when
we mortals have to do with more than man.
You came and by your coming saved our city,
freed us from tribute which we paid of old   40
to the Sphinx, cruel singer. This you did
in virtue of no knowledge we could give you,
in virtue of no teaching; it was God
that aided you, men say, and you are held
with God's assistance to have saved our lives.   45
Now Oedipus, Greatest in all men's eyes,
here falling at your feet we all entreat you,
find us some strength for rescue.
Perhaps you'll hear a wise word from some God,
perhaps you will learn something from a man   50
(for I have seen that for the skilled of practice
the outcome of their counsels live the most).
Noblest of men, go, and raise up our city,
go, – and give heed. For now this land of ours
calls you its savior since you saved it once.   55
So, let us never speak about your reign
as of a time when first our feet were set
secure on high, but later fell to ruin.
Raise up our city, save it and raise it up.
Once you have brought us luck with happy omen;   60
be no less now in fortune.
If you will rule this land, as now you rule it,
better to rule it full of men than empty.
For neither tower nor ship is anything
when empty, and none live in it together.   65

OEDIPUS

I pity you, children. You have come full of longing,
but I have known the story before you told it
only too well. I know you are all sick,
yet there is not one of you, sick though you are,
that is as sick as I myself.   70
Your several sorrows each have single scope
and touch but one of you. My spirit groans

for city and myself and you at once.
You have not roused me like a man from sleep;
know that I have given many tears to this,   75
gone many ways wandering in thought,
but as I thought I found only one remedy
and that I took. I sent Menoeceus' son
Creon, Jocasta's brother, to Apollo,
to his Pythian temple,   80
that he might learn there by what act or word
I could save this city. As I count the days,
it vexes me what ails him; he is gone
far longer than he needed for the journey.
But when he comes, then, may I prove a villain,   85
if I shall not do all the God commands.

PRIEST

Thanks for your gracious words. Your servants here
signal that Creon is this moment coming.

OEDIPUS

His face is bright. O holy Lord Apollo,
grant that his news too may be bright for us   90
and bring us safety.

PRIEST

It is happy news,
I think, for else his head would not be crowned
with sprigs of fruitful laurel.

OEDIPUS

We will know soon,
he's within hail. Lord Creon, my good brother,   95
what is the word you bring us from the God?

(Creon enters.)

CREON

A good word, – for things hard to bear themselves
if in the final issue all is well
I count complete good fortune.

OEDIPUS

What do you mean?
What you have said so far   100
leaves me uncertain whether to trust or fear.

CREON
  If you will hear my news before these others
  I am ready to speak, or else to go within.

OEDIPUS
  Speak it to all;
  the grief I bear, I bear it more for these   105
  than for my own heart.

CREON
                        I will tell you, then,
  what I heard from the God.
  King Phoebus in plain words commanded us
  to drive out a pollution from our land,
  pollution grown ingrained within the land;   110
  drive it out, said the God, not cherish it,
  till it's past cure.

OEDIPUS
                        What is the rite
  of purification? How shall it be done?

CREON
  By banishing a man, or expiation
  of blood by blood, since it is murder guilt   115
  which holds our city in this destroying storm.

OEDIPUS
  Who is this man whose fate the God pronounces?

CREON
  My Lord, before you piloted the state
  we had a king called Laius.

OEDIPUS
  I know of him by hearsay. I have not seen him.   120

CREON
  The God commanded clearly: let some one
  punish with force this dead man's murderers.

OEDIPUS
  Where are they in the world? Where would a trace
  of this old crime be found? It would be hard
  to guess where.

CREON

     The clue is in this land;   125
 that which is sought is found;
 the unheeded thing escapes:
 so said the God.

OEDIPUS

     Was it at home,
 or in the country that death came upon him,
 or in another country travelling?   130

CREON

 He went, he said himself, upon an embassy,
 but never returned when he set out from home.

OEDIPUS

 Was there no messenger, no fellow traveller
 who knew what happened? Such a one might tell
 something of use.   135

CREON

 They were all killed save one. He fled in terror
 and he could tell us nothing in clear terms
 of what he knew, nothing, but one thing only.

OEDIPUS

 What was it?
 If we could even find a slim beginning   140
 in which to hope, we might discover much.

CREON

 This man said that the robbers they encountered
 were many and the hands that did the murder
 were many; it was no man's single power.

OEDIPUS

 How could a robber dare a deed like this   145
 were he not helped with money from the city,
 money and treachery?

CREON

      That indeed was thought.
 But Laius was dead and in our trouble
 there was none to help.

OEDIPUS

> What trouble was so great to hinder you 150
> inquiring out the murder of your king?

CREON

The riddling Sphinx induced us to neglect
mysterious crimes and rather seek solution
of troubles at our feet.

OEDIPUS

> I will bring this to light again. King Phoebus 155
> fittingly took this care about the dead,
> and you too fittingly.
> And justly you will see in me an ally,
> a champion of my country and the God.
> For when I drive pollution from the land 160
> I will not serve a distant friend's advantage,
> but act in my own interest. Whoever
> he was that killed the king may readily
> wish to dispatch me with his murderous hand;
> so helping the dead king I help myself. 165
>
> Come, children, take your suppliant boughs and go;
> up from the altars now. Call the assembly
> and let it meet upon the understanding
> that I'll do everything. God will decide
> whether we prosper or remain in sorrow. 170

PRIEST

> Rise, children – it was this we came to seek,
> which of himself the king now offers us.
> May Phoebus who gave us the oracle
> come to our rescue and stay the plague.

(*Exeunt all but the Chorus.*)

CHAPTER 14

JOB (BIBLICAL): TRAGIC HERO

INTRODUCTION

The difference between Job and Oedipus is that Job has done nothing to warrant his fall. It is not only Job who proclaims his blamelessness. So does God, so does Satan, and so does the book itself. Job loses his children, his possessions, and his health not as punishment but as a test of his loyalty to God. Only the friends who come to "comfort" Job insist that he must be getting what he deserves, and they say so on the basis of their naive faith in the justice of God, not from any knowledge of Job's behavior. The comforters argue that Job must have sinned because, after all, he is only human. Job's actual innocence thereby elevates him on at least that count to the status of a god. Ironically, God, finally granting Job his day in court, justifies the suffering not on the grounds that Job has deserved it but on the grounds that Job is a mere human being and so dare not challenge the right of God to do as God wishes. God invokes not his own superior morality but his own superior power. Like Oedipus, Job has presumed to act like a god, though in Job's case only in reaction to his fall and not as the cause of it. Both Job and Oedipus are heroic in coming to accept their lowly, human place in the world. Unlike Oedipus, Job is restored to his pre-fallen state, albeit with a new set of children rather than with his dead ones resurrected. Joseph Campbell briefly discusses the case of Job, to which René Girard devotes an entire book (*Job, the Victim of His People,* tr. Yvonne Freccero [London: Athlone Press; Stanford: Stanford University Press, 1987]). On Job, see *The Book of Job,* ed. Paul S. Sanders, Twentieth Century Interpretations (Englewood Cliffs, NJ: Prentice-Hall, 1968). For a view that biblical justice precludes tragedy, see George Steiner, *The Death of Tragedy* (New York: Knopf, 1961,

Original publication: Book of Job, Revised Standard Version, chs. 1–2, 13, 38, 42.

ch. 1). The following excerpt presents Job at the beginning of the Book of Job and at the end.

THE NEW OXFORD ANNOTATED BIBLE WITH THE APOCRYPHA

Edited by Herbert G. May and Bruce M. Metzger

1 There WAS A MAN IN THE LAND OF Uz, whose name was Job; and that man was blameless and upright, one who feared God, and turned away from evil.[2]There were born to him seven sons and three daughters.[3]He had seven thousand sheep, three thousand camels, five hundred yoke of oxen, and five hundred she-asses, and very many servants; so that this man was the greatest of all the people of the east.[4]His sons used to go and hold a feast in the house of each on his day; and they would send and invite their three sisters to eat and drink with them.[5]And when the days of the feast had run their course, Job would send and sanctify them, and he would rise early in the morning and offer burnt offerings according to the number of them all; for Job said, "It may be that my sons have sinned, and cursed God in their hearts." Thus Job did continually.

6 Now there was a day when the sons of God came to present themselves before the LORD, and Satan also came among them.[7]The LORD said to Satan, "Whence have you come?" Satan answered the LORD, "From going to and fro on the earth, and from walking up and down on it."[8]And the LORD said to Satan, "Have you considered my servant Job, that there is none like him on the earth, a blameless and upright man, who fears God and turns away from evil?"[9]Then Satan answered the LORD, "Does Job fear God for nought?[10]Hast thou not put a hedge about him and his house and all that he has, on every side? Thou hast blessed the work of his hands, and his possessions have increased in the land.[11]But put forth thy hand now, and touch all that he has, and he will curse thee to thy face."[12]And the LORD said to Satan, "Behold, all that he has is in your power; only upon himself do not put forth your hand." So Satan went forth from the presence of the LORD.

13 Now there was a day when his sons and daughters were eating and drinking wine in their eldest brother's house;[14]and there came a messenger to Job, and said, "The oxen were plowing and the asses feeding beside them;[15]and the Sabe'ans fell upon them and took them, and slew the

servants with the edge of the sword; and I alone have escaped to tell you."[16]While he was yet speaking, there came another, and said, "The fire of God fell from heaven and burned up the sheep and the servants, and consumed them; and I alone have escaped to tell you."[17]While he was yet speaking, there came another, and said, "The Chalde'ans formed three companies, and made a raid upon the camels and took them, and slew the servants with the edge of the sword; and I alone have escaped to tell you."[18]While he was yet speaking, there came another, and said, "Your sons and daughters were eating and drinking wine in their eldest brother's house;[19]and behold, a great wind came across the wilderness, and struck the four corners of the house, and it fell upon the young people, and they are dead; and I alone have escaped to tell you."

20 Then Job arose, and rent his robe, and shaved his head, and fell upon the ground, and worshiped.[21]And he said, "Naked I came from my mother's womb, and naked shall I return; the LORD gave, and the LORD has taken away; blessed be the name of the LORD."

22 In all this Job did not sin or charge God with wrong.

2 Again there was a day when the sons of God came to present themselves before the LORD, and Satan also came among them to present himself before the LORD.[2]And the LORD said to Satan, "Whence have you come?" Satan answered the LORD, "From going to and for on the earth, and from walking up and down on it."[3]And the LORD said to Satan, "Have you considered my servant Job, that there is none like him on the earth, a blameless and upright man, who fears God and turns away from evil? He still holds fast his integrity, although you moved me against him, to destroy him without cause."[4]Then Satan answered the LORD, "Skin for skin! All that a man has he will give for his life.[5]But put forth thy hand now, and touch his bone and his flesh, and he will curse thee to thy face."[6]And the LORD said to Satan, "Behold, he is in your power; only spare his life."

7 So Satan went forth from the presence of the LORD, and afflicted Job with loathsome sores from the sole of his foot to the crown of his head. [8]And he took a potsherd with which to scrape himself, and sat among the ashes.

9 Then his wife said to him, "Do you still hold fast your integrity? Curse God, and die."[10]But he said to her, "You speak as one of the foolish women would speak. Shall we receive good at the hand of God, and shall we not receive evil?" In all this Job did not sin with his lips.

11 Now when Job's three friends heard of all this evil that had come upon him, they came each from his own place, Eli'phaz the Te'manite, Bildad the Shuhite, and Zophar the Na'amathite. They made an appointment together to come to condole with him and comfort him.[12]And when

they saw him from afar, they did not recognize him; and they raised their voices and wept; and they rent their robes and sprinkled dust upon their heads toward heaven. ¹³And they sat with him on the ground seven days and seven nights, and no one spoke a word to him, for they saw that his suffering was very great.

13 "Lo, my eye has seen all this, my ear has heard and understood it. ² What you know, I also know; I am not inferior to you.

³ But I would speak to the Almighty, and I desire to argue my case with God.

⁴ As for you, you whitewash with lies; worthless physicians are you all.

⁵ Oh that you would keep silent, and it would be your wisdom!

⁶ Hear now my reasoning, and listen to the pleadings of my lips.

⁷ Will you speak falsely for God, and speak deceitfully for him?

⁸ Will you show partiality toward him, will you plead the case for God?

⁹ Will it be well with you when he searches you out? Or can you deceive him, as one deceives a man?

¹⁰ He will surely rebuke you if in secret you show partiality.

¹¹ Will not his majesty terrify you, and the dread of him fall upon you?

¹² Your maxims are proverbs of ashes, your defenses are defenses of clay.

¹³ "Let me have silence, and I will speak, and let come on me what may.

¹⁴ I will take my flesh in my teeth, and put my life in my hand.

¹⁵ Behold, he will slay me; I have no hope; yet I will defend my ways to his face.

¹⁶ This will be my salvation, that a godless man shall not come before him.

¹⁷ Listen carefully to my words, and let my declaration be in your ears.

¹⁸ Behold, I have prepared my case; I know that I shall be vindicated.

¹⁹ Who is there that will contend with me? For then I would be silent and die.

²⁰ Only grant two things to me, then I will not hide myself from thy face:

²¹ withdraw thy hand far from me, and let not dread of thee terrify me.

²² Then call, and I will answer; or let me speak, and do thou reply to me.

²³ How many are my iniquities and my sins? Make me know my transgression and my sin.

²⁴ Why dost thou hide thy face, and count me as they enemy?

²⁵ Wilt thou frighten a driven leaf and pursue dry chaff?

²⁶ For thou writest bitter things against me, and makest me inherit the iniquities of my youth.

²⁷ Thou puttest my feet in the stocks, and watchest all my paths; thou settest a bound to the soles of my feet.

²⁸ Man wastes away like a rotten thing, like a garment that is moth-eaten."

38 Then the LORD answered Job out of the whirlwind:
² "Who is this that darkens counsel by words without knowledge?
³ Gird up your loins like a man, I will question you, and you shall declare to me.
⁴ "Where were you when I laid the foundation of the earth? Tell me, if you have understanding.
⁵ Who determined its measurements – surely you know! Or who stretched the line upon it?
⁶ On what were its bases sunk, or who laid its cornerstone,
⁷ when the morning stars sang together, and all the sons of God shouted for joy?
⁸ "Or who shut in the sea with doors, when it burst forth from the womb;
⁹ when I made clouds its garment, and thick darkness its swaddling band,
¹⁰ and prescribed bounds for it, and set bars and doors,
¹¹ and said, 'Thus far shall you come, and no farther, and here shall your proud waves be stayed'?
¹² "Have you commanded the morning since your days began, and caused the dawn to know its place,
¹³ that it might take hold of the skirts of the earth, and the wicked be shaken out of it?
¹⁴ It is changed like clay under the seal, and it is dyed like a garment.
¹⁵ From the wicked their light is withheld, and their uplifted arm is broken.
¹⁶ "Have you entered into the springs of the sea, or walked in the recesses of the deep?
¹⁷ Have the gates of death been revealed to you, or have you seen the gates of deep darkness?
¹⁸ Have you comprehended the expanse of the earth? Declare, if you know all this.
¹⁹ "Where is the way to the dwelling of light, and where is the place of darkness,
²⁰ that you may take it to its territory and that you may discern the paths to its home?
²¹ You know, for you were born then, and the number of your days is great!
²² "Have you entered the storehouses of the snow, or have you seen the storehouses of the hail,

²³ which I have reserved for the time of trouble, for the day of battle and war?

²⁴ What is the way to the place where the light is distributed, or where the east wind is scattered upon the earth?

²⁵ "Who has cleft a channel for the torrents of rain, and a way for the thunderbolt,

²⁶ to bring rain on a land where no man is, on the desert in which there is no man;

²⁷ to satisfy the waste and desolate land, and to make the ground put forth grass?

²⁸ "Has the rain a father, or who has begotten the drops of dew?

²⁹ From whose womb did the ice come forth, and who has given birth to the hoarfrost of heaven?

³⁰ The waters become hard like stone, and the face of the deep is frozen.

³¹ "Can you bind the chains of the Plei′ades, or loose the cords of Orion?

³² Can you lead forth the Maz′zaroth in their season, or can you guide the Bear with its children?

³³ Do you know the ordinances of the heavens? Can you establish their rule on the earth?

³⁴ "Can you lift up your voice to the clouds, that a flood of waters may cover you?

³⁵ Can you send forth lightnings, that they may go and say to you, 'Here we are'?

³⁶ Who has put wisdom in the clouds, or given understanding to the mists?

³⁷ Who can number the clouds by wisdom? Or who can tilt the waterskins of the heavens,

³⁸ when the dust runs into a mass and the clods cleave fast together?

³⁹ "Can you hunt the prey for the lion, or satisfy the appetite of the young lions,

⁴⁰ when they crouch in their dens, or lie in wait in their covert?

⁴¹ Who provides for the raven its prey, when its young ones cry to God, and wander about for lack of food?"

42 Then Job answered the LORD:
² "I know that thou canst do all things, and that no purpose of thine can be thwarted.

³ 'Who is this that hides counsel without knowledge?'
Therefore I have uttered what I did not understand, things too wonderful for me, which I did not know.

⁴ 'Hear, and I will speak; I will question you, and you declare to me.'

⁵ I had heard of thee by the hearing of the ear, but now my eye sees thee;

⁶ therefore I despise myself, and repent in dust and ashes."

7 After the LORD had spoken these words to Job, the LORD said to Eli'phaz the Te'manite: "My wrath is kindled against you and against your two friends; for you have not spoken of me what is right, as my servant Job has. ⁸Now therefore take seven bulls and seven rams, and go to my servant Job, and offer up for yourselves a burnt offering; and my servant Job shall pray for you, for I will accept his prayer not to deal with you according to your folly; for you have not spoken of me what is right, as my servant Job has." ⁹So Eli'phaz the Te'manite and Bildad the Shuhite and Zophar the Na'amathite went and did what the LORD had told them; and the LORD accepted Job's prayer.

10 And the LORD restored the fortunes of Job, when he had prayed for his friends; and the LORD gave Job twice as much as he had before. ¹¹Then came to him all his brothers and sisters and all who had known him before, and ate bread with him in his house; and they showed him sympathy and comforted him for all the evil that the LORD had brought upon him; and each of them gave him a piece of money and a ring of gold. ¹²And the LORD blessed the latter days of Job more than his beginning; and he had fourteen thousand sheep, six thousand camels, a thousand yoke of oxen, and a thousand she-asses. ¹³He had also seven sons and three daughters. ¹⁴And he called the name of the first Jemi'mah; and the name of the second Kezi'ah; and the name of the third Ker'enhap'puch. ¹⁵And in all the land there were no women so fair as Job's daughters; and their father gave them inheritance among their brothers. ¹⁶And after this Job lived a hundred and forty years, and saw his sons, and his sons' sons, four generations. ¹⁷And Job died, an old man, and full of days.

CHAPTER 15

JOAN OF ARC (FRENCH): HERO AS SAINT/HERO AS MARTYR/FEMALE HERO AS MALE

INTRODUCTION

Joan of Arc (c.1412–31) was born just after the Hundred Years' War between England and France (1337–1453) had resumed, with King Henry V of England taking advantage of the civil war in France to invade and to win the famous battle of Agincourt. In alliance with one of the French factions (the Burgundians), the English occupied most of northern France, and Henry VI was proclaimed King of both England and France. The leader of the other French faction, which was now the nationalist party, was the disinherited dauphin son of King Charles VI of France. At the age of thirteen, Joan began hearing voices from several saints instructing her to go to the aid of the dauphin. After the English lay siege to the key city of Orleans, she sought an audience with the dauphin and persuaded him to allow her to fulfill her mission to relieve the siege, to have him crowned at Reims, and to drive the English out of France. Under Joan, the French drove the English from Orleans, and she accompanied the dauphin to his coronation as King Charles VII at Reims. Joan then sought to capture Paris but failed. In a subsequent campaign she was captured by the French faction allied to the English and was turned over to the English, who then turned her over to the ecclesiastical court at Rouen, where French clerics allied to the English tried and convicted her of heresy. When she rescinded her recantation, which would have commuted her death sentence to life imprisonment, she was turned over to the

Original publication: Frances Gies, *Joan of Arc* (New York: Harper & Row, 1981), pp. 1–2, 23–4, 79–82.

secular court and burned at the stake as a relapsed heretic. The following selection describes Joan's voices and then jumps to her liberation of Orleans. Like Penthesilea, Joan assumes a consummately masculine role and is triumphant at it. The spectacular successes to which she leads the army mark the turning point in the Hundred Years' War. Yet she is also a martyr, dying for the sake of France. Like Christ, albeit on a national rather than cosmic scale, she is rejected by those she serves and even wonders whether her supernatural voices have deceived her. Among the thousands of books on Joan, see, for example, Edward Lucie-Smith, *Joan of Arc* (New York: Norton, 1977); and Marina Warner, *Joan of Arc* (London: Wiedenfeld & Nicolson, 1981).

JOAN OF ARC: THE LEGEND AND THE REALITY

Frances Gies

Joan of Arc was born in Domremy, in northeastern France, into a prosperous peasant family, probably in the year 1412, at the moment of the resumption of the devastating Hundred Years' War. Suspended by a truce in 1395, the fighting recommenced in 1411 in the form of a civil war between two factions, Burgundians and Orleanists (later called Armagnacs), rivals for control of the government of mentally ill King Charles VI.

English king Henry V took advantage of the civil strife to renew his dynasty's claim to the French throne, invading France in 1415 and winning the battle of Agincourt. In 1418 the Burgundians seized Paris, and in 1419 the assassination of the duke of Burgundy drove his son Philip the Good into alliance with the English. The following year Charles VI signed the treaty of Troyes disinheriting his son, the dauphin Charles, and making Henry V heir to the French throne. When both kings died in 1422, Henry's infant son Henry VI was proclaimed king of England and France, while the dauphin, assuming the title of Charles VII, became leader of the Armagnacs, now the national party. In the early 1420s Anglo-Burgundian forces conquered and occupied most of northern France.

In 1425, when she was thirteen, Joan began to hear voices, which she identified as those of Saints Michael, Margaret, and Catherine. They told

147

her about the "great misery in the kingdom of France" and that she must go to the aid of Charles VII. After the English began the siege of strategically crucial Orleans, on the Loire, in the fall of 1428, Joan went to the nearby royal stronghold of Vaucouleurs and persuaded Robert de Baudricourt, captain of the royal garrison, to give her an escort to the king. Arriving at the royal castle of Chinon at the end of February 1429, Joan revealed her mission: to relieve Orleans, have the king crowned at Reims, and drive the English out of France. She persuaded the king, his council, and a commission of prelates and theologians to give her a chance to fulfill it.

Led by Joan, French forces drove the English from Orleans and the Loire, won the battle of Patay, and triumphantly escorted the king to his coronation at Reims. After the coronation, the royal army liberated several more towns and assaulted but did not capture Paris, where Joan was wounded.

In April 1430 Joan undertook her last campaign and in May was captured by Burgundians in a sally from the besieged town of Compiègne. For seven months she was moved from prison to prison before finally being turned over to the English, who brought her to Rouen, in English-occupied Normandy. There she was tried as a heretic by a Church court on the grounds that her visions were diabolical and her deeds evil. The trial began February 21, 1431, and lasted three months. On May 24, taken to the cemetery of the abbey of St. Ouen, in Rouen, to be sentenced, Joan signed a last-minute abjuration, agreeing to submit to the judgment of the Church. Four days later she withdrew her abjuration and on May 30, 1431, was burned at the stake as a heretic. [...]

Voices

In 1425, the year that *routier* Henri d'Orly carried off the villagers' cattle and goods, Joan had her first vision. It was summer, "at about the hour of noon," and she was in her father's garden when she heard a voice, "on the right side, toward the church." With it was a light coming from the same direction as the voice. The first time she was "much afraid." But she knew at once that it was "a worthy voice...sent by God," and when she had heard it three times, she knew that it was "the voice of an angel." When the voice returned, it was almost always with an accompanying light, "usually a great light."

At first the voice simply advised her how to behave, and told her to be good and go to church. But later it began to tell her that she must "go to

France." Although Domremy was part of the kingdom of France, its geographic isolation was such that to Joan going to France meant going to the central part of the realm, where the king was.

Joan soon identified the voice as that of St. Michael; he spoke "the speech and language of angels." She saw him before her own eyes, "the eyes of my body," she emphasized. He was accompanied by other angels. He told her that St. Catherine and St. Margaret would come to her, and that she should follow their counsel, and he told her about the great misery *(grand pitié)* that was in the kingdom of France. After St. Michael and his accompanying angels had left, she "kissed the ground on which they had stood, doing them reverence."

As St. Michael had promised, St. Catherine and St. Margaret soon appeared. Their heads were "crowned with beautiful crowns, very rich and precious." At her trial Joan refused to describe the saints further, saying only that they spoke "most excellently and beautifully, and that she understood them perfectly."

The first time Joan heard the voice of St. Michael, she vowed her virginity "as long as it should be pleasing to God."

Few religious experiences have been subjected to as extensive examination and analysis as has the phenomenon of Joan's voices. At her trial at Rouen in 1431 the judges questioned her shrewdly about her mystical experiences, almost like modern psychologists diagnosing a crisis of adolescence. Was she fasting when she first heard the voices? No. Did she ever kiss or embrace St. Catherine or St. Margaret? Yes, she had embraced them both. What part did she embrace, the upper or lower? It was more fitting to embrace them below than above. Was St. Michael naked or was he clothed? – which provoked Joan's famous answer, "Do you think that our Lord has not wherewithal to clothe him?"

Yet Joan's judges made no serious attempt to prove that her voices and visions were hallucinations. They themselves believed in the possibility of supernatural revelation, as did most of Joan's contemporaries. The crucial question was not so much the genuineness of the experience as the origin of the revelations. People who communicated with the supernatural outside normal Church channels were necessarily suspect. Mystics were often critical of the Church, and almost every saint who was a mystic came at some time into conflict with Church authority. But the difficulty was not merely that mystics undermined authority. On the face of it, such irregular communications seemed far likelier to originate with demonic than with divine sources, which might reasonably be expected to transmit their messages through the Church rather than through eccentrics and neurotic women. [...]

149

Liberation of Orleans

Once more crossing the river and reaching the Augustins, Joan summoned "all the lords and captains," according to Jean d'Aulon, to plan the attack, first against the great outwork – palisade, moat, and earthworks – which the English had built to protect the drawbridge leading to the Tourelles. The French surrounded the rampart and assaulted it from three sides. The English above showered them with arrows, missiles, and cannonballs. As the French placed their scaling ladders, the defenders hurled the assailants down and battled them with axes, lances, maces, guisarmes, and even with their fists. Early in the fighting, Joan was wounded, as she had foretold, by an arrow that pierced her shoulder. She "was afraid, and wept, and was comforted," Pasquerel reported, as the wound was dressed with olive oil and lard. Some soldiers wanted to use a spell to heal the wound, but she refused, saying that it was a sin to use magical cures.

Dunois and the other captains advised suspending the assault until the next day. Joan would hear none of it. "In the name of God, you will soon enter the fortress, never doubt it, and the English will have no more strength against you. Rest for a while, eat and drink." They did as she bade; after which she told them, "Return to the assault, before God, for the English will have no more will to defend themselves, and their Tourelles and their ramparts will be taken."

The attack was renewed. The English fought, said the *Journal du Siège*, as if they believed they were immortal. At sunset the leaders of the army were once more ready to sound retreat. Exactly what followed is uncertain in detail but clear enough in its general sense. According to Dunois, Joan again asked him to wait. Mounting her horse, she withdrew into a nearby vineyard, where she prayed for eight minutes. Returning, she seized her standard and took up her position on the outer edge of the moat, declaring (as Louis de Coutes reported) that when the wind blew her standard toward the rampart, it would be theirs.

Jean d'Aulon gave a somewhat different and very circumstantial account: retreat had already been sounded and the army was withdrawing, when he saw Joan's standard-bearer, exhausted, hand her standard to a man known as the Basque. D'Aulon conceived the idea that if Joan's standard were carried forward, the French would rally behind it and might still succeed in taking the fortification that night. He asked the Basque if he would follow him if he ran toward the rampart, and the Basque promised to do so. Leaping into the moat, d'Aulon approached the farther bank, holding his shield to ward off the English missiles, and expecting the Basque to follow. But when Joan saw her standard in the Basque's hands, she seized the shaft, crying, "My standard! My standard!" and shook it so vigorously that d'Aulon believed the others must think she was signaling. He shouted, "Oh, Basque! Is this how you keep your promise?" Whereupon the Basque wrenched the standard from Joan's hands and brought it to d'Aulon, while Joan's company rallied again and stormed the rampart.

The *Journal du Siège* reported that Joan said to a knight who was standing nearby, "Watch for the moment when the tip of my standard touches the wall." When he cried, "Joan, the tip is touching!" she replied, "It's all yours, go in." And the troops burst into the rampart.

The English tried to retreat into the Tourelles, but the French attack now closed in on them from both directions. Some of the Orleans militia that had remained in the city had organized an assault from the northern bank. They moved onto the bridge, bringing ladders and pieces of troughs (perhaps from the eaves of houses) to rig a temporary span over the broken arches and threaten the Tourelles from this side. The troughs proved too short, but a carpenter fashioned a scaffold that reached the farther arch, and a knight of the order of Rhodes ventured out on it. His example was at once followed – "a greater miracle than any other performed by our Lord that day," the *Journal du Siège* thought, considering that the scaffold was "marvelously long and narrow, and high in the air, without any support."

Simultaneously, as the French poured into the outwork from the southern bank, the English tried to retreat across the drawbridge, but the French had set fire to a boat and floated it down the river. It came accurately to rest against the drawbridge, setting it ablaze. Many of the English (four or five hundred, said the *Journal du Siège*) fell into the river and were drowned, among them Sir William Glasdale, the commander of the Tourelles. The handful of remaining defenders were soon compelled to surrender.

Pasquerel, in an echo of his story about the soldier at Chinon who had insulted Joan and later drowned, reported with satisfaction that Joan had shouted to Glasdale, "Clasdas, Clasdas, yield to the King of Heaven! You have called me a whore, but I have great pity for your soul and the souls of your men." When Glasdale and his men drowned, Joan wept for their souls. The *Journal du Siège* expressed a more practical regret: all the enemy lords were killed, leaving only common soldiers to be taken prisoner, which was a great misfortune, since they brought no ransom.

The dramatic reversal of the war's fortune, swiftly reported in Paris, struck dismay to the hearts of the Anglo-Burgundians, and lent credence to the idea that Joan was a witch. "It was said that she told an English

151

captain to leave the siege with his company or evil would come to them all," recorded the *Journal d'un Bourgeois de Paris*. "He cursed her, calling her whore and tart; she told him that in spite of themselves they would all very soon depart, but that he would not see it, and that many of his men would be killed. And so it happened." The Bourgeois added funerary details: "Afterwards [Glasdale] was fished up, cut in quarters, and boiled, and embalmed"; the body spent a week in a chapel in Paris before it was shipped to England for burial.

In Orleans the bells rang, and clergy and people sang the "Te Deum Laudamus." The *Journal du Siège* reported that Joan remained with a part of the army that camped south of the river, but more probably, as Dunois says, she returned with him to Orleans by the bridge, as she had promised they would. They were received with "transports of joy and thanksgiving." Joan went to her lodging to have her wound dressed, and supped on bread dipped in wine mixed with water – the first meal she had eaten all day. [...]

Early on Sunday, May 8, the English in the western forts at last stirred. Abandoning their forts, they assembled in battle array in the open, as if to challenge the French. Joan donned a coat of mail – her wound prevented her from wearing her plate armor – and rode out of town with the other captains and knights, men-at-arms, and citizens of Orleans, ranging themselves in order of battle facing the enemy. The English, practicing their usual tactic of standing on the defensive, awaited attack, perhaps hoping to retrieve their defeat with an eleventh-hour Agincourt. But Joan (undoubtedly in agreement with Dunois, Gaucourt, and the others) forbade the French to charge, and for an hour the two forces faced each other without a blow being struck. The *Journal du Siège* attributed Joan's prudence to her reluctance to fight on the Sabbath, but on other occasions she did not scruple to fight on holy days.

The *Chronique de la Pucelle*, a compilation of other chronicles made some twenty years after the event, described Joan as sending for an altar and vestments and having two masses said for the French army. Then she asked whether the English were still facing them. "No, they are turned toward Meung." She is supposed to have replied, "Let them go – our Lord does not want us to fight them today; you will have them another time." Eyewitnesses, however, merely say that after an hour the English began to depart – Jean d'Aulon says "discomfited and in confusion," the *Journal du Siège*, more credibly, in good order, to take refuge in Meung and Beaugency, the two towns they held on the river west of Orleans. The French harried their rear guard and captured bombards, cannons, bows, and crossbows. The *Journal du Siège* added a symbolic incident: among the retreating English was an Augustinian monk, Talbot's confessor, who dragged a French prisoner in fetters. The Frenchman overpowered the monk and forced him to carry him on his shoulders back to Orleans "and thus escaped his ransom."

Miraculously, as it seemed, the siege of Orleans was raised. Joan, the captains, and the soldiers returned triumphantly to the city, where the day was celebrated with "a solemn procession and a sermon." The joy and the solemnity were justified. The turning point in the Hundred Years' War had at last arrived.

CHAPTER 16

GALILEO (ITALIAN): INTELLECTUAL HERO

INTRODUCTION

The persecution of intellectual heroes goes all the way back to Socrates, who was charged with corrupting the youth of Athens because of his questioning of conventional morality. The astronomer Galileo Galilei (1564–1642) was tried by the Inquisition for advocating the Copernican view that the earth revolves around the sun rather than the biblical view that the sun and the rest of the cosmos revolve around a stationary earth. Galileo based his views on the discoveries he had made with his telescope, especially the discovery that the planet Jupiter has stars revolving around it. To be sure, he did not go so far as to pit science against the Bible. On the contrary, he maintained that the Bible does not primarily teach cosmogony and that it accords with science whenever it does. The view that Galileo, in the name of truth, was willing to confront the authority of the Bible, the Church, and reigning Aristotelian philosophy is popularized in the play *Galileo* by Bertolt Brecht, from which the following selection is taken. Yet Brecht's hero is no saint. He loves food and drink as much as science. At his trial, he recants when shown the instruments of torture he will face if he does not. Still, he heroically manages to finish in secret his greatest work, *The Discorsi*, and to get it smuggled abroad. For Brecht, Galileo is an inspiration for defenders of truth against totalitarian systems anywhere, not least Nazi Germany and Stalinist Russia. For less one-sided views of Galileo, see Giorgio de Santillana, *The Crime of Galileo* (Alexandria, VA: Time-Life Books, 1962 [1955]); Stillman Drake, *Galileo at Work* (Chicago: University of Chicago Press, 1978); and *The Cambridge Companion to Galileo*, ed. Peter Machamer (Cambridge:

Original publication: Bertolt Brecht, *The Life of Galileo* (originally published in German in 1955), tr. Desmond I. Vesey, in *Bertolt Brecht: Plays* (London: Methuen, 1961 [1960]), vol. I, pp. 265–7, 276–7, 282–4, 316–19, 326–31.

Cambridge University Press, 1998). For a selection of Galileo's own writings, see *Discoveries and Opinions of Galileo* ed. Stillman Drake (Garden City, NY: Doubleday Anchor Books, 1957). On Brecht, see Martin Esslin, *Brecht* (Garden City, NY: Doubleday, 1960).

BERTOLT BRECHT, PLAYS, VOLUME I: THE LIFE OF GALILEO

Translated by Desmond I. Vesey

CHARACTERS

Galileo Galilei: Andrea Sarti: Signora Sarti, Galileo's housekeeper and Andrea's mother: Ludovico Marsili, a rich young man: the Curator of the University of Padua, Signor Priuli: Sagredo, Galileo's friend: Virginia, Galileo's daughter: Federzoni, a lens-grinder, Galileo's collaborator: the Doge: senators: Cosimo dé Medici, Grand Duke of Florence: the Court Chamberlain: the theologian: the philosopher: the mathematician: the older court lady: the younger court lady: the Grand Duke's lackey: two nuns: two soldiers: the old lady: a fat prelate: two scholars: two monks: two astronomers: a very thin monk: the very old cardinal: Father Christopher Clavius, astronomer: the little monk: the Cardinal Inquisitor: Cardinal Barberini, later Pope Urban VIII: Cardinal Bellarmin: two ecclesiastical secretaries: two young ladies: Filippo Mucius, a scholar: Signor Gaffone, Rector of the University of Pisa: the ballad-singer: his wife: Vanni, an iron-founder: an official: a high official: an individual: a monk: a peasant: a frontier guard: a scribe: men, women, children.

THE MATHEMATICIAN: Why mince matters? Sooner or later Signor Galilei will have to reconcile himself with the facts. His planets of Jupiter would break through the crystal spheres. It is quite simple.

FEDERZONI: You'll be astonished! There are no crystal spheres.

THE PHILOSOPHER: Every school-book will tell you they exist, my good man.

FEDERZONI: Then hurrah for new school-books.

THE PHILOSOPHER: Your Highness, my worthy colleague and I rely on the authority of none less than the divine Aristotle himself.

GALILEO *almost obsequiously*: Gentlemen, belief in the authority of Aristotle is one thing; facts, tangible facts, are another. You say that according to Aristotle there are crystal spheres up there and therefore certain movements cannot take place because the stars would have to break through those spheres. But what if you can confirm those movements? Perhaps that will persuade you that those crystal spheres simply don't exist. Gentlemen, I beseech you in all humility to trust your eyes.

THE MATHEMATICIAN: My dear Galileo, old-fashioned though it may sound to you, I am accustomed among other things to read Aristotle, and I can assure you that there I do trust my eyes.

GALILEO: I am used to seeing members of all faculties shutting their eyes against every fact and behaving as though nothing has happened. I offer my observations, and they smile. I place my telescope at their disposal so that they can convince themselves, and they quote Aristotle. But the man had no telescope!

THE MATHEMATICIAN: Certainly not. Certainly not.

THE PHILOSOPHER *sweepingly*: If Aristotle – an authority recognised not only by the entire learning of antiquity but also by the Holy Fathers of the Church – if Aristotle is to be dragged through the mud, then it seems, to me at least, that a continuation of this discussion is superfluous. I avoid pointless discussion. Enough!

GALILEO: Truth is the child of time, not of authority. Our ignorance is infinite, so let us diminish it by a fraction. Why try to be so clever now, when at last we can become a little less stupid? I have had the unbelievable good fortune to lay my hands on a new instrument by means of which one can see one tiny corner of the universe a little clearer. Not much – but a little. Make use of it!

THE PHILOSOPHER: Your Highness, ladies and gentlemen, I am just asking myself where all this may lead.

GALILEO: I would suggest that as scientists it is not for us to ask where the truth may lead us.

THE PHILOSOPHER *furiously*: Signor Galilei, the truth may lead us to absolutely anything.

GALILEO: Your Highness. On nights such as these, all over Italy telescopes are being turned towards the Heavens. Jupiter's moons will not make milk any cheaper. But they have never been seen before, and they are there. From that the man in the street draws the conclusion that there may be many more things to see if only he opens his eyes. You owe him that confirmation. It is not the movements of a few distant stars that make all Italy prick up its ears, but the news that opinions hitherto held inviolable have now begun to totter – and everyone knows there are too many of those. Gentlemen, let us not defend dying teachings.

FEDERZONI: You, as teachers, should hasten their end.

THE PHILOSOPHER: I should prefer your man not to proffer advice in a scientific disputation.

GALILEO: Your Highness. My work in the Great Arsenal of Venice brought me into daily contact with draughtsmen, builders and instrument-makers. These people taught me many a new way of doing things. Illiterate, they relied on the evidence of their five senses, in most cases regardless of where such evidence might lead them...

THE PHILOSOPHER: Oho!

GALILEO: Very like our mariners, who a hundred years ago left our shores without knowing what sort of other shores they might reach, if any at all. It seems that today, in order to find that high curiosity which made the true greatness of ancient Greece, one has to resort to the shipyards.

THE PHILOSOPHER: After all that we have heard here, I have no longer any doubt that Signor Galilei will find admirers in the shipyards. [...]

Enter a very old cardinal supported by a monk. Everyone respectfully makes way for him.

THE VERY OLD CARDINAL: Are they still in there? Can they really not dispose of this triviality more quickly? Clavius ought to understand his own astronomy. I hear that this Signor Galilei banishes mankind from the centre of the universe to somewhere at the edge. He is, therefore, plainly an enemy of the human race. And he should be treated as such. Man is the crown of creation, every child knows that, God's highest and most beloved creature. How could He place such a miracle, such a masterpiece, on a little remote and forever wandering star? Would He have sent His Son to such a place? How can there be people so perverse as to believe in these slaves of their own mathematical tables? Which of God's creatures would submit to such a thing?

THE FAT PRELATE *sotto voce*:   The gentleman is present.

THE VERY OLD CARDINAL *to Galileo*:   So you are the person? I no longer see very well, but what I can see is enough to show me that you are remarkably like that man we burnt here in his time. What was his name?

THE MONK: Your Eminence should not excite himself. The doctor...

THE VERY OLD CARDINAL *shaking him off, to Galileo*:   You wish to degrade the earth, although you live on it and receive everything from it. You would foul your own nest! But I at least will have none of it! *He pushes the monk away and begins proudly pacing up and*

157

down. I am not just any being on just any little star circling round somewhere for a short time. I tread the firm earth, with a sure step; it is at rest; it is the centre of the universe; I am at the centre, and the eye of the Creator rests on me and on me alone. Around me revolve, attached to eight crystalline spheres, the fixed stars and the mighty sun which was created to shed light upon my surroundings. And upon me too, in order that God may see me. And so, visibly and irrefutably, everything depends on me, on Man, the masterpiece of God, the centre of Creation, the very image of God, immortal and...*He collapses.* [...]

BARBERINI: No? He insists on a serious conversation. All right. Are you sure, friend Galileo, that you astronomers are not simply concerned with making your astronomy more manageable? *He leads him to the front again.* You think in terms of circles and ellipses and equal velocities, simple movements that your mind can grasp. But what if it had pleased God to make his stars move like this? *With his finger moving at varying speeds he describes in the air an extremely complicated track.*

GALILEO: Your Eminence, if God had constructed the universe like that – *he repeats Barberini's track* – then he would also have constructed our brains like that – *he repeats the same track* – so that they would recognise these very tracks as the simplest possible. I believe in reason.

BARBERINI: I hold reason to be inadequate. – He is silent. He is too polite to say now that he holds me to be inadequate. *He laughs and returns to the balustrade at the back.*

BELLARMIN: Reason, my friend, does not reach very far. All around we see nothing but crookedness, crime and weakness. Where is truth?

GALILEO *angrily*: I believe in reason.

BARBERINI *to the clerks*: There is no need to take this down. This is a scientific conversation between friends.

BELLARMIN: Consider for a moment all the trouble and thought it cost the Fathers of the Church, and so many after them, to bring a little sense into this world (is it not a little repellent?). Consider the brutality of the landlords in the Campagna who have their peasants whipped half-naked over their estates, and the stupidity of those poor people who kiss their feet in return.

GALILEO: Horrible! On my journey here I saw...

BELLARMIN: We have placed the responsibility for the meaning of such happenings as we cannot comprehend – life consists of them – on a higher Being, and we have explained that such things are the result of certain intentions, that all this happens according to one great plan. Not that this has brought about complete reassurance; but now you have to accuse this supreme Being of not knowing for certain how the stars move, a matter on which *you* are perfectly clear. Is that wise?

GALILEO *preparing to explain*: I am a true son of the Church...

BARBERINI: He is incorrigible. In all innocence he tries to prove God a complete fool on the subject of astronomy! Do you mean that God did not study astronomy sufficiently before he indited the Holy Scriptures? My dear friend!

BELLARMIN: Does it not appear probable to you that the Creator knows more about His own handiwork than does the handiwork itself?

GALILEO: But, gentlemen, man can misinterpret not only the movements of the stars, but the Bible too.

BELLARMIN: But the interpretation of the Bible is, after all, the business of the theologians of the Holy Church, eh?

Galileo is silent.

BELLARMIN: You see. You are silent now. *He makes a sign to the clerks.* Signor Galilei, tonight the Holy Office has decided that the teachings of Copernicus, according to which the sun is the centre of the universe and motionless, while the earth is not the centre of the universe and is moving, are futile, foolish and heretical. I have been entrusted with the duty of informing you of this decision. *To the first clerk*: Repeat that.

FIRST CLERK: His Eminence Cardinal Bellarmin to the aforementioned Galileo Galilei: The Holy Office has decided that the teachings of Copernicus, according to which the sun is the centre of the universe and motionless, while the earth is not the centre of the universe and is moving, are futile, foolish and heretical. I have been entrusted with the duty of informing you of this decision.

GALILEO: What does that mean?

From the ballroom can be heard boys' voices singing another verse of the poem:

> 'I said: the lovely season flieth fast;
> So pluck the rose – it still is May.'

Barberini gestures Galileo to be silent while the song lasts. They listen.

GALILEO: But the facts? I understood that the astronomers of the Collegium Romanum had accepted my observations.

BELLARMIN: With the expression of the deepest satisfaction, which does you the greatest honour.

GALILEO: But the satellites of Jupiter, the phases of Venus...

BELLARMIN: The Holy Congregation has made its decision without considering these details.

GALILEO: That means that all further scientific research...

BELLARMIN: Is well assured, Signor Galilei. And that, in conformity with the Church's view that we cannot know, but we may research. *He again greets a guest in the ballroom.* You are at liberty to expound even this teaching through mathematical hypotheses. Science is the legitimate and dearly beloved daughter of the Church, Signor Galilei. Not one of us seriously believes that you desire to undermine the authority of the Church.

GALILEO *angrily*:   Authority grows feeble from being abused.

BARBERINI: Does it? *He claps him on the shoulder, laughing loudly. Then he looks sharply at him and says, not unkindly*:   Don't throw out the baby with the bath-water, friend Galileo. We don't do that either. We need you, more than you need us.

BELLARMIN: I am burning to present the greatest mathematician in Italy to the President of the Holy Office, who regards you with the utmost admiration. [...]

In the Palace of the Florentine Ambassador in Rome

Galileo's pupils are waiting for news. The little monk and Federzoni are playing the new form of chess with its extended moves. In a corner Virginia is kneeling and praying.

THE LITTLE MONK: The Pope has not received him. No more scientific discussions.

FEDERZONI: He was his last hope. It was true what he said years ago in Rome, when he was still Cardinal Barberini: 'We need you'. Now they have him.

ANDREA: They will destroy him. The Discorsi will never be finished.

FEDERZONI *looks at him furtively*:   Do you think so?

ANDREA: Because he will never recant.

Pause.

THE LITTLE MONK: You always get distracted with trivial thoughts when you lie awake at nights. Last night, for example, I kept thinking: he should never have left the Republic.

ANDREA: He could not write his book there.

FEDERZONI: And in Florence he could not publish it.

Pause.

THE LITTLE MONK: I also wondered whether they would leave him his little stone which he always carries round with him in his pocket. His touch-stone.

FEDERZONI: To that place where they are taking him, one goes without pockets.

ANDREA *shouting*: They won't dare! And even if they do it to him, he would never recant. 'He who does not know the truth is merely an idiot, but he who knows it and calls it a lie, is a criminal.'

FEDERZONI: I do not think he will, either; and I would rather not live if he did; but they have force on their side.

ANDREA: Not everything can be accomplished by force.

FEDERZONI: Perhaps not.

THE LITTLE MONK *softly*: He has been in prison for twenty-three days. Yesterday was the great cross-examination. And today is the sitting. *Loudly, since Andrea is listening.* The time when I visited him here two days after the decree, we sat over there, and he pointed out to me the little figure of Priapus by the sundial in the garden – you can see it from here – and he compared his work to a poem by Horace in which nothing can be changed either. He spoke of his feeling for beauty which made him search for the truth. And he quoted a motto: hieme et aestate, et prope et procul, usque dum vivam et ultra. And he meant the truth.

ANDREA *to the little monk*: Have you told him how he stood in the Collegium Romanum when they were testing his telescope? Tell him. *The little monk shakes his head.* He behaved just as usual. He stood with his hands on his buttocks, stuck out his stomach and said: 'I ask only for commonsense, gentlemen!' *Laughing, he imitates Galileo.*

Pause.

ANDREA *speaking of Virginia*: She is praying that he will recant.

FEDERZONI: Leave her. She is almost out of her mind since they spoke to her. They have summoned her Father Confessor from Florence.

Enter the individual from the Grand Duke's Palace in Florence.

THE INDIVIDUAL: Signor Galilei will soon be here. He may require a bed.

FEDERZONI: Has he been released?

THE INDIVIDUAL: It is expected that, at five o'clock at a session of the Inquisition, Signor Galilei will recant. The great bell of St. Mark's will be rung and the wording of the recantation will be publicly proclaimed.

ANDREA: I don't believe it.

THE INDIVIDUAL: Because of the crowds collecting in the streets, Signor Galilei will be brought here through the garden door at the back of the palace.

Exit.

ANDREA *suddenly shouting*:   The moon is an earth and has no light of its own. Neither has Venus its own light and like the earth it revolves round the sun. And four moons revolve round the planet Jupiter, which is in the region of the fixed stars and is not attached to any crystal sphere. And the sun is the centre of the universe and motionless in its place, and the earth is *not* the centre and is *not* motionless. And he is the one who showed it to us.

THE LITTLE MONK: And force cannot make unseen what has already been seen.

Silence.

FEDERZONI *looks at the sundial in the garden*:   Five o'clock.

Virginia prays louder.

ANDREA: I cannot wait any longer. They are killing the truth.

He stops up his ears, as does the little monk. But the bell does not toll. After a pause, filled by Virginia's murmured prayers, Federzoni shakes his head in negation. The others let their hands drop.

FEDERZONI *hoarsely*:   Nothing. It is three minutes past five.

ANDREA: He resists.

THE LITTLE MONK: He does not recant.

FEDERZONI: No! Oh, we blessed ones!

They embrace. They are overjoyed.

ANDREA: Well! Force has not prevailed! It cannot do everything! Therefore, stupidity is conquered; it is not invulnerable! Therefore, man is not afraid of death!

FEDERZONI: Now the age of science has really begun. This is the hour of its birth. And think, if he had recanted!

THE LITTLE MONK: I did not say it, but I was filled with fear. I, of so little faith!

ANDREA: But I knew it.

FEDERZONI: It would have been as if night had fallen again just after the sun rose.

ANDREA: As if the mountain had said: I am a sea.

THE LITTLE MONK *kneels down, crying*:   Lord, I thank Thee!

ANDREA: But everything has been changed today! Man, tortured man, lifts up his head and says: I can live. So much is gained when only one man stands up and says 'No'.

At this moment the bell of St. Mark's begins to toll. All stand rigid.

VIRGINIA *stands up*:   The bell of Saint Mark's. He is not damned!

From the street outside can be heard the voice of the crier reading Galileo's recantation.

VOICE OF THE CRIER: 'I, Galileo Galilei, teacher of mathematics and physics at the University of Florence, renounce what I have taught, that the sun is the centre of the universe and motionless in its place, and that the earth is not the centre and not motionless. I renounce, abhor and curse, with all my heart and with sincere faith, all these falsehoods and heresies, as well as every other falsehood and every other opinion which is contrary to the teachings of the Holy Church.'

The stage grows dark.
When it grows light again the bell is still tolling, and then stops. Virginia has gone. Galileo's pupils are still there.

FEDERZONI: He never paid you properly for your work. You could neither buy hose nor publish your own work. You suffered because it was 'working for science'.

ANDREA *loudly*:   Unhappy the land that has no heroes! [...]

GALILEO: I have finished writing the 'Discorsi'.

ANDREA: What? 'The Conversations between two Branches of Science: Mechanics and the Laws of Falling Bodies'? Here?

GALILEO: Oh, they give me paper and quills. My superiors are no fools. They know that ingrained vices cannot be cured overnight. They protect me from unfortunate results by locking it away page by page.

ANDREA: Oh God!

GALILEO: Did you say anything?

ANDREA: They're making you plough water! They give you paper and quills just to soothe you! How could you ever write anything with that prospect before your eyes?

GALILEO: Oh, I am the slave of my habits.

ANDREA: The 'Discorsi' in the hands of the monks! And Amsterdam and London and Prague hungry for them!

GALILEO: I can hear Fabricius wailing, insisting on his pound of flesh, while he sits safely in Amsterdam.

ANDREA: Two new branches of science as good as lost!

GALILEO: It will doubtless cheer him and some others to hear that I risked the last miserable remains of my peace of mind by making a copy, behind my own back so to speak, using up the last ounce of light of the bright nights for the last six months.

ANDREA: You have a copy?

GALILEO: My vanity has hitherto restrained me from destroying it.

ANDREA: Where is it?

GALILEO: 'If thine eye offend thee, pluck it out.' Whoever wrote that knew more about comfort than I. I call it the height of stupidity to hand it over. But since I have never managed to keep myself away from scientific work you might as well have it. The copy is in the globe. If you were to risk taking it to Holland, you would of course have to shoulder full responsibility. In that case you would have bought it from someone who had access to the original in the Holy Office.

Andrea walks across to the globe and takes out the manuscript.

ANDREA: The 'Discorsi'!

He thumbs through the pages.

ANDREA *reads*: 'My project is to establish an entirely new science dealing with a very old subject – Motion. Through experiments I have discovered some of its properties which are worth knowing.'

GALILEO: I had to do something with my time.

ANDREA: This will found a new science of physics.

GALILEO: Stuff it under your coat.

ANDREA: And we thought you had become a renegade! My voice was raised loudest against you!

GALILEO: And quite right, too. I taught you science and I denied the truth.

ANDREA: This changes everything, everything.

GALILEO: Yes?

ANDREA: You concealed the truth. From the enemy. Even in the field of ethics you were a thousand years ahead of us.

GALILEO: Explain that, Andrea.

ANDREA: In common with the man in the street, we said: he will die, but he will never recant. – You came back: I have recanted, but I shall live. – Your hands are tainted, we said. – You say: better tainted than empty.

GALILEO: Better tainted than empty. Sounds realistic. Sounds like me. New science, new ethics.

ANDREA: I of all people ought to have known. I was eleven years old when you sold another man's telescope to the Venetian Senate. And I saw you make immortal use of that instrument. Your friends shook their heads when you bowed before a child in Florence, but science caught the public fancy. You always laughed at our heroes. 'People that suffer bore me', you said. 'Misfortune comes from insufficient foresight.' And: 'Taking obstacles into account, the shortest line between two points may be a crooked one.'

GALILEO: I recollect.

ANDREA: Then, in 1633, when it suited you to retract a popular point in your teachings, I should have known that you were only withdrawing from a hopeless political squabble in order to be able to carry on with your real business of science.

GALILEO: Which consists in...

ANDREA: ...The study of the properties of motion, mother of machines, which will make the earth so inhabitable that heaven can be demolished.

GALILEO: Aha.

ANDREA: You thereby gained the leisure to write a scientific work which only you could write. Had you ended in a halo of flames at the stake, the others would have been the victors.

GALILEO: They are the victors. And there is no scientific work which only one man can write.

ANDREA: Then why did you recant?

GALILEO: I recanted because I was afraid of physical pain.

ANDREA: 'No!'

GALILEO: I was shown the instruments.

ANDREA: So there was no plan?

GALILEO: There was none.

Pause.

ANDREA *loudly*:   Science knows only one commandment: contribute to science.

GALILEO: And that I have done. Welcome to the gutter, brother in science and cousin in treachery! Do you eat fish? I've got fish. What stinks is not fish but me. I sell cheap; you are a buyer. Oh irresistible sight of a book, the sacred goods! Mouths water, and curses drown. The Great Babylonian, the murderous cow, the scarlet woman, opens her thighs and everything is different! Hallowed be our haggling, whitewashing, death-fearing society!

ANDREA: Fear of death is human! Human weaknesses are no concern of science.

GALILEO: No! My dear Sarti, even in my present situation I still feel capable of giving you a few tips about science in general, in which you have involved yourself.

A short pause.

GALILEO: *academically, his hands folded over his stomach*:   During my free hours, of which I have many, I have gone over my case and have considered how the world of science, in which I no longer count myself, will judge it. Even a wool-merchant, apart from buying cheaply and selling dear, must also be concerned that trade in wool can be carried on unhindered. In this respect the pursuit of science seems to me to require particular courage. It is concerned with knowledge, achieved through doubt. Making knowledge about everything available for everybody, science strives to make sceptics of them all. Now the greater part of the population is kept permanently by their princes, landlords and priests in a nacreous haze of superstition and outmoded words which obscure the machinations of these characters. The misery of the multitude is as old as the hills, and from pulpit and desk is proclaimed as immutable as the hills. Our new device of doubt delighted the great public, which snatched the telescope from our hands and turned it on its tormentors. These selfish and violent men, who greedily exploited the fruits of science to their own use, simultaneously felt the cold eye of science turned on a thousand-year-old, but artificial misery which clearly could be eliminated by eliminating them. They drenched us with their threats and bribes, irresistible to weak souls. But could we deny ourselves to the crowd and still remain scientists? The movements of the stars have become clearer; but to the mass of the people the movements of their masters are still incalculable. The fight over the measurability of the heavens has been won through doubt; but the fight of the Roman housewife for milk is ever and again lost through faith. Science, Sarti, is concerned with both battle-fronts. A humanity which stumbles in this age-old milky mist of superstition and outmoded words, too ignorant to develop fully its own powers, will not be capable of developing the powers of nature which you reveal. What are you working for? I maintain that the only purpose of science is to ease the hardship of human existence. If scientists, intimidated by self-seeking people in power, are content to amass knowledge for the sake of knowledge, then science can become crippled, and your new machines will represent nothing but new means of oppression. With time you may discover all that is to be discovered, and your progress will only be a progression away from mankind. The gulf between you and them can one day become so great that your cry of jubilation over some new achievement may be answered by a universal cry of horror. – I, as a scientist, had a unique opportunity. In my days astronomy reached the market-places. In these quite exceptional circumstances, the steadfastness of one man could have shaken the world. If only I had resisted, if only the natural scientists had been able to evolve something like the Hippocratic oath of the doctors, the vow to devote their knowledge wholly to the benefit of mankind! As things now stand, the best one can hope for is for a race of inventive dwarfs who can be hired for anything. Moreover, I am now convinced, Sarti, that I never was in real danger. For a few years I was as strong as the authorities. And I surrendered my knowledge to those in power, to use, or not to use, or to misuse, just as suited their purposes. *Virginia has entered with a dish and stops still.* I have betrayed my profession. A man who does what I have done cannot be tolerated in the ranks of science.

VIRGINIA: You have been received into the ranks of the faithful.

She walks forward and places the dish upon the table.

GALILEO: Right. – I must eat now.

Andrea holds out his hand. Galileo looks at his hand without taking it.

GALILEO: You yourself are a teacher, now. Can you bring yourself to take a hand such as mine? *He walks over to the table.* Someone passing through sent me geese. I still enjoy my food.

ANDREA: So you are no longer of the opinion that a new age has dawned?

GALILEO: I am. Take care when you go through Germany. – Hide the truth under your coat.

CHAPTER 17

ARJUNA (INDIAN): RELUCTANT HERO

INTRODUCTION

The vast Hindu epic *The Mahabharata* (completed about 400 AD) centers on the civil war in Hastinapura, northern India, between branches of the royal family, the Kauravas and the Pandavas. The Kauravas are led by Duryodhana, the eldest of a hundred brothers. Their cousins, the Pandavas, are led by Yudhistira, the eldest of five brothers. As the first battle is about to begin, Arjuna, one of Yudhistira's brothers, throws down his arms in despair at the prospect of killing the kinsmen arrayed against him. Krishna, an incarnation of the god Vishnu, appears to Arjuna and delivers a philosophical discourse to persuade him to fight. That discourse, summarized in the following selection, is known as the *Bhagavadgita*, one of the most popular and best loved of Indian sacred scriptures. Krishna, who serves as charioteer to Arjuna, offers him many reasons to fight: that Arjuna will be seen as a coward if he does not; that Arjuna, as a member of the warrior class, has a duty to fight; that Arjuna's failure to do his duty will encourage others to fail to do theirs; that duty (*dharma*) should be undertaken with detachment rather than with desire; and above all that in reality no one kills or is killed, for at death the soul (*Atman*) is simply incarnated in another body. Krishna's preaching is directed to all, not merely to Arjuna, who heeds it and proceeds to lead his army to victory in an eighteen-day battle. Joseph Campbell discusses the case of Arjuna. On the *Bhagavadgita*, see Eliot Deutsch and Lee Siegel, "Bhagavadgita," *Encyclopedia of Religion*, ed. Mircea Eliade (New York: Macmillan; London: Collier Macmillan, 1987), vol. II, 124–8.

Original publication: *The Mahabharata*, tr. R. K. Narayan (London: Heinemann, 1978), pp. 145–9.

The Mahabharata: A Shortened Modern Prose Version of the Indian Epic

R. K. Narayan

When Krishna came back and reported the results of his mission, Yudhistira turned to his brothers and said, "You have heard the final word from the other side. We have assembled seven akshaunis of troops. We have seven distinguished warriors who could each lead a division: Drupada, Virata, Dhrishtadyumna, Sikandi, Satyaki, Chekithana, and Bhima; all of them conversant with the Vedas, brave, and accomplished in the science of warfare; all of them familiar with the use of every kind of weapon. Now I want your advice as to who should be the Commander-in-Chief. On the other side, Bhishma is certain to be the Generalissimo." Many names were suggested, but finally, on Krishna's advice, Draupadi's brother, Dhrishtadyumna, was made the Supreme Commander.

As the time for battle approached, troop movements began, creating a tremendous din – horses neighing, elephants trumpeting, their riders shouting and urging them on over the noise of drums, conchs, and rolling chariot wheels. Yudhistira personally supervised the transportation of food supplies and fodder. He gathered a stock of tents, cash chests, war machines, weapons, and medicines, and made arrangements for surgeons and physicians to follow the army. He left Draupadi behind at Upaplavya, with a strong contingent to guard her.

Yudhistira marched at the head of the advancing troops. In the rear were Virata, Dhrishtadyumna, Virata's sons, forty thousand chariots, cavalry and infantry. Yudhistira encamped on the levelled part of a field called Kurukshetra, which was at a fair distance from cemeteries, temples, and other consecrated ground. Krishna dammed a little river nearby for water storage, and stationed a strong body of troops to protect it. Thousands of tents were pitched all around, stocked with plenty of food and drink. Huge quantities of weapons and coats of mail were heaped in mounds.

At Hastinapura, the troops were mustered in millions and moved to the front. Duryodhana arranged his eleven akshaunis of troops – men, elephants, chariots, and horses – into three classes – superior, middling, and inferior. In addition to normal weapons, his military store consisted of earthen pots filled with poisonous snakes or inflammable material, strange devices for throwing hot treacle, poison darts, and huge syringes for shooting boiling oil. He placed akshaunis of troops under Kripa, Drona, Salya, Dussasana, and others. His Supreme Commander, as expected, was Bhishma. Karna reminded everyone of his vow not to fight until Bhishma should be slain in battle.

Duryodhana ordered musicians to play their instruments, sound the drums, and blow conchs. Suddenly, amid these celebrations, there were bad omens. The sky was cloudless, but blood-coloured showers fell and made the ground slushy. Whirlwinds and earthquakes occurred. Meteors fell. Jackals howled.

Dhritarashtra received a description of the armies through Sanjaya, who had been granted an extraordinary vision by which he could watch the progress of the battle from his seat in the palace hall. Sanjaya reported on the formations of troops facing each other on the east and west of Kurukshetra Field. At dawn all the arrangements were complete and both sides were ready to fight.

Piloted by Krishna, Arjuna's chariot was stationed at a strategic point in the front line from which he could survey fully the personalities opposite. He recognized each one, and suddenly lost heart. All his kins-men, his guru, his uncle, grandfather, and cousins were there waiting to be hurt and killed. He suddenly felt weak and irresolute. He confessed to Krishna, "I cannot go on with this war. My grasp on Gandiva slips, my mind wanders; how can I slaughter my kith and kin? I do not want the kingdom; I do not want anything. Leave me alone. Let me go away." The Gandiva slipped from his hand, and he sat down on the floor of his chariot and began to sob. "How can I direct my arrow at Bhishma or Drona, whom I ought to worship? I do not know if any kingdom is worth winning after so much bloodshed. What is that gain worth?" Thus he lamented.

When Arjuna fell into a silence after exhausting his feelings, Krishna quietly said, "You are stricken with grief at the thought of those who deserve no consideration."

Krishna then began to preach in gentle tones, a profound philosophy of detached conduct. He analysed the categories and subtle qualities of the mind that give rise to different kinds of action and responses. He defined the true nature of personality, its scope and stature in relation to society, the world, and God, and of existence and death. He expounded yoga of different types, and how one should realize the deathlessness of the soul encased in the perishable physical body. Again and again Krishna emphas-ized the importance of performing one's duty with detachment in a spirit of dedication. Arjuna listened reverently, now and then interrupting to clear a doubt or to seek an elucidation. Krishna answered all his questions with the utmost grace, and finally granted him a grand vision of his real stature. Krishna, whom he had taken to be his companion, suddenly stood transformed – he was God himself, multidimensional and all-pervading.

Time, creatures, friends and foes alike were absorbed in the great being whose stature spanned the space between sky and earth, and extended from horizon to horizon. Birth, death, slaughter, protection, and every activity seemed to be a part of this being, nothing existed beyond it. Creation, destruction, activity and inactivity all formed a part and parcel of this grand being, whose vision filled Arjuna with terror and ecstasy. He cried out, "Now I understand!"

The God declared, "I am death, I am destruction. These men who stand before you are already slain through their own karma, you will be only an instrument of their destruction."

"O Great God," said Arjuna, "my weakness has passed. I have no more doubts in my mind." And he lifted his bow, ready to face the battle. Krishna then resumed his mortal appearance.

When Arjuna was seen to take up his bow again, great relief swept through the ranks of the Pandavas. Just when this happened and the battle was about to begin, much to everyone's surprise, Yudhistira was seen crossing over to the other side, after taking off his armor and mail coat. The Kauravas thought at first that he was approaching to sue for peace, having become nervous at the last moment. But Yudhistira went directly to his master, Drona, and bowed to him, touched the feet of his grand-uncle, Bhishma, and the other elders, and returned to his post. Wearing again his coat of mail and armour, he gave the signal for attack.

The battle was to rage for eighteen days on the field of Kurukshetra, sometimes in favour of one side and sometimes in favour of the other. It was strictly understood that action should begin at sunrise and end with the setting sun, but as the days passed this restriction was not always observed. Sometimes battle was prolonged into the night when the armies fought with the help of flares and torches. Normally they ceased to fight at sunset, and retreated to their respective tents to assess the day's action and plan the following day's strategy. The soldiers relaxed at night with song and dance.

Each day the troop formations were altered. Both sides tried to obtain information as to the intentions of the other and plan a counter-move. Several types of troop formations were ordered by the generals according to the need of the hour. If the troops on one side were formed in makara, the fish, the other adopted the form of krauncha, the heron, so that the formation and the attack thereon might follow a logistical law. The commanders chose how the troops should be placed, deployed, or formed. Each unit commander had to decide for himself how best to act under a given circumstance. On the third day, Bhishma had the Kaurava army in the eagle formation. For this the antidote was the crescent formation, with Bhima and Arjuna at each tip of the crescent, which could close from both sides in a pincer movement.

Each day there was exultation on one side and despair on the other – a see-saw of hope and despair. Counting their losses, the Pandavas sometimes felt hopeless, but Krishna, always beside Arjuna, kept up their spirits with his encouraging words. Every day on both sides there were disheartening losses of men, horses, and leaders, and the ground became soaked with blood.

CHAPTER 18

GILGAMESH (SUMERIAN): FAILED HERO

INTRODUCTION

The Sumerian hero Gilgamesh, reigning supreme as King of Uruk, never confronts his own mortality until the wasting away of his equal in strength, Enkidu. In desperation, Gilgamesh treks to the end of the earth in search of the fabled Utnapishtim, who has somehow achieved immortality. When Gilgamesh, after much travail, finally reaches Utnaphistim, he learns that Utnapishtim and his wife have discovered no secret of immortality but have alone been granted immortality by the god Enlil, who felt guilty for having sent a flood that had destroyed the rest of humanity and who also wanted to receive sacrifices. Gilgamesh almost secures a chance at, if not immortality, at least rejuvenation, but it is snatched from him by, fittingly, a snake. Gilgamesh returns home less reconciled than resigned to his mortality, and indeed does die. Despite his failure, he is heroic in his attempt to secure immortality, which, as in the Bible, is limited to the gods – Utnapishtim and his wife constituting exceptions. Gilgamesh is two-thirds divine, evinced in his strength, energy, and drive, but he is still mortal. Joseph Campbell discusses Gilgamesh not only in *Hero with a Thousand Faces* but even more in *The Masks of God: Occidental Mythology* (New York: Viking, 1964). On Gilgamesh, see N. K. Sandars' introduction to the translation from which the excerpt is taken; Alexander Heidel, *The Gilgamesh Epic and Old Testament Parallels*, 2nd edn. (Chicago: University of Chicago Press, 1949 [1st edn. 1946]); and "The Epic of Gilgamesh," tr. E. A. Speiser, in *Ancient Near Eastern Texts Relating to the Old Testament*, ed. James B. Pritchard, 3rd edn. (Princeton: Princeton University Press, 1969 [1st edn. 1950), 72–99.

Original publication: *The Epic of Gilgamesh*, tr. N. K. Sandars, 3rd edn. (Harmondsworth: Penguin Books, 1972 [1st edn. 1960]), pp. 97–108, 112–17.

The Epic of Gilgamesh

Translated by N. K. Sandars

BITTERLY Gilgamesh wept for his friend Enkidu; he wandered over the wilderness as a hunter, he roamed over the plains; in his bitterness he cried, "How can I rest, how can I be at peace? Despair is in my heart. What my brother is now, that shall I be when I am dead. Because I am afraid of death I will go as best I can to find Utnapishtim whom they call the Faraway, for he has entered the assembly of the gods." So Gilgamesh travelled over the wilderness, he wandered over the grasslands, a long journey, in search of Utnapishtim, whom the gods took after the deluge; and they set him to live in the land of Dilmun, in the garden of the sun; and to him alone of men they gave everlasting life.

At night when he came to the mountain passes Gilgamesh prayed: "In these mountain passes long ago I saw lions, I was afraid and I lifted my eyes to the moon; I prayed and my prayers went up to the gods, so now, O moon god Sin, protect me." When he had prayed he lay down to sleep, until he was woken from out of a dream. He saw the lions round him glorying in life; then he took his axe in his hand, he drew his sword from his belt, and he fell upon them like an arrow from the string, and struck and destroyed and scattered them.

So at length Gilgamesh came to Mashu, the great mountains about which he had heard many things, which guard the rising and the setting sun. Its twin peaks are as high as the wall of heaven and its paps reach down to the underworld. At its gate the Scorpions stand guard, half man and half dragon; their glory is terrifying, their stare strikes death into men, their shimmering halo sweeps the mountains that guard the rising sun. When Gilgamesh saw them he shielded his eyes for the length of a moment only; then he took courage and approached. When they saw him so undismayed the Man-Scorpion called to his mate, "This one who comes to us now is flesh of the gods." The mate of the Man-Scorpion answered, "Two thirds is god but one third is man."

Then he called to the man Gilgamesh, he called to the child of the gods: "Why have you come so great a journey; for what have you travelled so far, crossing the dangerous waters; tell me the reason for your coming?" Gilgamesh answered, "For Enkidu; I loved him dearly, together we endured all kinds of hardships; on his account I have come, for the common lot of man has taken him. I have wept for him day and night,

174

I would not give up his body for burial, I thought my friend would come back because of my weeping. Since he went, my life is nothing; that is why I have travelled here in search of Utnapishtim my father; for men say he has entered the assembly of the gods, and has found everlasting life. I have a desire to question him concerning the living and the dead." The Man-Scorpion opened his mouth and said, speaking to Gilgamesh, "No man born of woman has done what you have asked, no mortal man has gone into the mountain; the length of it is twelve leagues of darkness; in it there is no light, but the heart is oppressed with darkness. From the rising of the sun to the setting of the sun there is no light." Gilgamesh said, "Although I should go in sorrow and in pain, with sighing and with weeping, still I must go. Open the gate of the mountain." And the Man-Scorpion said, "Go, Gilgamesh, I permit you to pass through the mountain of Mashu and through the high ranges; may your feet carry you safely home. The gate of the mountain is open."

When Gilgamesh heard this he did as the Man-Scorpion had said, he followed the sun's road to his rising, through the mountain. When he had gone one league the darkness became thick around him, for there was no light, he could see nothing ahead and nothing behind him. After two leagues the darkness was thick and there was no light, he could see nothing ahead and nothing behind him. After three leagues the darkness was thick, and there was no light, he could see nothing ahead and nothing behind him. After four leagues the darkness was thick and there was no light, he could see nothing ahead and nothing behind him. At the end of five leagues the darkness was thick and there was no light, he could see nothing ahead and nothing behind him. At the end of six leagues the darkness was thick and there was no light, he could see nothing ahead and nothing behind him. When he had gone seven leagues the darkness was thick and there was no light, he could see nothing ahead and nothing behind him. When he had gone eight leagues Gilgamesh gave a great cry, for the darkness was thick and he could see nothing ahead and nothing behind him. After nine leagues he felt the north wind on his face, but the darkness was thick and there was no light, he could see nothing ahead and nothing behind him. After ten leagues the end was near. After eleven leagues the dawn light appeared. At the end of twelve leagues the sun streamed out.

There was the garden of the gods; all round him stood bushes bearing gems. Seeing it he went down at once, for there was fruit of carnelian with the vine hanging from it, beautiful to look at; lapis lazuli leaves hung thick with fruit, sweet to see. For thorns and thistles there were haematite and rare stones, agate, and pearls from out of the sea. While Gilgamesh walked in the garden by the edge of the sea Shamash saw him, and he saw that he was dressed in the skins of animals and ate their flesh. He was distressed, and he spoke and said, "No mortal man has gone this way before, nor will, as long as the winds drive over the sea." And to Gilgamesh he said, "You will never find the life for which you are searching." Gilgamesh said to glorious Shamash, "Now that I have toiled and strayed so far over the wilderness, am I to sleep, and let the earth cover my head for ever? Let my eyes see the sun until they are dazzled with looking. Although I am no better than a dead man, still let me see the light of the sun."

Beside the sea she lives, the woman of the vine, the maker of wine; Siduri sits in the garden at the edge of the sea, with the golden bowl and the golden vats that the gods gave her. She is covered with a veil; and where she sits she sees Gilgamesh coming towards her, wearing skins, the flesh of the gods in his body, but despair in his heart, and his face like the face of one who has made a long journey. She looked, and as she scanned the distance she said in her own heart, "Surely this is some felon; where is he going now?" And she barred her gate against him with the cross-bar and shot home the bolt. But Gilgamesh, hearing the sound of the bolt, threw up his head and lodged his foot in the gate; he called to her, "Young woman, maker of wine, why do you bolt your door; what did you see that made you bar your gate? I will break in your door and burst in your gate, for I am Gilgamesh who seized and killed the Bull of Heaven, I killed the watchman of the cedar forest, I overthrew Humbaba who lived in the forest, and I killed the lions in the passes of the mountain."

Then Siduri said to him, "If you are that Gilgamesh who seized and killed the Bull of Heaven, who killed the watchman of the cedar forest, who overthrew Humbaba that lived in the forest, and killed the lions in the passes of the mountain, why are your cheeks so starved and why is your face so drawn? Why is despair in your heart and your face like the face of one who has made a long journey? Yes, why is your face burned from heat and cold, and why do you come here wandering over the pastures in search of the wind?"

Gilgamesh answered her, "And why should not my cheeks be starved and my face drawn? Despair is in my heart and my face is the face of one who has made a long journey, it was burned with heat and with cold. Why should I not wander over the pastures in search of the wind? My friend, my younger brother, he who hunted the wild ass of the wilderness and the panther of the plains, my friend, my younger brother who seized and killed the Bull of Heaven and overthrew Humbaba in the cedar forest, my friend who was very dear to me and who endured dangers beside me, Enkidu my brother, whom I loved, the end of mortality has overtaken him. I wept for him seven days and nights till the worm fastened on him. Because of my brother I am afraid of death, because of my brother I stray through the wilderness and cannot rest. But now, young woman, maker of wine, since I have seen your face do not let me see the face of death which I dread so much."

She answered, "Gilgamesh, where are you hurrying to? You will never find that life for which you are looking. When the gods created man they allotted to him death, but life they retained in their own keeping. As for you, Gilgamesh, fill your belly with good things; day and night, night and day, dance and be merry, feast and rejoice. Let your clothes be fresh, bathe yourself in water, cherish the little child that holds your hand, and make your wife happy in your embrace; for this too is the lot of man."

But Gilgamesh said to Siduri, the young woman, "How can I be silent, how can I rest, when Enkidu whom I love is dust, and I too shall die and be laid in the earth. You live by the sea-shore and look into the heart of it; young woman, tell me now, which is the way to Utnapishtim, the son of Ubara-Tutu? What directions are there for the passage; give me, oh, give me directions. I will cross the Ocean if it is possible; if it is not I will wander still farther in the wilderness." The wine-maker said to him, "Gilgamesh, there is no crossing the Ocean; whoever has come, since the days of old, has not been able to pass that sea. The Sun in his glory crosses the Ocean, but who beside Shamash has ever crossed it? The place and the passage are difficult, and the waters of death are deep which flow between. Gilgamesh, how will you cross the Ocean? When you come to the waters of death what will you do? But Gilgamesh, down in the woods you will find Urshanabi, the ferryman of Utnapishtim; with him are the holy things, the things of stone. He is fashioning the serpent prow of the boat. Look at him well, and if it is possible, perhaps you will cross the waters with him; but if it is not possible, then you must go back."

When Gilgamesh heard this he was seized with anger. He took his axe in his hand, and his dagger from his belt. He crept forward and he fell on them like a javelin. Then he went into the forest and sat down. Urshanabi saw the dagger flash and heard the axe, and he beat his head, for Gilgamesh had shattered the tackle of the boat in his rage. Urshanabi said to him, "Tell me, what is your name? I am Urshanabi, the ferryman of Utnapishtim the Faraway." He replied to him, "Gilgamesh is my name, I am from Uruk, from the house of Anu." Then Urshanabi said to him, "Why are your cheeks so starved and your face drawn? Why is despair in your heart and your face like the face of one who has made a long journey; yes, why is your face burned with heat and with cold, and why do you come here wandering over the pastures in search of the wind?"

177

Gilgamesh said to him, "Why should not my cheeks be starved and my face drawn? Despair is in my heart, and my face is the face of one who has made a long journey. I was burned with heat and with cold. Why should I not wander over the pastures? My friend, my younger brother who seized and killed the Bull of Heaven, and overthrew Humbaba in the cedar forest, my friend who was very dear to me, and who endured dangers beside me, Enkidu my brother whom I loved, the end of mortality has overtaken him. I wept for him seven days and nights till the worm fastened on him. Because of my brother I am afraid of death, because of my brother I stray through the wilderness. His fate lies heavy upon me. How can I be silent, how can I rest? He is dust and I too shall die and be laid in the earth for ever. I am afraid of death, therefore, Urshanabi, tell me which is the road to Utnapishtim? If it is possible I will cross the waters of death; if not I will wander still farther through the wilderness."

Urshanabi said to him, "Gilgamesh, your own hands have prevented you from crossing the Ocean; when you destroyed the tackle of the boat you destroyed its safety." Then the two of them talked it over and Gilgamesh said, "Why are you so angry with me, Urshanabi, for you yourself cross the sea by day and night, at all seasons you cross it." "Gilgamesh, those things you destroyed, their property is to carry me over the water, to prevent the waters of death from touching me. It was for this reason that I preserved them, but you have destroyed them, and the *urnu* snakes with them. But now, go into the forest, Gilgamesh; with your axe cut poles, one hundred and twenty, cut them sixty cubits long, paint them with bitumen, set on them ferrules and bring them back."

When Gilgamesh heard this he went into the forest, he cut poles one hundred and twenty; he cut them sixty cubits long, he painted them with bitumen, he set on them ferrules, and he brought them to Urshanabi. Then they boarded the boat, Gilgamesh and Urshanabi together, launching it out on the waves of Ocean. For three days they ran on as if it were a journey of a month and fifteen days, and at last Urshanabi brought the boat to the waters of death. Then Urshanabi said to Gilgamesh, "Press on, take a pole and thrust it in, but do not let your hands touch the waters. Gilgamesh, take a second pole, take a third, take a fourth pole. Now, Gilgamesh, take a fifth, take a sixth and seventh pole. Gilgamesh, take an eighth, and ninth, a tenth pole. Gilgamesh, take an eleventh, take a twelfth pole." After one hundred and twenty thrusts Gilgamesh had used the last pole. Then he stripped himself, he held up his arms for a mast and his covering for a sail. So Urshanabi the ferryman brought Gilgamesh to Utnapishtim, whom they call the Faraway, who lives in Dilmun at the place of the sun's transit, eastward of the mountain. To him alone of men the gods had given everlasting life.

178

Now Utnapishtim, where he lay at ease, looked into the distance and he said in his heart, musing to himself, "Why does the boat sail here without tackle and mast; why are the sacred stones destroyed, and why does the master not sail the boat? That man who comes is none of mine; where I look I see a man whose body is covered with skins of beasts. Who is this who walks up the shore behind Urshanabi, for surely he is no man of mine?" So Utnapishtim looked at him and said, "What is your name, you who come here wearing the skins of beasts, with your cheeks starved and your face drawn? Where are you hurrying to now? For what reason have you made this great journey, crossing the seas whose passage is difficult? Tell me the reason for your coming."

He replied, "Gilgamesh is my name. I am from Uruk, from the house of Anu." Then Utnapishtim said to him, "If you are Gilgamesh, why are your cheeks so starved and your face drawn? Why is despair in your heart and your face like the face of one who has made a long journey? Yes, why is your face burned with heat and cold; and why do you come here, wandering over the wilderness in search of the wind?"

Gilgamesh said to him, "Why should not my cheeks be starved and my face drawn? Despair is in my heart and my face is the face of one who has made a long journey. It was burned with heat and with cold. Why should I not wander over the pastures? My friend, my younger brother who seized and killed the Bull of Heaven and overthrew Humbaba in the cedar forest, my friend who was very dear to me and endured dangers beside me, Enkidu, my brother whom I loved, the end of mortality has overtaken him. I wept for him seven days and nights till the worm fastened on him. Because of my brother I am afraid of death; because of my brother I stray through the wilderness. His fate lies heavy upon me. How can I be silent, how can I rest? He is dust and I shall die also and be laid in the earth for ever." Again Gilgamesh said, speaking to Utnapishtim, "It is to see Utnapishtim whom we call the Faraway that I have come this journey. For this I have wandered over the world, I have crossed many difficult ranges, I have crossed the seas, I have wearied myself with travelling; my joints are aching, and I have lost acquaintance with sleep which is sweet. My clothes were worn out before I came to the house of Siduri. I have killed the bear and hyena, the lion and panther, the tiger, the stag and the ibex, all sorts of wild game and the small creatures of the pastures. I ate their flesh and I wore their skins; and that was how I came to the gate of the young woman, the maker of wine, who barred her gate of pitch and bitumen against me. But from her I had news of the journey; so then I came to Urshanabi the ferryman, and with him I crossed over the waters of death. Oh, father Utnapishtim, you who have entered the assembly of the gods, I wish to question you concerning

179

the living and the dead, how shall I find the life for which I am searching?"

Utnapishtim said, "There is no permanence. Do we build a house to stand for ever, do we seal a contract to hold for all time? Do brothers divide an inheritance to keep for ever, does the flood-time of rivers endure? It is only the nymph of the dragon-fly who sheds her larva and sees the sun in his glory. From the days of old there is no permanence. The sleeping and the dead, how alike they are, they are like a painted death. What is there between the master and the servant when both have fulfilled their doom? When the Anunnaki, the judges, come together, and Mammetun the mother of destinies, together they decree the fates of men. Life and death they allot but the day of death they do not disclose."

Then Gilgamesh said to Utnapishtim the Faraway, "I look at you now, Utnapishtim, and your appearance is no different from mine; there is nothing strange in your features. I thought I should find you like a hero prepared for battle, but you lie here taking your ease on your back. Tell me truly, how was it that you came to enter the company of the gods and to possess everlasting life?" Utnapishtim said to Gilgamesh, "I will reveal to you a mystery, I will tell you a secret of the gods."

"You know the city Shurrupak, it stands on the banks of Euphrates? That city grew old and the gods that were in it were old. There was Anu, lord of the firmament, their father, and warrior Enlil their counsellor, Ninurta the helper, and Ennugi watcher over canals; and with them also was Ea. In those days the world teemed, the people multiplied, the world bellowed like a wild bull, and the great god was aroused by the clamour. Enlil heard the clamour and he said to the gods in council, "The uproar of mankind is intolerable and sleep is no longer possible by reason of the babel." So the gods agreed to exterminate mankind. Enlil did this, but Ea because of his oath warned me in a dream. He whispered their words to my house of reeds, "Reed-house, reed-house! Wall, O wall, hearken reed-house, wall reflect; O man of Shurrupak, son of Ubara-Tutu; tear down your house and build a boat, abandon possessions and look for life, despise worldly goods and save your soul alive. Tear down your house, I say, and build a boat. These are the measurements of the barque as you shall build her: let her beam equal her length, let her deck be roofed like the vault that covers the abyss; then take up into the boat the seed of all living creatures." [...]

"When Enlil had come, when he saw the boat, he was wrath and swelled with anger at the gods, the host of heaven, 'Has any of these mortals escaped? Not one was to have survived the destruction.' Then the god of the wells and canals Ninurta opened his mouth and said to the

warrior Enlil, 'Who is there of the gods that can devise without Ea? It is
Ea alone who knows all things.' Then Ea opened his mouth and spoke to
warrior Enlil, 'Wisest of gods, hero Enlil, how could you so senselessly
bring down the flood?

> *Lay upon the sinner his sin,*
> *Lay upon the transgressor his transgression,*
> *Punish him a little when he breaks loose,*
> *Do not drive him too hard or he perishes;*
> *Would that a lion had ravaged mankind*
> *Rather than the flood,*
> *Would that a wolf had ravaged mankind*
> *Rather than the flood,*
> *Would that famine had wasted the world*
> *Rather than the flood,*
> *Would that pestilence had wasted mankind*
> *Rather than the flood.*

It was not I that revealed the secret of the gods; the wise man learned it in
a dream. Now take your counsel what shall be done with him.'

"Then Enlil went up into the boat, he took me by the hand and my wife
and made us enter the boat and kneel down on either side, he standing
between us. He touched our foreheads to bless us saying, 'In time past
Utnapishtim was a mortal man; henceforth he and his wife shall live in
the distance at the mouth of the rivers.' Thus it was that the gods took me
and placed me here to live in the distance, at the mouth of the rivers."

Utnapishtim said, "As for you, Gilgamesh, who will assemble the gods
for your sake, so that you may find that life for which you are searching?
But if you wish, come and put it to the test: only prevail against sleep for
six days and seven nights." But while Gilgamesh sat there resting on his
haunches, a mist of sleep like soft wool teased from the fleece drifted over
him, and Utnapishtim said to his wife, "Look at him now, the strong man
who would have everlasting life, even now the mists of sleep are drifting
over him." His wife replied, "Touch the man to wake him, so that he may
return to his own land in peace, going back through the gate by which he
came." Utnapishtim said to his wife, "All men are deceivers, even you he
will attempt to deceive; therefore bake loaves of bread, each day one loaf,
and put it beside his head; and make a mark on the wall to number the
days he has slept."

So she baked loaves of bread, each day one loaf, and put it beside his
head, and she marked on the wall the days that he slept; and there came a
day when the first loaf was hard, the second loaf was like leather, the

third was soggy, the crust of the fourth had mould, the fifth was mildewed, the sixth was fresh, and the seventh was still on the embers. Then Utnapishtim touched him and he woke. Gilgamesh said to Utnapishtim the Faraway, "I hardly slept when you touched and roused me." But Utnapishtim said, "Count these loaves and learn how many days you slept, for your first is hard, your second like leather, your third is soggy, the crust of your fourth has mould, your fifth is mildewed, your sixth is fresh and your seventh was still over the glowing embers when I touched and woke you." Gilgamesh said, "What shall I do, O Utnapishtim, where shall I go? Already the thief in the night has hold of my limbs, death inhabits my room; wherever my foot rests, there I find death."

Then Utnapishtim spoke to Urshanabi the ferryman: "Woe to you Urshanabi, now and for ever more you have become hateful to this harbourage; it is not for you, nor for you are the crossings of this sea. Go now, banished from the shore. But this man before whom you walked, bringing him here, whose body is covered with foulness and the grace of whose limbs has been spoiled by wild skins, take him to the washing-place. There he shall wash his long hair clean as snow in the water, he shall throw off his skins and let the sea carry them away, and the beauty of his body shall be shown, the fillet on his forehead shall be renewed, and he shall be given clothes to cover his nakedness. Till he reaches his own city and his journey is accomplished, these clothes will show no sign of age, they will wear like a new garment." So Urshanabi took Gilgamesh and led him to the washing-place, he washed his long hair as clean as snow in the water, he threw off his skins, which the sea carried away, and showed the beauty of his body. He renewed the fillet on his forehead, and to cover his nakedness gave him clothes which would show no sign of age, but would wear like a new garment till he reached his own city, and his journey was accomplished.

Then Gilgamesh and Urshanabi launched the boat on to the water and boarded it, and they made ready to sail away; but the wife of Utnapishtim the Faraway said to him, "Gilgamesh came here wearied out, he is worn out; what will you give him to carry him back to his own country?" So Utnapishtim spoke, and Gilgamesh took a pole and brought the boat in to the bank. "Gilgamesh, you came here a man wearied out, you have worn yourself out; what shall I give you to carry you back to your own country? Gilgamesh, I shall reveal a secret thing, it is a mystery of the gods that I am telling you. There is a plant that grows under the water, it has a prickle like a thorn, like a rose; it will wound your hands, but if you succeed in taking it, then your hands will hold that which restores his lost youth to a man."

When Gilgamesh heard this he opened the sluices so that a sweet-water current might carry him out to the deepest channel; he tied heavy stones to his feet and they dragged him down to the water-bed. There he saw the plant growing; although it pricked him he took it in his hands; then he cut the heavy stones from his feet, and the sea carried him and threw him on to the shore. Gilgamesh said to Urshanabi the ferryman, "Come here, and see this marvellous plant. By its virtue a man may win back all his former strength. I will take it to Uruk of the strong walls; there I will give it to the old men to eat. Its name shall be 'The Old Men Are Young Again'; and at last I shall eat it myself and have back all my lost youth." So Gilgamesh returned by the gate through which he had come, Gilgamesh and Urshanabi went together. They travelled their twenty leagues and then they broke their fast; after thirty leagues they stopped for the night.

Gilgamesh saw a well of cool water and he went down and bathed; but deep in the pool there was lying a serpent, and the serpent sensed the sweetness of the flower. It rose out of the water and snatched it away, and immediately it sloughed its skin and returned to the well. Then Gilgamesh sat down and wept, the tears ran down his face, and he took the hand of Urshanabi; "O Urshanabi, was it for this that I toiled with my hands, is it for this I have wrung out my heart's blood? For myself I have gained nothing; not I, but the beast of the earth has joy of it now. Already the stream has carried it twenty leagues back to the channels where I found it. I found a sign and now I have lost it. Let us leave the boat on the bank and go."

After twenty leagues they broke their fast, after thirty leagues they stopped for the night; in three days they had walked as much as a journey of a month and fifteen days. When the journey was accomplished they arrived at Uruk, the strong-walled city. Gilgamesh spoke to him, to Urshanabi the ferryman, "Urshanabi, climb up on to the wall of Uruk, inspect its foundation terrace, and examine well the brickwork; see if it is not of burnt bricks; and did not the seven wise men lay these foundations? One third of the whole is city, one third is garden, and one third is field, with the precinct of the goddess Ishtar. These parts and the precinct are all Uruk."

This too was the work of Gilgamesh, the king, who knew the countries of the world. He was wise, he saw mysteries and knew secret things, he brought us a tale of the days before the flood. He went a long journey, was weary, worn out with labour, and returning engraved on a stone the whole story.

CHAPTER 19

SISYPHUS (ANCIENT GREEK): ABSURD HERO

INTRODUCTION

Among the figures that Odysseus sees in Tantalus, the part of Hades reserved for those who have offended Zeus, is Sisyphus, whose eternal punishment is to have to push a huge stone up a steep hill, only for it every time to roll back down just as he nears the top. As Odysseus describes the sight, "Also I saw Sisyphos. He was suffering strong pains, and with both arms embracing the monstrous stone, struggling with hands and feet alike, he would try to push the stone upward to the crest of the hill, but when it was on the point of going over the top, the force of gravity turned it backward, and the pitiless stone rolled back down to the level. He then tried once more to push it up, straining hard, and sweat ran all down his body, and over his head a cloud of dust rose" (Homer, *The Odyssey*, tr. Richmond Lattimore [New York: Harper Torchbooks, 1968 (1965)], p. 183, lines 593–600). Homer does not say what Sisyphus' misdeed was, and ancient mythographers differ. For all ancients, Sisyphus was to be pitied, and he was as far from a hero as one could get. But for Albert Camus, he is to be admired. Rather than embodying the fate that awaits those who defy the gods, Sisyphus for Camus symbolizes the fate of all human beings in a world without gods. Sisyphus is admirable because he accepts the absurdity of human existence, which is less unfair than pointless. Instead of giving up and committing suicide, Sisyphus toils on, even while aware that his every attempt will prove futile. His is the only kind of heroism that a meaningless world allows. The following interpretation of the myth comes at the end of Camus' philosophical essay on "The Myth of Sisyphus." On Camus, see

Original publication: Albert Camus, *The Myth of Sisyphus and Other Essays*, tr. Justin O'Brien (New York: Vintage Books, 1960 [1955]), pp. 88–91.

Conor Cruise O'Brien, *Albert Camus*, Modern Masters Series (New York: Viking, 1970).

THE MYTH OF SISYPHUS

Albert Camus

The gods had condemned Sisyphus to ceaselessly rolling a rock to the top of a mountain, whence the stone would fall back of its own weight. They had thought with some reason that there is no more dreadful punishment than futile and hopeless labor.

If one believes Homer, Sisyphus was the wisest and most prudent of mortals. According to another tradition, however, he was disposed to practice the profession of highwayman. I see no contradiction in this. Opinions differ as to the reasons why he became the futile laborer of the underworld. To begin with, he is accused of a certain levity in regard to the gods. He stole their secrets. Ægina, the daughter of Æsopus, was carried off by Jupiter. The father was shocked by that disappearance and complained to Sisyphus. He, who knew of the abduction, offered to tell about it on condition that Æsopus would give water to the citadel of Corinth. To the celestial thunderbolts he preferred the benediction of water. He was punished for this in the underworld. Homer tells us also that Sisyphus had put Death in chains. Pluto could not endure the sight of his deserted, silent empire. He dispatched the god of war, who liberated Death from the hands of her conqueror.

It is said also that Sisyphus, being near to death, rashly wanted to test his wife's love. He ordered her to cast his unburied body into the middle of the public square. Sisyphus woke up in the underworld. And there, annoyed by an obedience so contrary to human love, he obtained from Pluto permission to return to earth in order to chastise his wife. But when he had seen again the face of this world, enjoyed water and sun, warm stones and the sea, he no longer wanted to go back to the infernal darkness. Recalls, signs of anger, warnings were of no avail. Many years more he lived facing the curve of the gulf, the sparkling sea, and the smiles of earth. A decree of the gods was necessary. Mercury came and seized the impudent man by the collar and, snatching him from his joys, led him forcibly back to the underworld, where his rock was ready for him.

You have already grasped that Sisyphus is the absurd hero. He *is*, as much through his passions as through his torture. His scorn of the gods, his hatred of death, and his passion for life won him that unspeakable penalty in which the whole being is exerted toward accomplishing nothing. This is the price that must be paid for the passions of this earth. Nothing is told us about Sisyphus in the underworld. Myths are made for the imagination to breathe life into them. As for this myth, one sees merely the whole effort of a body straining to raise the huge stone, to roll it and push it up a slope a hundred times over; one sees the face screwed up, the cheek tight against the stone, the shoulder bracing the clay-covered mass, the foot wedging it, the fresh start with arms outstretched, the wholly human security of two earth-clotted hands. At the very end of his long effort measured by skyless space and time without depth, the purpose is achieved. Then Sisyphus watches the stone rush down in a few moments toward that lower world whence he will have to push it up again toward the summit. He goes back down to the plain.

It is during that return, that pause, that Sisyphus interests me. A face that toils so close to stones is already stone itself! I see that man going back down with a heavy yet measured step toward the torment of which he will never know the end. That hour like a breathing-space which returns as surely as his suffering, that is the hour of consciousness. At each of those moments when he leaves the heights and gradually sinks toward the lairs of the gods, he is superior to his fate. He is stronger than his rock.

If this myth is tragic, that is because its hero is conscious. Where would his torture be, indeed, if at every step the hope of succeeding upheld him? The workman of today works every day in his life at the same tasks, and this fate is no less absurd. But it is tragic only at the rare moments when it becomes conscious. Sisyphus, proletarian of the gods, powerless and rebellious, knows the whole extent of his wretched condition: it is what he thinks of during his descent. The lucidity that was to constitute his torture at the same time crowns his victory. There is no fate that cannot be surmounted by scorn.

If the descent is thus sometimes performed in sorrow, it can also take place in joy. This word is not too much. Again I fancy Sisyphus returning toward his rock, and the sorrow was in the beginning. When the images of earth cling too tightly to memory, when the call of happiness becomes too insistent, it happens that melancholy rises in man's heart: this is the rock's victory, this is the rock itself. The boundless grief is too heavy to bear. These are our nights of Gethsemane. But crushing truths perish from being acknowledged. Thus, Oedipus at the outset obeys fate without knowing it. But from the moment he knows, his tragedy begins. Yet at the same moment, blind and desperate, he realizes that the only bond linking him to the world is the cool hand of a girl. Then a tremendous remark rings out: "Despite so many ordeals, my advanced age and the nobility of my soul make me conclude that all is well." Sophocles' Oedipus, like Dostoevsky's Kirilov, thus gives the recipe for the absurd victory. Ancient wisdom confirms modern heroism.

One does not discover the absurd without being tempted to write a manual of happiness. "What! by such narrow ways – ?" There is but one world, however. Happiness and the absurd are two sons of the same earth. They are inseparable. It would be a mistake to say that happiness necessarily springs from the absurd discovery. It happens as well that the feeling of the absurd springs from happiness. "I conclude that all is well," says Oedipus, and that remark is sacred. It echoes in the wild and limited universe of man. It teaches that all is not, has not been, exhausted. It drives out of this world a god who had come into it with dissatisfaction and a preference for futile sufferings. It makes of fate a human matter, which must be settled among men.

All Sisyphus' silent joy is contained therein. His fate belongs to him. His rock is his thing. Likewise, the absurd man, when he contemplates his torment, silences all the idols. In the universe suddenly restored to its silence, the myriad wondering little voices of the earth rise up. Unconscious, secret calls, invitations from all the faces, they are the necessary reverse and price of victory. There is no sun without shadow, and it is essential to know the night. The absurd man says yes and his effort will henceforth be unceasing. If there is a personal fate, there is no higher destiny, or at least there is but one which he concludes is inevitable and despicable. For the rest, he knows himself to be the master of his days. At that subtle moment when man glances backward over his life, Sisyphus returning toward his rock, in that slight pivoting he contemplates that series of unrelated actions which becomes his fate, created by him, combined under his memory's eye and soon sealed by his death. Thus, convinced of the wholly human origin of all that is human, a blind man eager to see who knows that the night has no end, he is still on the go. The rock is still rolling.

I leave Sisyphus at the foot of the mountain! One always finds one's burden again. But Sisyphus teaches the higher fidelity that negates the gods and raises rocks. He too concludes that all is well. This universe henceforth without a master seems to him neither sterile nor futile. Each atom of that stone, each mineral flake of that night-filled mountain, in itself forms a world. The struggle itself toward the heights is enough to fill a man's heart. One must imagine Sisyphus happy.

CHAPTER 20

DON QUIXOTE (SPANISH): HERO AS MADMAN

INTRODUCTION

We are told by Cervantes that his character Don Quixote became so smitten with the tales he continually read of chivalrous knights of days of old that he imagined himself a knight and sought to fulfill the role by obtaining armor, a horse, a squire, and above all a lady, on whose behalf he risked his life redressing wrongs and thereby winning honor. Don Quixote misinterprets every situation he encounters, turning ordinary activities into grand ones requiring the services of a knight. He is more than idealistic. He is mad. He does not merely ask others to live by his own ideals. He assumes that they do. He does not merely seek chivalric encounters. He assumes that he has found them. At most, only his squire, Sancho Panza, is motivated by nobility. Everyone else acts out of crass self-interest or else sheer love – for example, his niece and the priest. Yet it is far from clear that Cervantes is mocking Don Quixote, who over the centuries since the publication of the book (in two parts, in 1604 and 1614) has been taken as, alternatively, a fool, a tragic hero, and an existentialist hero. Don Quixote is heroic in refusing to accept the every-day world and in instead insisting on changing it or at least treating it as if it were otherwise. The following excerpt begins with the most famous of Don Quixote's many adventures, or misadventures: his mistaking wind-mills for giants, whom he must rid the world of. The excerpt then describes his mistaking an innocent journey by two monks riding along-side a coach with a lady en route to join her husband for the kidnapping of her by highwaymen. René Girard discusses Don Quixote (*Deceit, Desire, and the Novel*, tr. Yvonne Freccero [Baltimore: Johns Hopkins University Press, 1966], chs. 1, 4). On Don Quixote as a modern hero, see

Original publication: Miguel de Cervantes, *The Adventures of Don Quixote*, tr. J. M. Cohen (Harmondsworth: Penguin Books, 1950), pp. 68–74.

Ian Watt, *Myths of Modern Individualism* (Cambridge: Cambridge University Press, 1996), ch. 3.

THE ADVENTURES OF DON QUIXOTE

Miguel de Cervantes

At that moment they caught sight of some thirty or forty windmills, which stand on that plain, and as soon as Don Quixote saw them he said to his squire: "Fortune is guiding our affairs better than we could have wished. Look over there, friend Sancho Panza, where more than thirty monstrous giants appear. I intend to do battle with them and take all their lives. With their spoils we will begin to get rich, for this is a fair war, and it is a great service to God to wipe such a wicked brood from the face of the earth."

"What giants?" asked Sancho Panza.

"Those you see there," replied his master, "with their long arms. Some giants have them about six miles long."

"Take care, your worship," said Sancho; "those things over there are not giants but windmills, and what seem to be their arms are the sails, which are whirled round in the wind and make the millstone turn."

"It is quite clear," replied Don Quixote, "that you are not experienced in this matter of adventures. They are giants, and if you are afraid, go away and say your prayers, whilst I advance and engage them in fierce and unequal battle."

As he spoke, he dug his spurs into his steed Rocinante, paying no attention to his squire's shouted warning that beyond all doubt they were windmills and no giants he was advancing to attack. But he went on, so positive that they were giants that he neither listened to Sancho's cries nor noticed what they were, even when he got near them. Instead he went on shouting in a loud voice: "Do not fly, cowards, vile creatures, for it is one knight alone who assails you."

At that moment a slight wind arose, and the great sails began to move. At the sight of which Don Quixote shouted: "Though you wield more arms than the-giant Briareus, you shall pay for it!" Saying this, he commended himself with all his soul to his Lady Dulcinea, beseeching her aid in his great peril. Then, covering himself with his shield and putting his lance in the rest, he urged Rocinante forward at a full gallop and attacked the nearest windmill, thrusting his lance into the sail. But the wind turned it with such violence that it shivered his weapon in pieces, dragging the horse and his rider with it, and sent the knight rolling badly injured across the plain. Sancho Panza rushed to his assistance as fast as his ass could trot, but when he came up he found that the knight could not stir. Such a shock had Rocinante given him in their fall.

"O my goodness!" cried Sancho. "Didn't I tell your worship to look what you were doing, for they were only windmills? Nobody could mistake them, unless he had windmills on the brain."

"Silence, friend Sancho," replied Don Quixote. "Matters of war are more subject than most to continual change. What is more, I think – and that is the truth – that the same sage Friston who robbed me of my room and my books has turned those giants into windmills, to cheat me of the glory of conquering them. Such is the enmity he bears me; but in the very end his black arts shall avail him little against the goodness of my sword."

"God send it as He will," replied Sancho Panza, helping the knight to get up and remount Rocinante, whose shoulders were half dislocated.

As they discussed this last adventure they followed the road to the pass of Lapice where, Don Quixote said, they could not fail to find many and various adventures, as many travellers passed that way. He was much concerned, however, at the loss of his lance, and, speaking of it to his squire, remarked: "I remember reading that a certain Spanish knight called Diego Perez de Vargas, having broken his sword in battle, tore a great bough or limb from an oak, and performed such deeds with it that day, and pounded so many Moors, that he earned the surname of the Pounder, and thus he and his descendants from that day onwards have been called Vargas y Machuca. I mention this because I propose to tear down just such a limb from the first oak we meet, as big and as good as his; and I intend to do such deeds with it that you may consider yourself most fortunate to have won the right to see them. For you will witness things which will scarcely be credited."

"With God's help," replied Sancho, "and I believe it all as your worship says. But sit a bit more upright, sir, for you seem to be riding lop-sided. It must be from the bruises you got when you fell."

"That is the truth," replied Don Quixote. "And if I do not complain of the pain, it is because a knight errant is not allowed to complain of any wounds, even though his entrails may be dropping out through them."

"If that's so, I have nothing more to say," said Sancho, "but God knows I should be glad if your worship would complain if anything hurt you. I must say, for my part, that I have to cry out at the slightest twinge, unless this business of not complaining extends to knights errants' squires as well."

Don Quixote could not help smiling at his squire's simplicity, and told him that he could certainly complain how and when he pleased, whether he had any cause or no, for up to that time he had never read anything to the contrary in the law of chivalry.

Sancho reminded him that it was time for dinner, but his master replied that he had need of none, but that his squire might eat whenever he pleased. With this permission Sancho settled himself as comfortably as he could on his ass and, taking out what he had put into the saddle-bags, jogged very leisurely along behind his master, eating all the while; and from time to time he raised the bottle with such relish that the best-fed publican in Malaga might have envied him. Now, as he went along like this, taking repeated gulps, he entirely forgot the promise his master had made him, and reckoned that going in search of adventures, however dangerous, was more like pleasure than hard work.

They passed that night under some trees, from one of which our knight tore down a dead branch to serve him as some sort of lance, and stuck into it the iron head of the one that had been broken. And all night Don Quixote did not sleep but thought about his Lady Dulcinea, to conform to what he had read in his books about knights errant spending many sleepless nights in woodland and desert dwelling on the memory of their ladies. Not so Sancho Panza; for, as his stomach was full, and not of chicory water, he slept right through till morning. And, if his master had not called him, neither the sunbeams, which struck him full on the face, nor the song of the birds, who in great number and very joyfully greeted the dawn of the new day, would have been enough to wake him. As he got up he made a trial of his bottle, and found it rather limper than the night before; whereat his heart sank, for he did not think they were taking the right road to remedy this defect very quickly. Don Quixote wanted no breakfast for, as we have said, he was determined to subsist on savoury memories. Then they turned back on to the road they had been on before, towards the pass of Lapice, which they sighted about three in the afternoon.

"Here," exclaimed Don Quixote on seeing it, "here, brother Sancho Panza, we can steep our arms to the elbows in what they call adventures. But take note that though you see me in the greatest danger in the world, you must not put your hand to your sword to defend me, unless you know that my assailants are rabble and common folk; in which case you may come to my aid. But should they be knights, on no account will it be legal or permissible, by the laws of chivalry, for you to assist me until you are yourself knighted."

"You may be sure, sir", replied Sancho, "that I shall obey your worship perfectly there. Especially as I am very peaceable by nature and all against shoving myself into brawls and quarrels. But as to defending myself, sir, I shan't take much notice of those rules, because divine law and human law allow everyone to defend himself against anyone who tries to harm him."

"I never said otherwise," replied Don Quixote, "but in the matter of aiding me against knights, you must restrain your natural impulses."

"I promise you I will," replied Sancho, "and I will observe this rule as strictly as the Sabbath."

In the middle of this conversation two monks of the order of St. Benedict appeared on the road, mounted on what looked like dromedaries; for the two mules they were riding were quite as big. They were wearing riding-masks against the dust and carrying sunshades. And behind them came a coach, with four or five horsemen escorting it, and two muleteers on foot.

In the coach, as it afterwards turned out, was a Basque lady travelling to Seville to join her husband, who was going out to take up a very important post in the Indies. The monks were not of her company, but merely journeying on the same road.

Now no sooner did Don Quixote see them in the distance than he said to his squire: "Either I am much mistaken, or this will prove the most famous adventure ever seen. For those dark shapes looming over there must, beyond all doubt, be enchanters bearing off in that coach some princess they have stolen; and it is my duty to redress this wrong with all my might."

"This will be a worse job than the windmills," said Sancho. "Look, sir, those are Benedictine monks, and the coach must belong to some travellers. Listen to me, sir. Be careful what you do, and don't let the Devil deceive you."

"I have told you," replied Don Quixote, "that you know very little of this subject of adventures. What I say is true, and now you will see it."

So saying, he rode forward and took up his position in the middle of the road along which the monks were coming; and when they got so near that he thought they could hear him, he called out in a loud voice: "Monstrous and diabolical crew! Release immediately the noble princesses whom you are forcibly carrying off in that coach, or prepare to receive instant death as the just punishment for your misdeeds."

The monks reined in their mules, and stopped in astonishment at Don Quixote's appearance and at his speech.

"Sir Knight," they replied, "we are neither monstrous nor diabolical, but two monks of St Benedict travelling about our business, nor do we know whether there are any princesses being carried off in that coach or not."

"No fair speeches for me, for I know you, perfidious scoundrels!" cried Don Quixote. Then, without waiting for their reply, he spurred Rocinante and, with his lance lowered, charged at the foremost monk with such vigour and fury that, if he had not slid from his mule, he would have been thrown to the ground and badly hurt, if not killed outright. The second monk, on seeing his companion so treated, struck his heels into his stout mule's flanks and set her galloping over the plain fleeter than the wind itself. When Sancho Panza saw the monk on the ground, he got down lightly from his ass, ran up and started to strip him of his clothes. Upon this, two servants of the monks arrived and asked him why he was stripping their master. Sancho replied that the clothes fell rightly to his share as spoils of the battle which his master, Don Quixote, had won. The lads, who did not get the joke nor understand this talk of spoils and battles, saw that Don Quixote had gone off and was talking with the ladies in the coach, and so fell upon Sancho and knocked him down. And, pulling every hair from his beard, they kicked him mercilessly, and left him stretched on the ground, breathless and stunned. Then, without a moment's hesitation, the monk remounted his mule, trembling, terrified and as white as a sheet; and as soon as he was up he spurred after his comrade, who was waiting for him some distance off, watching to see the upshot of this sudden attack. But without caring to wait for the end of the adventure, they went on their way, crossing themselves more often than if they had had the Devil himself at their backs.

Don Quixote, as we have said, was talking with the lady in the coach: "Your fair ladyship may now dispose of yourself as you desire, for now the pride of your ravishers lies in the dust, overthrown by this strong arm of mine. And lest you be racked with doubt as to the name of your deliverer, know that I am Don Quixote de la Mancha, knight errant, adventurer and captive to the peerless and beautiful lady, Dulcinea del Toboso. And in requital of the benefit you have received from me, I would ask no more of you than to go to El Toboso and present yourself on my behalf before that lady, telling her what I have done for your deliverance."

All that Don Quixote said was overhead by one of the squires accompanying the coach, a Basque. And when he saw that the knight would not let them pass, but was talking of their turning back at once to El Toboso, he went up to Don Quixote and, grasping his lance, addressed him in bad Castilian and worse Basque.

"Get along, you ill-gotten knight. By God who made me, if you do not leave coach I kill you, sure as I be Basque."

Don Quixote understood him very well, and replied with great calm: "If you were a knight, as you are not, I should have punished your rash insolence by now, you slavish creature."

"I not gentleman? I swear you liar, as I am a Christian. You throw down lance and draw sword, and you will see you are carrying the water to the cat. Basque on land, gentleman at sea. A gentleman, by the devil, and you lie if you say otherwise!"

"'Now you shall see,' said Agrages," quoted Don Quixote, and threw his lance down on the ground. Then, drawing his sword and grasping his shield, he rushed at his antagonist, determined to take his life. When the Basque saw him coming he would have liked to get down from his mule, as it was a poor sort of hired beast and not to be trusted, but there was nothing for it but to draw his sword. He was, however, lucky enough to be near the coach, from which he was able to snatch a cushion to serve as a shield; whereupon they immediately fell to, as if they had been two mortal enemies. The rest of the party tried to pacify them, but could not; for the Basque swore in his uncouth language that if they did not let him finish the battle, he would himself kill his mistress and all who hindered him.

The lady in the coach, amazed and terrified at the sight, made the coachman drive off a little way, and sat watching the deadly struggle from a distance. In the course of the fight the Basque dealt Don Quixote a mighty blow on one shoulder, thrusting above his shield, and had our knight been without defence he would have been cleft to the waist. When Don Quixote felt the weight of that tremendous stroke he cried out aloud: "O lady of my soul, Dulcinea, flower of beauty, come to the aid of this your knight, who for the sake of your great goodness is now in this dire peril!"

To speak, to raise his sword, to cover himself with his shield and attack the Basque: all this was the work of a moment. For he had resolved to risk everything upon a single stroke. The Basque, seeing him come on, judged Don Quixote's courage by his daring, and decided to do the same as he. So he covered himself well with his cushion and waited, unable to turn his mule in either direction, for the beast was now dead weary, and not being made for such games, could not budge a step.

Don Quixote, as we have said, rushed at the wary Basque with sword aloft, determined to cleave him to the waist; and the Basque watched, with his sword also raised and well guarded by his cushion; while all the by-standers trembled in terrified suspense, hanging upon the issue of the dreadful blows with which they threatened one another. And the lady of the coach and her waiting-women offered a thousand vows and prayers to all the images and places of devotion in Spain, that God might deliver their squire and them from the great peril they were in.

CHAPTER 21

DAVY CROCKETT (AMERICAN): COMIC HERO

INTRODUCTION

During his lifetime Davy Crockett (1786–1836) became a figure of myth and even mythicized his own life. An American frontiersman from Tennessee, he became a state legislator and a member of Congress. He was best known for his bravery at the Texas fort known as the Alamo, whose American defenders died rather than surrender to the army of the Mexican General Santa Anna. But Crockett was legendary as much for his homespun ways as for his courage. He was seen as an uncouth, rustic, uneducated man of nature who lived by his agility. He idealized the frontiersman – an honest, uncomplicated, self-reliant man who helped pave the way westward for his fellow Americans. He was praised for his independence of mind, for his representation in the legislature of small farmers and new settlers, and for his skill as a hunter and an Indian fighter. While Crockett's self-deprecating humor hardly suggests divinity, his feasts against bears, alligators, buffalo, and forces of nature like the sun border on the superhuman. The sightings of him after his apparent death bespeak of immortality. The following tales, while somewhat tongue-in-cheek, describe Crockett's "posthumous" as well as living feats. On Crockett as figure of both history and myth, see *Davy Crockett*, ed. Richard M. Dorson (New York: Arno Press, 1973 [1939]); Walter Blair, *Davy Crockett – Frontier Hero* (New York: Coward-McCann, 1955); James Atkins Shackford, *David Crockett: The Man and the Legend*, ed. John B. Shackford (Chapel Hill: University of North Carolina Press, 1956); Richard Boyd Hauck, *Crockett: A Bio-Bibliography* (Westport, CT: Greenwood Press, 1982). See also David Crockett, *A Narrative of the Life of David Crockett*, eds. James A. Shackford and Stanley J. Fulmsbee

Original publication: Constance Rourke, *Davy Crockett* (New York: Harcourt, Brace, 1934), ch. 12 (pp. 225–43).

(Nashville: University of Tennessee Press, 1973 [1834]). On other American frontier heroes, see Kent Ladd Steckmesser, *The Western Hero in History and Legend* (Norman: University of Oklahoma Press, 1965). On American folk heroes generally, see Richard M. Dorson, *American Folklore* (Chicago: University of Chicago Press, 1959), ch. 6.

DAVY CROCKETT

Constance Rourke

A FEW men had gathered about the fire in a tavern on the Forked Deer River in western Tennessee. The winter dusk had fallen. An old hunter was speaking, mournfully.

"Thar's a great rejoicing among the bears of the river country and the alligators of the Mississippi are rolling up their shining ribs to the sun. The rattlesnakes has been coming out of their holes this autumn to frolic in the clearings, and the foxes goes to sleep in the goose pens. It's because the rifle of Crockett is silent forever, and the print of his moccasins is found no more in our woods."

"The painters and bears will miss him," said another hunter.

"He never missed *them*," said a man with red hair who was bending over the barrel of a flintlock, oiling it.

"I heard Davy never died at all," said a hunter.

"I heard he was a roaming over the prairies of Texas with a bear," said a traveler.

"Named Death Hug," said the red-haired man.

"He was carrying messages for Sam Houston," said the traveler, "and he was stopped by a big party of Mexican scouts. Quick as lightning Crockett mounted Death Hug and leapt clean over their heads." There was a pause. "Another time when he was carrying those messages he met a squad of Mexicans just as he came up to a grove of oaks and Death Hug ran right up one of the oaks with Crockett on his back and then out on a limb as slick as a panther going to roost, and over to the limb of another oak, and another, and then they were down and away."

"And once he sighted a stallion on the prairie," said the old hunter, "wild as the whirlwind, and tall and strong. Crockett came within a hundred yards of him, and the stallion threw back his ears, spread his jaws, and came snorting at him. As the horse reared to plunge Crockett seized his mane and mounted him as easy as a cow bird sits on the back of a brindle bull. The stallion made off like lightning and a big thunderstorm came up. Lightning struck all around but it flashed to either side of the horse as he ran and never struck him. The horse was off to the west and Crockett thought he was going to be flung against the Rocky Mountains. He ran for three days and three nights until he came to the Mad River, that poured down the mountainside boiling and hissing. There the horse ran under a tree, trying to brush Crockett off his back, but Crockett pulled his mane and that stallion leapt over the tree and the boiling river besides. Then he stopped quiet and Crockett got off."

For twenty years after his death stories were told of Davy Crockett as though he were still alive. It was said that he had been shot by a silver bullet that had made no wound and left no trace, and that he had feigned death at the Alamo, and had concealed himself when the battle was over. Then – in the story – he had set out to avenge the death of the five prisoners whom the Mexicans had put to the sword. He had found the slayers and had killed them with his hunting knife. Afterwards he was seen on the prairies far to the north, hunting buffalo.

"Sometimes Crockett rides wild horses, sometimes he rides Death Hug when he goes hunting buffalo," said the traveler. "Once he got trace of two mammoth buffaloes from the wilds of Oregon that snorted blue fire and bellowed small thunder. When they got in a particular passion they used to butt trees down and bore a hole in the earth twenty feet deep before they could cool off their dispositions. Crockett put off to the spot where they were and found them just as the hurricane of their temper was up and they were snorting young lightning and roaring bass music and had uprooted a few trees and tossed them into the air for practice. They were going to play toss with Crockett too, but he slipped round and tied their tails fast together, got between them with their tails like traces and with each of his arms over their flanks drove them a hundred miles, and they were as tame as sucking sheep."

He went on: "Another buffalo was so big and noisy and kept up such a continual thunderstorm of roaring that he used to scare away the sunrise, and the prairies was dark for days, but Crockett shot him on the wing and invited some Comanche warriors to the feast. It was night, and as they were making ready a great light appeared on the horizon. The light came nearer and nearer, and it was a prairie fire with billows of smoke and flame a foaming and a tossing in the air like waves at sea and a roaring like the sea. It came nearer and nearer to where Crockett was with the Comanches, as if it were going to sweep right over them, but a breeze came up and the fire swayed away a little. The breeze got to be a great wind and the fire turned and went off in another direction. Away went Davy after it with all those buffalo steaks in his hands holding them out in front of him and he kept on going until the steaks was well roasted. Then he came back to the Comanches and they had their feast."

"They was one buffalo Crockett captured out on the prairies and he tamed him," said the man with red hair, "and he called him Mississippi. When Crockett came to one of those border towns Mississippi was with him, and Mississippi would go to meeting every Sunday morning. He sang the bass of 'Old Hundred,' never missing a note, and that same critter would even lend the leader his horn for a tuning fork!"

"It's a caution what will happen in those border towns out on the wild prair*ee*."

It was not only hunters of the Great Valley who told stories about Crockett. Trappers from the far west said that they had seen him in the mountains of California, hunting grizzlies. Sailors back from long voyages in the South Seas declared that he was there, hunting pearls.

"Out there in the South Seas he was a diving," said a sailor, "and he came to a cave. He crawled till he came to dry land under the deepest water of the ocean. It was dark, so he made a lampwick out of his hair and soaked it with elbow grease and made a light by striking his knuckles on a rock.

"Crockett looked around and discovered that he had got in among thousands and thousands of pearl oysters that were fast asleep in their beds. He sang a song and danced a measure or two, and the oysters woke up. They all opened their shells for him and he came ashore with sacks and sacks of pearls."

Someone repeated this story in a stage coach that was traveling slowly at night in western Kentucky. The light in the coach was dim, showing the dark figures of men in every seat.

Other tales about Crockett were told as the coach rumbled, the wheels creaked, and the hooves of the horses thudded against hard clay first at a walk, then at a trot, then at a walk again.

"I understand," said a man in a tall beaver hat, "I understand that Crockett has not lingered in the Far East but has returned to the great prairies of North America to hunt the buffalo, the deer, and the elk. Only the other day I learned that he had crossed the Cannon Ball River and was following the crooked courses of the Missouri."

"I am credibly informed that Davy Crockett has now reached the Mississippi," said a small man with an air of importance. "In fact a friend of mine who has a dwelling on its banks witnessed a curious adventure of his. Crockett was out hunting one day when he noticed a wing-broken goose riding on the surface of the river. He struck out after it. You know that Davy Crockett can swim faster, dive deeper, stay down longer, and come out dryer than any man in all creation. Just as he was about to seize the goose a loud howl rose suddenly near him. Crockett jumped up out of the water like a sturgeon. It was a wolf, only a few feet away. At the same moment an alligator swam toward him from another direction and from overhead the whole flock of wild geese flew down upon him, hissing and flapping their wings.

"Davy dove down slantwise so as to come up far beyond the reach of all these critters, but when he struck the bottom of the river he was chased by a river calf and had to swim straight up to the surface again. The wolf, the alligator, the geese, were still there and the river calf was hot foot after him besides! Crockett struck out for a sawyer and just then a little steamboat came whistling and tooting along with fire and black smoke, and scared all the critters away. Crockett asked for a passage on board. Death Hug came along at this moment, swimming in easy water, and Crockett requested a berth for him too. The captain was a fussy man and he refused to give a berth to Death Hug, so Crockett and his tame bear walked out of the water and into the woods where they cut down a very ancient hollow gum tree, hewed it open on one side with Crockett's knife, corked up both ends, and launched their canoe into the river just as the steamer got out of sight. Old Death Hug sat in the stern and steered with his tail. He lit a pipe and so did Crockett. Death Hug paddled with his paws and Crockett with his hands. Smoking like smokestacks, they made that hollow log canoe walk in and out and along the water until the fishes stared, and soon they passed the steamboat. After a while Death Hug wanted to go ashore, so the canoe was drawn up on a bank. Crockett took a log for a pillow and floated downstream, and was soon fast asleep.

"I suppose you gentlemen have heard what happened to him next," queried the little man as though he hoped they had not.

From the darkest corner of the coach a traveler spoke up. "I reckon it's just about there he met up with Ben Hardin!"

Now a certain Ben Hardin was a member of Congress from Kentucky, an orator, and a good deal of a humorist. Ben Hardin in the stories was a different figure altogether. Many tales were told of the frolics and adventures of Crockett and this curious personage in the Shakes and on the Mississippi – "the backbone of North America" – where Crockett had once traveled with his staves. These stories are full of wind, earthquakes, hurricanes, lightning. Not all of them could have been related in a single evening, no matter how long the journey.

Here are a few of them, set down as they were told in the talk of the day.

As Davy Crockett was drifting downstream, asleep on his log pillow, he was wakened by bumping into something. Before him was a strange equipage for river travel. In the center of a log three kegs had been fastened one on top of another, and on the topmost keg was sitting a fat little man wearing a snug tarpaulin hat that looked as bright as a new dollar. His trousers were of sailcloth, his shoes thin and light with ribbons on them. He wore a big black patch over one eye.

"Well, stranger," said Crockett, "you must have robbed a peddler and got off with all his flashy trumpery."

"Why," said the fat little man, "the critter's got the lingo of a Christian. I thought I had spoke to a catfish. I've plowed salt water for forty year and I've seen porpoises and dolphins and mermaids, and I've took many a Nantucket sleighride, but you're the queerest looking sea craft I ever come across, on soundings or off. Where you cruising, old rusty bottom?"

The little man's voice grew deeper and rougher as he spoke. He had a voice so rough it couldn't be written down but would have to be shown in a picture.

"You infernal heathen," said Crockett, "I suppose you're new down this way, but I'll tell you I'm a snorter by birth and education, and if you don't go floating along and leave me to finish my nap I'll give you a taste of my breed, beginning with the snapping turtle!"

At this rejoinder the fat little stranger looked as mad as a shovel full of hot coals. He took a string of tobacco out of his pocket and bit into it savagely. He bit off a string long and big enough to hang a buffalo with, and roared out, "I'll shiver your mizzen, you landlubber! You rock crab! You deck sweeper!"

Crockett's steam was up. "I'll double you up like a spare shirt. My name is Crockett – "

With this the stranger roared with laughter, and his laugh was as rough and noisy as his talk. Stooping down he reached out his hand. "Give us your flipper. I wouldn't hurt a hair of your head for all the world. I've been cruising up and down this river a looking for you. Hurrah for Davy Crockett!"

The stranger explained that his name was Ben Hardin and that he was a man who had seen great times. "My business is seeing," he said jovially, and added that he had been told he could see more with the black patch over one eye than any other man could see with it off. He said he had been captain of ships that had turned bottom upward and sailed along to their destinations on their masts. He said that he had leaned his back against a hurricane. He said that he drank bitters made out of whiskey and rusty cannon balls, and slept coiled up like a cable. The last time he counted he was going on into his ninety-ninth year.

As Hardin was talking a noise was heard like low thunder, then a distant roaring like the voice of old Niagara.

"Hello," said Crockett, "there's a storm coming."

"No, it's a steamer," said Ben Hardin.

"Maybe it's the echo of our voices," said Crockett.

The noise grew louder, the water began to squirm about, and Crockett's log and Hardin's little craft began playing see-saw. Then came a sudden roaring blast that would have made Niagara sound like a kitten. The trees on shore walked out by the roots and danced about. Houses came apart. Two boats on the river crashed into each other, and their ribs were stove in to the boilers. Crockett and Hardin thought it was time to be off.

When a streak of lightning glanced by, Crockett seized it by the fork and sprang upon it. For a man who had leaned his back against a hurricane Ben seemed in a hurry to leave. He gave a leap and seized Crockett's hair. Crockett greased the lightning with some rattlesnake oil he happened to have along and the way they left the tornado behind and slid across the land was astonishing to all nature.

When this feat became known people talked about greased lightning. They still do. "Quick as greased lightning."

When this adventure was over Crockett landed with his new friend in the woods, and he felt as good-natured as a soaped eel. He invited Hardin to come along to his cabin, where he promised him a bear steak, and the two went along through the woods as good friends as a tame hawk and a blind rooster.

But the way Ben walked was a caution, for he was used to the decks of a ship. When it came to walking among the tall masts of the backwoods he turned every way but the right way. He swung about like a bearskin hung to the limb of a tree.

One morning Ben wanted to go out hunting. So out they went and away went Ben, whistling and swinging his tarpaulin hat at every little creature that happened to be in sight. At last they got under an oak that was famous for breeding many generations of wildcats. Even its knots looked like wildcats' eyes. Just as they got beneath it and were going to take a seat on a root they heard something above them give a scratch and a grunt. Ben ran up the tree as light as a monkey up a ship's ladder. He hadn't gone further than heels out of sight when Crockett heard a sailor's regular rough language with all the trimmings. He looked up and saw a bear, and the creature had grabbed Ben by the shoulder. The way the old sea serpent fought back was a caution. Down they came to the ground, Ben and the bear, and rolled over and over. The leaves began to turn claret color so Crockett stepped up, squeezed the breath out of the bear, and gave Ben a swallow out of the lightning bottle. Ben swore that every claw of that bear was a whaler's harpoon.

Ben Hardin told Crockett that he was a whole squall and a hurricane at a frolic. Old sailors used to say that he could dance all the girls in all the seaports from Cadiz to Cape Cod out of their stockings. He danced till he wore away the stone steps in front of Crockett's cabin.

"Well, old Salt-Rope," said Crockett, "I'll give you a frolic that'll last you for a seven years' cruise."

Now Ben had said that Crockett's daughter was as pretty as a dolphin. "I've seen dolphins and mermaids too," he added. The story was that she had once been captured by Indians who carried her away and tied her to a tree, and meant to kindle a fire about her. But while they were gone for wood, panthers came and gnawed the ropes and set her free, and gathered about her as she ran through the forest and escorted her most of the way home.

"Anyway she's the true grit," said Crockett, "and she can dance anything from an earthquake reel to a square-toed double trouble shiver."

They all went to the Asphaltum Flats where lightning couldn't strike because the Flats were so hard. An old man with a hemlock fiddle played new tunes that went so fast a humming-bird's wing couldn't keep time with them. Crockett set Ben and the girl at it, and away they went, and the Asphaltum Flats looked like a prairie on fire. "After the first three tunes," Crockett said, "Old Ben began to grunt like a saw going through a pine knot. Then he staggered. My girl said nothing but kept on leading out every new tune. After the hundred and fifteenth tune Ben began to roll like a ship in a sea-storm and finally he fell over and curled up in his pigtail. But my girl was ready to go on."

Strange tales were told of Crockett's hunting exploits in wild country of the Northwest and of his encounters with Indians. One evening about dark Crockett and Hardin came to the great Indian Rock, which was the hardest stone in all creation.

"It was so 'tarnal high and so all flinty hard," said Crockett, "that it would turn off a common ordinary everyday streak of lightning and make it point down and look flat as a cow's tail."

They got under a shelf of this great rock, and Crockett struck a little fire from it with his knuckles to light their pipes, and they began puffing. They looked up and the whole stone around and on both ends was alive and red with Indians, all with guns and tomahawks. Ben reached for his flintlock but Crockett saw that lightning would be the only thing so he rubbed himself against the shelf of the rock and struck his left eye two or three times. Then he stepped back and with a single wink sent such a blasting streak of hot lightning into the great rock that it parted into forty thousand pieces. There were red Indians shooting up into the sky like rockets and landing way out on the prairie. "We cut stick in such a shower of red Indians as was never seen before," said Crockett.

Another time Crockett and Ben Hardin were having a feast of roasted buffalo with some friendly Indians near one of their lodges. Afterwards Crockett danced a breakdown on a great flat rock nearby. He rattled off some clear music as he danced and all the Indians came out and sat around in a circle to watch him – all but the Indian chief who began a regular Indian war dance in opposition. The Indians began to shout and whoop. Crockett went at it harder and danced until the old rock began to snap and smoke like a hemlock back log. Fire began to fly about, the Indian chief's feet began to singe, and the blankets of the others were all in a light blaze. Just as the Indians were all going to run off Crockett finished with a regular old "Grind the Bottle," and stamped the whole fire out again.

Farther to the north Crockett and Ben Hardin went wolf hunting. After the hunt one day when Crockett was feeling hot and lazy, the old sailor bantered him for a race on the frozen river. Now Crockett was a rocket on skates. Skating, he could pass the swiftest Indians, and Indians could go fast as thought on their bone runners made of buffalo ribs. Up and down the frozen rivers of the north Crockett would go, leaping great air holes twenty feet or more across and skating on without losing a stroke. Death Hug was also a prime skater, though not so good as Crockett. For the race Death Hug started off ahead while Davy and Ben started even. They went so fast they struck fire against the wind. Sparks flew out of the ice and made Crockett's gun go off so he lost a stroke but he skated ahead and grabbed Death Hug's tail. At the same moment Ben fell. He caught hold of the tail of Crockett's hunting shirt and down the river went the three for a hundred miles like a toboggan, with Death Hug in the lead.

Traveling over the country in winter Davy and Death Hug came to the Niagara River, which was frozen. They were cutting all sorts of frolic flourishes on the ice when suddenly the great piece on which they were skating parted from the rest and headed toward the Falls. There were people all along the banks and Crockett waved at them. Suddenly Crockett and his bear were left on only a small wedge of ice that was sharp at one end. Death Hug put his paw to his nose, Crockett raised Uncle Sam's starry handkerchief, and they steered over the great hill of water as easy as though they were on a greased ship.

Then Crockett mounted his old pet alligator and steered right back up the roaring thunder-water as slick as a stream of wind going up a chimney.

"My old alligator walked up that monstrous great hill of water as easy as a wildcat goes up a white oak," said Crockett. "And my alligator opened his mouth as wide as the Black Cave, and the people were all astonished."

On the Upper Lower Fork of the Great Little Deep Shallow River Davy gathered all his animals around him. Death Hug was there, and Mississippi, the buffalo that could sing "Old Hundred," and a cougar, a fox, a wolf, and a hyena. Crockett's pet hyena could outlaugh an earthquake, and he was so wild that the northeast wind couldn't reach him and even the lightning couldn't catch up with him.

"The lightning put out after him once," said Davy, "but he laughed it out of countenance and ran away, and when I followed him I had to run for seven days and seven nights. Then he turned round and came home with me as docile as a kitten."

Crockett gathered them all together under the Liberty Tree. It was the Fourth of July, so he took out his bag of patriotism and gave them an oration. "When I began my oration," said Crockett, "they opened their eyes and ears in the most teetotal attentive manner and showed a 'tarnal sight more respect than the members of Congress show one another during their speeches, and when I concluded by lifting my cap with twenty-six cheers for Uncle Sam and his states, with a little thrown in for Texas and Oregon, why choke me if those critters didn't follow with such a shout as set all the trees to shaking!"

Then Crockett taught all the animals the polka. Death Hug and the buffalo Mississippi and the old alligator could wear down an oak floor in a single night, all flipping their heels in regular polka step while Ben Hardin whistled the tunes. Ben could outwhistle the prettiest clarionette that ever talked music.

Stories about Crockett are still told in Kentucky and Tennessee and in the Ozark Mountains. Even now people in the Ozarks talk about him as though he were still living just over the next ridge.

They say that once he went bear hunting in the fall up on Whangdoodle Knob. At sundown he was tired out so he lay down under a big old dead cedar tree and went to sleep. In his sleep he rolled over and nearly broke his powder horn. Above him was a little curved yellow branch and he hung his horn on it. The next morning the horn was gone and he couldn't find the branch. That night he came back to the Knob and soon the little crescent moon came up, riding low over the mountain. It came so close and looked so yellow it nearly blinded him, and there was his powder horn hanging from the tip. He reached it down and went along home to his cabin.

In the Ozarks they tell of another time when Crockett was out hunting and traveled far from his cabin and spent the night in the woods. The next morning at daybreak he took a far jump and landed on the sun, thinking that he would be carried over the mountain to his cabin. But he had forgotten that he was west of his cabin instead of east. So, traveling with the sun for twenty-four hours, he saw the whole world, and dropped off the next morning and landed on his own doorstep.

During his own lifetime Crockett had been spoken of as consorting on easy terms with the moon, with shooting stars, a fiery comet, and the lightning. In all the stories his close companions were wind, water, fire, the earth, and the wild creatures of forest and prairie. In a last story he is portrayed as stronger than the sun, and he appears once more in the hunting country of Tennessee.

This story belongs to the Winter of the Big Snow, the winter of 1835, when Crockett set out for Texas, when snow fell early through the wide stretches of the North, crept farther and farther down through the hard wood forests of Michigan, then through the soft wood forests, through the long valleys of Wisconsin, down upon the prairie country of Illinois, into Kentucky and Tennessee. The story was told as if Crockett himself related it.

"On one of those winter mornings it was all screwen cold," said Crockett. "The forest trees were so stiff they couldn't shake and the very daybreak froze fast as it was trying to dawn. The tinder-box in my cabin would no more catch fire than a sunk raft at the bottom of the sea. All creation was in a fair way for freezing fast, so I thought I must strike a little fire from my fingers and travel out a few leagues and see what I could do about it. I brought my knuckles together like two thunder-clouds, but the sparks froze up before I could collect 'em, so out I walked and tried to keep myself unfrozen by going along at a frolic gait, whistling the tune of 'Fire in the Mountains' and keeping going at three double quick time. Well, after I had walked about a hundred miles up Daybreak Hill I reached Peak o' Day, and there I discovered what was the matter. The earth had actually frozen fast on her axis and couldn't turn round, and the sun had got jammed between two cakes of ice under the wheels, and there he had been shining and working to get loose till he was frozen fast in his cold sweat.

"'C-R-E-A-T-I-O-N,' thought I, 'this is the toughest sort of suspension, and it mustn't be endured – something must be done or human creation is done for!' It was so premature and antediluvian cold on top of Peak o' Day that my upper and lower teeth were all collapsed together as tight as a frozen oyster. So I took a big bear off my back that I'd picked up on my road and threw him down on the ice and soon there was hot sweet bear oil on all sides. I took and squeezed him over the earth's axis until I'd thawed it loose, and I poured about a ton of sweet bear oil over the sun's face. Then I gave the earth's cog wheel one kick backward till I got the sun free and whistled 'Push Along, Keep Moving.' In about fifteen seconds the earth gave a grunt and began to roll around easy, and the sun walked up most beautiful, saluting me with such a wind of gratitude it made me sneeze.

"I lit my pipe by the blaze of his topknot and walked home, introducing people to the fresh daylight with a piece of sunrise in my pocket."

So when Davy Crockett set out for Texas the earth was no longer screwed up stiff and frozen fast, but rolled around. The sun walked up in the morning and down at night, though the days were bitter cold and the snow lay deep.

CHAPTER 22

ELVIS PRESLEY (AMERICAN): HERO AS ENTERTAINER

INTRODUCTION

Elvis Presley (1935–77) was the entertainer supreme. He had more fans than anyone else, his fans were more dedicated to him, and many of them refused to accept his death. Even more than other stars, Elvis lived like a god. At Graceland, which he left only for recordings, films, and appearances, he lived as a recluse in a womb-like world in which all of his wishes were immediately satisfied. While he considered himself a normal, even all-American boy, he was in fact a consummate mama's boy. The worst tragedy in his life, from which he never wholly recovered, was the death of his mother. His wife, Priscilla, was no substitute and was more friend than wife. Elvis traveled everywhere with his entourage of boyhood friends, who, together with his manager, shielded him from the travails of the real world. He lived the life of a perpetual adolescent, free to do as he pleased. What his fans wanted most was the same: a figure arrested sexually and emotionally at adolescence. During his life, his most loyal fans would follow him from city to city or wait to greet him upon his return to Memphis. After his death, his home became a shrine, to which followers still come like pilgrims. Visitors not only tour his house and bus and plane but also pray at his gravestone. His death continues to be commemorated. In light of the connection drawn by Lord Raglan between kingship and divinity, it is notable that Elvis was dubbed the "King" of Rock and Roll. Elvis was godlike in his capacity to forge a narcissistic world for himself, in his fans' "idolization" of him, and in his immortality. He lives on, not only in the popular belief that he is still alive

Original publication: Patsy Guy Hammontree, *Elvis Presley* (Westport, CT: Greenwood Press, 1985), pp. 3–4, 28–9, 29–30, 45–6, 56–7, 59, 78, 79–80.

but also in the impersonations of him. The following selection offers an impartial, factual account of the fantasy world that Elvis constructed. For a more sensationalistic exposé, see Albert Goldman, *Elvis* (New York: McGraw-Hill, 1981).

ELVIS PRESLEY: A BIO-BIBLIOGRAPHY

Patsy Guy Hammontree

Elvis Presley's life is more like fiction than fact. By American standards, his life was a success. He moved from an impoverished life to an extraordinarily wealthy existence; he was admired by literally millions; he was as sought after as any public figure of this century; and when he died at a relatively early age, his funeral attracted world attention. At his death, great furor arose over the autopsy. A literal report, it gave the technical cause of death – cardiac arrest. Many asserted his death was caused by drugs. In reality, Elvis died from detachment.

This is not to say that Elvis consciously willed his own death. On the contrary, he considered himself actively in pursuit of life. He was, in fact, on the very evening of his death, setting out on a two-week concert tour of the Northeast. The week preceding Elvis's death, Felton Jarvis, Elvis's record-production manager who made all road trips with the Elvis tour, told former back-up singer Gordon Stoker, "He is working us to death. All he wants to do is work, work, work." Elvis looked forward to road trips because they put him in touch with the metaphorical source of his life: he needed the stimulus of audience response.

Taking the term "entertainer" seriously, Elvis felt it to be his calling in life in the same sense that a minister or a spiritualist speaks of having a calling. And why not? His phenomenal success, which came so suddenly and so mysteriously, was more than he ever could comprehend. He never lost his apprehension that success could disappear as mysteriously and as suddenly as it appeared. Even the tension such anxiety caused, however, could not provide adequate excitement; tension motivated him, certainly, but it was not enough – finally – to insulate him from the routine of his life. Fans who supported him – and his fans were legion – would themselves have sacrificed anything to reassure him of his importance. But after so many years, there came to be a monotony even in fan response, and their often bizarre attempts to get to him became routine.

To fans, Elvis led a life too exciting to imagine. They longed to share in what Elvis himself once referred to as the "razzle dazzle." In comparison, their own lives seemed tedious and boring. But fans had Elvis to look forward to. He lifted their spirits and gave meaning to their lives. He inhabited both their reality and their fantasy. But Elvis had only himself. In the time he spent apart from fans, separated from the intensity of being center-stage he settled into a ritualized existence. Caught in a surrealistic paradox, Elvis became a living example of absurdism, equal to the drama of Beckett or Ionesco.

Elvis's success provided freedoms unavailable to the ordinary human and he enjoyed his life, but he understood that he was bound by certain circumstance. Edith Neeley, sister-in-law of Elvis's father, Vernon Presley, visited the Presley home frequently after Vernon's marriage to Dee Stanley. She saw Elvis there in a relaxed atmosphere, and she found him to be very down-to-earth. His courtesy toward her family and other guests impressed her. She did notice, however, a turbulence about him.

> Sometimes when we were up there, I saw him seem restless. Once he was sitting, pecking his fingers on a table. He looked up at me when I walked in and said, "You know what, Edith, when some people get down and out, they go out and get drunk and forget it all. Me – I just go out and buy another car." Then he laughed and said, "I've got money and I could buy anything there is to buy, but I still can't get out and mix with people like I'd like to."

His remark acknowledges both extremes of his life.

Much has been made of Elvis's being an isolated figure – a kind of modern Byronic hero who prowls around his castle, brooding and unhappy. Persons who had frequent contact with him, however, contend that he was an active and interested person who got around as much as he wanted to. And they are generally accurate. Elvis had restructured his life to such an extent that eventually he no longer considered moving freely among people in a shopping mall or grocery store to be an option for himself. He adapted to his separation from the public. At the same time, his life's predicability did make his existence routine, leaving little to anticipate. Finally, in insulating himself from the routine, he insulated himself from reality. His life became a half-life and ultimately no life.[...]

Elvis's intense need to surround himself with the familiar ironically contributed a destructive element to his life: he was too much insulated from reality. Already he was far removed from a traditional way of life, leading a kind of fantasy existence without financial worries or household worries of any kind. He never carried cash, and somebody took care of

209

everything for him. Further, he had more song hits in a year than many have in a lifetime.

It was from the point at which he turned his professional career over to Parker that Elvis began to have a distorted sense of reality, but in 1957 the far-reaching consequences of his life did not concern him. Daily excitement left little time for him to ponder the future. His energies focused on the immediate. He was an optimistic entertainer whose phenomenal success had brought him advantages previously unimagined. He had a spacious private home for himself and his parents. He could provide for his extended family. He had automobiles and motorcycles in abundance and he had an expensive wardrobe.

Further, he surrounded himself with the male camaraderie most often found in adolescent life, and his economic power enabled him to engage to excess in everything a traditional adolescent enjoyed. A surfeit of young women were ever present. He could rent a skating rink for the evening and invite as many or as few friends as he wished; he could rent amusement parks and restrict them to his friends; and he could rent movie theatres, scheduling films he specifically wanted to see, viewing them repeatedly as he wished. The personal appearances Parker scheduled for him were prestigious: he appeared to a capacity crowd at the Dallas Cotton Bowl; he appeared in the Pacific Northwest; and he appeared in Canada, filling a stadium at Vancouver, British Columbia. Of greatest importance to him, the first three films he made were box-office hits. All over the United States and even in Europe and Asia, young men emulated his hair style, his manner of talking, and his type of clothing. In short, he lived a satisfying – even hedonistic – kind of life. A disruption came with his draft notice. But even two years in the Army did not impinge greatly on his established way of life.

His draft notice, which came in late 1957, was disturbing news; the major worry for Elvis was that two years away from films, recordings, and personal appearances would destroy him as an entertainer. Beyond his professional worries, he disliked the idea of venturing away from his own controlled world. A young man who preferred being with his family and friends and who never liked to undertake things alone certainly would not find the prospects of giving his life over to a rigid military regimen a pleasant proposition. [...]

He went through boot camp at Fort Hood, near Kileen, Texas. As soon as possible, Elvis rented a house in Kileen and moved his parents along with Lamar Fike, one of his live-in friends, to reside there the three months of his introductory training period. He spent his free time with his family. The opportunity to do so was not limited to Elvis. Any soldier who could bring his parents in could have had the same alternative. Not many GIs, however, could move their parents to the location of the boot camp. Before Elvis completed his training period, his mother became seriously ill and returned to Memphis for treatment. Shortly thereafter, she died, causing for Elvis the first real trauma of his life.

His mother had been an exceptionally strong influence in his life. Adjusting to her death was by far more difficult than anything else Elvis had attempted. He had kept in almost constant contact with his parents all the time he toured. According to Gordon Stoker, he called his mother each night. Harold Lloyd, Elvis's cousin who lived for extended periods with the Presleys while he was a youth, commented on Elvis and his mother's relationship, saying, "When those two were together, they could hardly keep their hands off each other. They were always petting and talking baby talk to each other." Elvis had pet names for his mother, among which was "Sattening," a family term of endearment. Relatives who attended Gladys Presley's funeral observed that Elvis was hardly able to tear himself away from the casket, one of elaborate design fitted with a glass top. Friends and family had to provide much emotional assistance for Elvis during the mourning period. [...]

The main factor making Elvis's life different was his coterie of companions. In a 1963 article in *McCalls*, reporter Vernon Scott commented on the group of men who surrounded Elvis saying, "The nine young men in dark clothes, who moved with practiced ease, [are] almost like secret service men guarding the President. The nine indeed were on guard duty... on a scale not seen in Hollywood since the days of Valentino and Fairbanks." In this way, Elvis sought to separate himself from the film colony largely because of his unease in social situations outside his own select environment. He was acutely aware of his lack of educational background and was sensitive to his awkwardness in such situations. Moreover, the traditional Hollywood life style did not interest him. Scott goes on to say that Elvis was "so involved with his own pals that contacts with other members of the cast and crew are necessarily restricted."

Scott touches the very nerve of the arrangement. When surrounded by his retinue, Elvis was protected from engaging in social situations – whether on the set or at typical Hollywood parties or premiers. At the same time, his contingent helped him create his own social structure because these men were the source of his recreation. They played games and practiced karate with each other, rode the "bump 'em" cars at amusement parks, rode their motorcycles, and played touch football. In Memphis they did all these things and additionally played "dodge 'em" on golf carts at the back of Graceland, rented roller-skating rinks, rented movie theatres for exclusive showings of films after regular hours, rented amusement parks, and, in later years, played racquetball. The director and others of the film crew accepted the presence of Elvis's retinue as if it were the traditional thing to do.

Writer C. Robert Jennings also described Elvis's association with his coterie. In a 1965 *Saturday Evening Post* article, Jennings states,

> Elvis relaxes by indulging in an almost continued round of playful pummeling with the eight young male assistants who live with him. He practices karate and water pistol marksmanship with them; then gathers them for close-harmony singing. Elvis handles his court with all the aplomb of a Renaissance prince.
>
> "I am the boss," he says. "I have to be. I have very specific uses for a highly trained CPA, another man to handle travel arrangements and make reservations, a wardrobe man, a confidential aide, and a man to handle security in crowds. This is my corporation."

Though these men afforded Elvis both the physical and psychological protection he needed, they also were detrimental to him.

Pat Boone, who had known Elvis since early on, remarked on Elvis's life in California, saying,

> We lived about five minutes drive from each other in Los Angeles. He came for chicken dinner at our house twice. We were friends, but not close friends. Once in our early days in Hollywood, he just drove up at our house – he and Charlie Hodge. Of course, we had known Charlie for a long time. He sang with Red Foley, Shirley's father, before he went into the Army. We were always glad to see them. . . . Elvis always seemed to envy mine and Shirley's family life. He was very nice to our children, the girls were very small at that time. He seemed to enjoy them, but he was awkward with them. In some ways, he was not too far beyond them. Elvis was a strange paradox. He was very keen, very sharp, but emotionally immature. Actually the events of his life stunted his emotional maturity. The men surrounding him bolstered his sense of identity and made him comfortable in that way, [but] they didn't help him to grow.

Boone is quite correct. Elvis's retainers helped satisfy his social needs, but they also caused him to remain socially restricted. [. . .]

Living as he did in an encapsulated world, Elvis created an environment so personal that he had his own standard of time and space, and his retinue adopted his way as their own. Elvis rose late in the afternoon and used the evening and most of the night as his time of leisure. He went to bed before sunrise and rose again the following afternoon. It became the schedule of his life, having been necessitated by his professional circumstances.

Entertainers work at night because that is when the public is ready to be entertained. Show business persons must therefore raise their adrenalin level to a high pitch just as others are winding down. Elvis carried the day-for-night schedule to its most extreme, maintaining it even when not working: it allowed him time to move about more easily. Although some of his fans were on watch twenty-four hours a day, they were fewer in number at night. Consequently, Elvis had more freedom to move about the city. [...]

Always present to provide diversion were the myriad young women. There was an assembly-line nature to their exits and entrances. Soon after Dee Presley became part of the family, Elvis showed her a picture of Priscilla, commenting that Priscilla was special to him. Dee reported that he then said he had had sexual intercourse with at least a thousand women, but that Priscilla was unlike any of them. Dee assumed that part of his motive for giving the statistic was for its shock potential. Yet it is entirely possible that he told her the truth.

Elvis's sexual potential was always part of his mystique. And though he did not appear at Hollywood functions with young starlets, publicity agents did not hesitate to link him with their starlet clients in newspapers and magazines. Elvis and women made good copy; reality or fiction did not matter. With each new picture, stories circulated of his "love affair" with his co-star.

It was impossible to enlarge on Elvis and his relationships with women. Women mailed themselves to him in boxes; they screamed at him from the highway a quarter mile from his house where they stood outside his gate, watching his every move as though he were a rare butterfly; they offered every possible inducement to his staff members and to his musicians in an attempt to get to him; and they enlisted the help of anyone remotely connected. They sent packages to Dr. Dan Cummins, minister of the Graceland Christian Church, begging him to carry them to Elvis. Later they besieged C. W. Bradley, minister of Wooddale Church of Christ, which Dee and Vernon attended, with gifts and messages for Elvis. Whatever he touched was sacred to them. During the 1968 NBC "Singer Christmas Special," Elvis mopped his face with a tissue and a portion remained on his face. Charlie Hodge stepped over to remove it and then let it waft out into the audience. A young woman snatched the lint-sized piece of tissue, wrapped it carefully in a handkerchief, and clutched it to herself. Elvis stood on the stage and watched, shook his head in bewilderment and remarked, "It never ceases to amaze me...." Wherever he traveled, women waited and thrust themselves at him, sometimes crying uncontrollably from overpowering emotion; sometimes shrieking his name over and over, hoping he would hear and turn their direction. Once during a motorcade to his motel, a woman threw herself on the hood of his fast-moving vehicle. The incident unnerved Elvis. These were all public manifestations. The compromises made in private in order to see Elvis are hard to measure.

Yet from 1961, Elvis had as a permanent house guest Priscilla Beaulieu. Then, on May 1, 1967, without advance publicity, Elvis and Priscilla married in a full-dress traditional wedding – except that it was a civil ceremony held at the Aladdin Hotel in Las Vegas. After their divorce, Priscilla told a reporter in a *Ladies Home Journal* interview that Elvis had very unceremoniously proposed marriage by giving her an elaborate ring for Christmas in 1966. [. . .]

Elvis's life changed only slightly with his marriage. He bought a 163-acre ranch in northern Mississippi and placed house trailers on it as homes for his closest retainers. He also bought horses for himself, Priscilla, and most of his retinue and their wives. Later, upon returning to California for a film, he bought an expensive house in the Trousdale Estates in Los Angeles. He and Priscilla made Los Angeles their home for the next two years, visiting the ranch on their Memphis vacations. In nine months, on February 1, Priscilla gave birth to their only child, Lisa Marie, at a Memphis hospital. Becoming a parent did not change Elvis's interests; he continued his social life with the same group of friends. Priscilla made no public complaint about the limited contacts she and Elvis had with others, but in an interview after his death she spoke with dismay of the stifling effects of "years and years and years [with] the same people." Her lack of privacy with Elvis was a source of endless frustration to her, having never gone anywhere without members of his retinue. Marty Lacker described a trip to Hawaii she and Elvis planned soon after they were married. Lacker noted that Priscilla was under the impression it would be for the two of them. Rather, it was for a party of eight, including three of Elvis's male companions and their wives.

Elvis also continued to make movies with the same worn-out plots. He recorded soundtracks but released no hit single. And he continued to keep an erratic schedule, traveling to Los Angeles or to Palm Springs – always accompanied by his retainers, but not always their wives. Priscilla acknowledged that she had expected to be with Elvis wherever he went and admitted having difficulty accepting the fact that she would not.

Lisa's birth did give Priscilla new focus for her life. And she adjusted herself to live in essentially the same way she had lived before the wedding ceremony. Elvis simply did not see marriage as anything to disrupt his life. Though he had particular expectations for Priscilla, he lived by his own dubious standards. There is no question that he had deep affection for Priscilla and Lisa, but he was addicted to his adolescent life style. [. . .]

In 1972, Elvis's career daily gained momentum, but his personal life with Priscilla daily deteriorated. She became increasingly alienated. Elvis's friends and family all attest to his exceedingly strong affection for Priscilla and Lisa. But Elvis wanted Priscilla to live in a romantic vacuum. He certainly did not consider his view of their life together as unrealistic, but his expectations of how they should respond to each other were those of a fantasy existence. He viewed himself as married when he was with Priscilla, but he saw himself as being beyond the conventions of marriage when he was in the world at large. He behaved accordingly. From the time they were married, Elvis continued to be surrounded by women of all ages. Wherever he went, they pursued him with a vengeance; some of them eagerly offered sexual favors while others simply wanted to adore him from afar. He was rarely separate from a varied collection of women, and he usually had a more select inner circle.

Clearly their attention flattered him. He thrived on the adulation, according to some reports, and his retinue of hired hands sought to keep the supply plentiful. If one can believe these reports, they surveyed the selection, making recommendations according to Elvis's particular taste in women. Meanwhile, Elvis counted on Priscilla's remaining almost virginal in her isolation, waiting for him to come back to Graceland or Beverly Hills. He expected her to be a traditional wife while he behaved as if his commitment to her remained in effect only in her immediate presence. After years of this restricted life, Priscilla grew tired. She later referred to the life as like being in a "cocoon," mentioning the "tight security" around her and Lisa in large part because Elvis feared kidnappers. She spoke of the boredom and how Elvis had controlled her life, choosing her clothing styles, her make-up and hair styles, and determining her activities. "He was not only a lover but a father to me, and as long as I stayed with him, I could never be anything but his little girl." Elvis quite possibly saw himself as her protector and guardian, more than he really felt himself to be her husband. Excerpts from Priscilla's book about Elvis reveal something of the nature of their relationship. Reports quote her as disclosing that Elvis rarely made love to her, specifying "no more than fifty times" during their marriage. [. . .]

Accepting Priscilla's decision to change the direction of her life was difficult for Elvis. Every book written about him after his death stresses Elvis's unhappiness about the separation. Priscilla's move to a small Los Angeles apartment in February started Elvis's year on a low emotional point. Shortly, however, George Klein, a long-time friend, introduced him to Linda Thompson, a Memphis resident and Miss Tennessee in the Miss

Universe Beauty Pageant. Aged twenty-one and ambitious, Thompson enjoyed publicity. She quickly understood that Elvis required a lot of attention and that she could benefit from seeing that he got it. She readily adapted to his controlled environment, accepting him as a law unto himself. Once, speaking to Rocky Barra, publisher of *Strictly Elvis*, Thompson remarked, "Elvis is a special person. He's different from other people and he doesn't have to live by the same rules that other people do." Like others in Elvis's inner circle, Thompson excluded Elvis from standard behavioral codes.

In spite of his authoritarianism, Elvis liked to be coddled and treated like a youngster needing protection. Thompson gladly behaved toward him in that way. In an article in *McCalls* magazine several years after Elvis died, Thompson described the relationship they had, pointing out that they were "lovers, friends, brother and sister, daddy and little girl, mommy and baby." According to Thompson, Elvis regularly called her "mommy" and she called him "Bunton" or "baby." She was with him twenty-four hours a day for three years, accompanying him on all tours and on his Las Vegas engagements. She remained with him off and on for an additional year.

INDEX

217

Index

Index